Ibsen: The Open Vision

John S. Chamberlain

ATHLONE
London

First published 1982 by The Athlone Press Limited
90–91 Great Russell Street, London WC1B 3PY

Distributor in USA and Canada
Humanities Press Inc
New Jersey

© John S. Chamberlain 1982

British Library Cataloguing in Publication Data

Chamberlain, John
    Ibsen: the open vision.
    1. Ibsen, Henrik – Criticism and interpretation
    I. Title
    839.8′226   PT8895

    ISBN 0-485-11227-2

Typeset by Inforum Ltd, Portsmouth
Printed in Great Britain by
The University Press, Cambridge

Ibsen: The Open Vision

Contents

For Marcella, Stephen and Hugh

Acknowledgements

My grateful thanks to the friends and Ibsen scholars who have taken an interest in my work. They have helped to ensure that this book grew from ideas that developed while I was, at the kind invitation of Professor James McFarlane, a Visiting Fellow at the University of East Anglia (1973–74). I am particularly indebted to Professor Inga-Stina Ewbank, of Bedford College, London; Dr. Katharine Worth, of Royal Holloway College, London; and Professor Charles Leland of St. Michael's College, Toronto, for their generous gifts of time and good advice.

In a more general way, the orientation of my critical attitudes was established during my doctoral studies of Ibsen (1967–70) with James Redmond, of Westfield College, London, and Torbjörn Stöverud, then W. P. Ker Lecturer in Norwegian at University College, London.

My Ibsen studies have been greatly facilitated by the financial assistance of the Canada Council (now the Social Sciences and Humanities Research Council of Canada), which has consistently encouraged my work. And I wish especially to acknowledge the generous contributions made by the University of Regina towards the preparation and publication of this book.

Prefatory Note

Except for *Peer Gynt*, for which the version by William and Charles Archer provided the kind of literalism I required, I have generally used *The Oxford Ibsen* for quotations from the plays in English. But I have frequently consulted Rolf Fjelde's equally outstanding translations. In deciding personal preferences for titles in *Peer Gynt*, I have drawn on *The Oxford Ibsen* (for the "Thin Man," for instance), the Archers (for the "Saeter-Girls," for example), and Fjelde, from whom I borrowed the "Troll King." Where the original Norwegian is quoted, I have used the Centennial Edition of the *Samlede Verker*, edited by Francis Bull, Halvdan Koht, and Didrik Arup Seip.

Matters of critical terminology requiring definition are, in general, discussed in Chapter One, but it is useful to observe here that I have used the word "endorse" in a manner which, though not specialized, may require some comment: it is used whenever it is necessary to speak of Ibsen's finding some means—or, more usually, avoiding any means—of implying definite personal support for ideas and attitudes expressed in his plays. Because his skill in withholding implicit support is considerable and still insufficiently recognized, comments on a lack of "endorsement" are frequent.

With regard to documentation, I have tried to avoid clutter: accordingly, the very numerous quotations from the plays are not documented, and in those cases in which a critical article or chapter of a critical work is quoted frequently because it advances a point of view I have considered in detail, a single identifying footnote is provided.

I have consistently spelt characters' names as they appear in the translations and critical works quoted. A considerable variety of spellings is evident in the case of *Ghosts*.

1

Some Fundamentals of Vision and Form in Ibsen

Ibsen's characteristically cryptic statement "I do but ask; my call is not to answer" is one of the best known and most widely quoted judgements of his work.[1] And an awareness of the multidimensional nature of his themes underlies much of the best Ibsen criticism and is reflected in the most successful productions of his plays. But the idea that, ultimately, the plays either individually or collectively endorse specific, clear-cut attitudes is persistent. *Peer Gynt*, for example, is regarded as endorsing the redemptive force of the Eternal Feminine, while *A Doll's House* and *Ghosts* are frequently interpreted as vindicating feminism (one recalls that the two films of *A Doll's House* were timed to coincide with International Women's Year). It is generally accepted that *The Wild Duck* discredits popular application of idealistic theories and prescribes "life-lies" for all but the sturdiest individualists—of whom the play appears to contain none. Sometimes rival interpretations of particular plays gain equal support: *Rosmersholm*, for instance, is seen by some as a tragedy of atonement and a vindication of the "higher love," but by others as almost a parody of such noble conceptions; *Little Eyolf* is interpreted either as a definite expression of hope or as a demonstration of Alfred Allmers's fraudulence. On the one hand, Ibsen's obvious fascination with the will to aspire—"Upwards, towards the bringer of light," as one of the notes for *Hedda Gabler* puts it[2]—exerts such a powerful appeal that it is not easy to respond to all the forces and implications which preclude fully endorsed positive judgements in the plays. On the other hand, once the nature and scope of Ibsen's irony is grasped, it is equally tempting to interpret his doubts as the expression of a comprehensive and systematic pessimism.

This study will attempt to demonstrate that there is a constant openness in Ibsen's work—that even when a prescriptive ideological or metaphysical element seems dominant, it is suffused with doubts of the most fundamental, though never utterly destructive, kinds; that the mock-heroic indications are almost invariably as powerful as the heroic; and that Ibsen's tragic themes are constantly established in contexts of ironic appraisal. Basically, I shall try to substantiate the view that the characteristic spirit of Ibsen's work arises from a dramatic exploitation of unresolved (and possibly unresolvable) thematic tensions to which no single tragic, comic, or even, in the more conventional senses, tragicomic mode can give full expression. Ibsen's "questions," as expressions of a complex and self-contradictory apprehension of life, required an original kind of tragicomic mode, which he pioneered in the theatre, assisted, especially in the closing decades of the nineteenth century, by Strindberg and Chekhov, bringing on to the stage some of the deeply felt ambivalences which had already found expression in nineteenth-century literature, in Kierkegaard's "meditations on the hero"[3] and the fiction of Stendhal and Flaubert, for instance.

Ibsen's ambivalence is now almost a household word, but its thoroughness and the extent of its implications are as yet far from widely appreciated. As Rolf Fjelde puts it in a comparison of Ibsen and Kierkegaard in the Introduction to an anthology illustrating diverse approaches to Ibsen: "Ibsen's concrete insight as an artist puts him even more in touch than his Danish counterpart with the psychological truth of man's existence, with the fact that propositions arising out of the depths of the self can often only be expressed paradoxically, as both/and statements, rather than those either/or formulations that are logical necessities on the plane of the reason and will."[4] While I would prefer "intimations" to his "propositions" and "implications" to his "statements," Fjelde clearly states here the nature of Ibsen's work as I understand it, and implies the kind of critical debate to which this book is meant to be a contribution.

In attempting to write about Ibsen, I am very conscious of my deep indebtedness to numerous critics who have written revealingly about the multidimensional nature of Ibsen's work and about its irony and tragicomic achievements. What I offer as an appreciation of at least the general topography of Ibsen's ambivalence has taken shape substantially in response to the criticism which has already mapped out several of its major features. It is appropriate, then, to begin with a discussion of the criticism which I have found most illuminating and with some statements about the ways in which this study seeks to follow paths now clearly sign-posted and to explore other relatively uncharted areas. It is probable that no critics have written more sensitively about Ibsen's ambiguity than Hermann Weigand, Alan Reynolds Thompson, John Northam, James McFarlane, and Jens Kruuse, while Karl Guthke and, to a lesser extent, Cyrus Hoy have done much to define Ibsen's place in modern tragicomic drama. It is to these writers that I am conscious of owing most, even at those points when my own opinions take appreciative leave of theirs.

Hermann J. Weigand's *The Modern Ibsen*, first published in 1925, is brilliant in its revelation of subtle contradictions in the plays: it detects, for example, the ludicrous element in Nora Helmer's apparent regeneration as well as the possibility that Alfred Allmers, having seemingly emerged strong and spiritually renewed from his ordeals, is still a "moral crank" and a "self-deluded fraud."[5] Weigand's attention to the psychology of motive is minute and illuminating: without formulating a comprehensive theory of tragicomedy, Weigand reveals sardonic ironies in play after play, and even when he accepts a standard interpretation of a character, as he does in the case of Consul Bernick (whose spiritual emancipation he regards as endorsed by Ibsen), he asks the right questions:

> In the light of the outcome, can one refrain from feeling *all* the complications of the plot to have been engineered by heaven in support of Lona's moral crusade? Surely this harrowing tale of suspense with its idyllic sequel is not realistic drama but pious comedy![6]

There is a deficiency in Weigand's approach, however, an emphasis on ironic negation which relegates characters all too certainly to a comic arena. We do not and cannot know that, for instance, Nora, having tried "desperately hard to grow up . . . will tire of the new game . . . and revert, imperceptibly, to her role of song-bird and charmer, as affording an unlimited range to the exercise of her inborn talents of coquetry and play-acting."[7] Not only is Weigand speculating about a character in terms of action assumed to occur beyond the play itself (a Bradleyan transgression!), he is also moving Ibsen much closer towards nihilistic determinism than is actually the case. The evidence will not support Weigand's view that Ibsen himself became (quite early in his career) that aspect of his own creation, Professor Arnold Rubek, which secretly gloats over the beastliness of mankind lying beneath the dignified exteriors of his portrait busts.

Alan Reynolds Thompson's commentary on Ibsen in *The Dry Mock* (1948)[8] is perhaps the most persuasively sustained study of Ibsen's irony available. It is the concluding section of Part Four, which is itself entitled "Mockery of Ideals: Tragic Irony" and deals with Aeschylus, Sophocles, and Euripides as well as with Ibsen. The argument is that of these four, Ibsen is the most consummate ironist. Interestingly, because he describes incontrovertible and important aspects of Ibsen's literary personality as much as his actual personality, Thompson gives a description of Ibsen's temperament:

> He was shy, yet assertive; introverted, yet moved by evangelical impulses; timid and even—in a physical sense—cowardly, yet as a dramatist undaunted by the harshest criticism; thin-skinned, yet satirical; idealistic and poetic, yet keenly observant of things as they are; self-critical, yet vain; stiff and reclusive toward society, yet hungry for

love and affection; without a faith, yet deeply religious. These contraries can be ranged on two opposing sides as belonging to two antagonistic persons or natures which dwelt and fought in his soul.

Pertinently, Thompson observes that Ibsen's ironic achievement is too little regarded by the world at large, and he draws the important conclusion that Ibsen does more than employ familiar forms of dramatic irony: he does, quite definitely and consistently, what, according to Thompson, Euripides only might have done—he exploits "the irony which uses a complete dramatic action to contrast the 'surface likeness' and the hidden truth."

Like Weigand's, Thompson's analyses of particular plays are extremely revealing (his discussions of *Brand* and *The Master Builder* are especially interesting). But, also like Weigand, Thompson finally comes down heavily in favour of an unmovable cynicism in Ibsen. Brand, for instance, is convicted, all too quickly, of vanity. The failure of the Emperor Julian (whose career undeniably turns into "a nightmare of cruel tyranny") to inaugurate the "third empire" is taken *tout court* as "Ibsen's climactic failure in his search for a faith" and, as Thompson sees it, after *Emperor and Galilean*, the "realistic satirist in [Ibsen] got the upper hand and kept it for the rest of his life." Although idealistic figures still dominate the plays, their worlds, according to Thompson, are negative and hopeless: "there is no real hope of victory for them and they are usually treated with a subtle scorn (really ironic self-condemnation) because their self-seeking, as the old poet came to view it, is essentially selfish." In stressing, quite rightly, that all Ibsen's heroic idealists both climb and fall, Thompson is surely incorrect to suggest that all the deaths in Ibsen are simply indications of despair and cynicism. The negative possibilities are always there, but so, almost always, is the implication that death, like the anguish endured by the young artist in the early poem "On the Heights", may in some sense offer meaningful freedom or even an insight into the divine. In Ibsen the agonies of estrangement and the egoism of personal assertion are rarely simply condemned. To claim, therefore, that Brand is damned "for lacking love," that Nora "merely play-acts the heroine," that Solness's fall "makes a ridiculous end to a life that was never anything but false and hollow," that Allmers is simply "boastful of creative achievements but actually sterile," and that Rosmer is no more than "a feeble soul, his nobility depleted by aristocratic inbreeding" is a too restrictive reading of Ibsen's irony. In *The Wild Duck* Ibsen did not 'capitulate," allowing the victory of cynicism over idealism to become complete. Like Weigand, then, Thompson suggestively analyses aspects of Ibsen's comparatively neglected irony but represents Ibsen's world as darker than it is. Ibsen the writer is like Rubek (Thompson repeats Weigand's analogue) only if it is remembered that Rubek may ultimately achieve the redemption to which he appears, with Irene, to be ascending, a possibility which neither Weigand nor Thompson concedes.

John Northam's much more recent book, *Ibsen A Critical Study* (1973), illustrates the nature of Ibsen's ambivalence in ways substantially opposed to those of Weigand and Thompson. Emphasis is still very properly placed on motive and on the states of mind of characters, but, in his sensitive examination of the theme of the heroic quest in Ibsen, Northam concentrates, without ignoring negative factors, on the positive aspects of the ethical and spiritual orientation of Ibsen's world. There are revealing and invaluable discussions of the ways in which Ibsen offers Falk, Hedvig, Hedda, and even Alfred Allmers as representatives of a "poetry of living." The struggles towards heroism of these aspiring figures may be immature, as with Falk, inarticulate and frustrated, as with Hedda, or ironically limited, as with Allmers, but there is a positive note of hope in the treatment of these characters, a concern for civilized values which always seems to be close to the heart of Ibsen's ambivalence. Ibsen's constant battle to define the nature of and possibilities for some kind of positive and enduring human achievement rightly emerges in Northam's study as a fundamental preoccupation which is as meaningful to contemporary as to late nineteenth-century Western societies.

This study departs from Northam's general view at one crucial point, however. It is indisputably true that Ibsen is profoundly concerned with the isolation and delineation of heroic potentialities appropriate to modern life and that he examines the quest motif as "the great poet of the contradictions inherent in modern society," but it is questionable whether Ibsen moved beyond despair to the kind of "finally convinced faith" (however circumspect and unsupported by a received body of beliefs) with which Northam ultimately credits him.[9] The note of possible despair, like those of the ironies which Weigand and Thompson detect, does not cease to sound because there may be reason to rejoice in a hero's cause and possible achievement. If the approaches of Weigand and Thompson are too negative, that of Northam, though much more broadly based, is ultimately too optimistic.

James McFarlane's lecture "Meaning and Evidence in Ibsen's Drama;" given at the first International Ibsen Conference in 1965,[10] is a richly suggestive discussion of Ibsen's ambivalence. Having spoken of the complexity of Ibsen's methods of presenting evidence about characters and situations in *Pillars of Society* and *Rosmersholm*, and demonstrated how "multilateral references" affect the audience's perception of, for instance, Consul Bernick and central figures from *Rosmersholm, Hedda Gabler* and *The Lady from the Sea*, McFarlane goes on to discuss the plight of the Emperor Julian, who, at the end of the *séance* with Maximos "seems balanced in a torment of doubt and uncertainty [and who] says, half sadly, half in despair: 'Tegn imot tegn' [sign against sign]!" McFarlane reminds us that Arnholm, in *The Lady from the Sea*, in a discussion of "the commonsensical as well as the more mystical" explanations of Ellida's fascination with the Stranger, uses the same phrase. McFarlane continues, in a passage that requires full quotation, to outline the nature of Ibsen's dramatic world as

> a composite construction of signs: signs coexistent and signs successive, signs seemingly contradictory, often apparently irreconcilable, signs reliable and deceptive: 'tegn imot tegn'. These signs and references are rarely simple indices of an evident truth, but are themselves in many instances 'interpretations' of what is actually 'the case'. He who then seeks for meaning in Ibsen's drama must always be ready to allow for the deceptively deceptive nature of these signs, if his grasp of the realities of this fictive world is to be what Ibsen requires of us.

McFarlane's definition of what is meant by "the case" is broad and inclusive—"I mean the state of [Ibsen's] fictional world as it really is"—and although the lecture is substantially devoted to a demonstration that certain objective judgements about character and situation may be made once the complexity of Ibsen's method is understood (and its excitement felt), it is implicit in McFarlane's argument that there is an element of the unknowable in Ibsen, a level at which the signs not only seem to be but are ultimately "contradictory," "irreconcilable," and "deceptive." (It is notable, for instance, that in reviewing the evidence for an ironic interpretation of *Pillars of Society*, McFarlane does not summarily dismiss other, more conventional interpretations: he speaks of other possibilities, not of any one certainty.) In seeking to demonstrate something of what can be known about Ibsen's unknowableness, I am deeply indebted to McFarlane's suggestive discussion of Ibsen's complex methods of expressing possibilities.

McFarlane, in both this lecture and the richly informative introductions to *The Oxford Ibsen*, probably takes non-Scandinavian Ibsen enthusiasts as close, in thematic and dramaturgical terms, to a general awareness of the "unknowable" element in Ibsen as is possible. Further explanation of his invaluable theories is, as I shall attempt to show, both possible and necessary: his approach generously invites others to share the riches he has discovered. But there are other areas of Ibsen's successful attempt to "speak the unspeakable,"[11] in terms of language and the poetic techniques dependent upon it, which are most suitably explored by those for whom the Scandinavian languages are a birthright. Like other intrigued non-Scandinavians who have felt Ibsen's power only in Norwegian, or, more correctly, Dano-Norwegian, learned in adulthood, I can only seek to appreciate what Scandinavians themselves have done and are doing in this field. There are whole areas of Ibsen's "poetry in the theatre"[12] which, for instance, Inga-Stina Ewbank has already described,[13] and which few non-Scandinavians could fully comprehend by their own efforts. My attempts to define and discuss some of the tragicomic mysteriousness (and, on occasion, deliberate ironic mystification) in Ibsen can, at best, only complement, with inevitable inadequacies, the assessments and reassessments of Ibsen's verbal and linguistic wealth by Norwegians and their fellow Scandinavians. The theories about Ibsen's ambivalence, and unknowability, in the present study, while appreciatively profiting from such work, are usually based rather on thematic and general dramaturgical considerations. Where multiplicity of meaning is considered as expressed primarily in specific words and phrases, the present study does not go beyond what a non-Scandinavian Ibsen enthusiast might reasonably be expected to gather from a basic knowledge of Dano-Norwegian and from accessible commentaries on textual subtleties, of which Henri Logeman's profusely documented study of *Peer Gynt* is an outstanding example.[14]

Jens Kruuse's comments in his lecture "The Functions of Humour in the Later Plays of Ibsen,"[15] given at the Second International Ibsen Conference in 1970, offer a bold and subtle appreciation of Ibsen's ironic ambivalence in *Rosmersholm* and *Hedda Gabler*. Although the idea of the complete fusion of tragic and comic elements is implicit in Kruuse's argument, the lecture concentrates on the separable (though mutually reinforcing) elements of tragedy and comedy in the plays. Humour is seen as having a highly specific function in each work: "in [*Rosmersholm*] we see the great protagonists tainted by ridicule, in [*Hedda Gabler*] we see the heroine fighting back against ludicrousness—using the weapon of comedy." Ultimately, Kruuse views Hedda as triumphing over the sordidness of her life in a Dionysian suicide. Her death is a grand romantic deed, the last action of a woman whose madness, both real and apparent, is quintessential sanity (related to that of "black comedy" or of Euripides' *The Bacchae*, as Kruuse suggests). In *Rosmersholm* comedy seizes upon figures who are mock-heroic rather than heroic: "Dramaturgically this means that the two idealists are under suspicion. Their naïveté and lack of realism has been established. They are slaves of comedy. In my opinion they never escape this bondage, not even in death."

In several ways Kruuse's points of reference in relation to Ibsen's humour are very similar to my own and I particularly appreciate the distinct identities which he defines for the tragic and comic elements in Ibsen's work as well as the fusion of the two which he implies. I do not agree with Kruuse, however, that *Rosmersholm* and *Hedda Gabler* belong, in the end, in the realms of elevated tragedy: "Lofty tragedy, indeed, for I would not have anybody believe that my preoccupation with humour makes me forget the kind of plays we are talking about." It is, moreover, difficult to reconcile Kruuse's actual analysis of *Rosmersholm* with this statement, and the commitment to the idea that Hedda's death is an unquestionable triumph is one that I cannot share. Here, as in almost every other Ibsen play, ironically ambivalent action culminates in an open ending: we know only what may be. It is true that Hedda uses her sense of the ludicrous to attack her world, but as, alone and with frightful deliberateness, she determines to kill herself "beautifully" she may or may not triumph. The play asks questions about the resurrection of Dionysus in modern life rather than ascribing him undisputed rights either in Mademoiselle Diana's brothel or the retiring room of the deceased general's daughter.

Jens Kruuse's discussion of the reciprocal relationship of tragedy and comedy in Ibsen naturally directs attention to recent critical appraisals of tragicomedy as a distinct and dominant mode in literature. Ibsen, as a progenitor of this literary kind, comments occasionally—always in a cryptic and guarded fashion—on some of the attitudes which underlie it. Writing in June 1882 to his publisher, Frederik Hegel, about *An Enemy of the People*, Ibsen observes that he is unsure whether to describe the work as comedy or a *drame*: "It has many of the characteristics of comedy but it also has a serious theme."[16] In 1898, having witnessed a performance of *The Wild Duck* at the Royal Theatre in Copenhagen in which the role of Hjalmar Ekdal was interpreted in a farcical manner, Ibsen said in an interview, "It [the play] is to be tragicomedy or else Hedvig's death is incomprehensible."[17] Perhaps Ibsen's most important comment on tragicomedy, however, is the one he had made much earlier, in 1875, in the preface to the revised edition of *Catiline*: "Much that my later work concerns itself with—the conflict between one's aims and one's abilities, between what man proposes and what is actually possible, constituting at once both the tragedy and comedy of mankind and of the individual—is already vaguely intimated in this work."[18]

Karl Guthke's isolation in *Modern Tragicomedy* (1966) of a specifically modern tragicomic form and vision is invaluable. One may entertain greater reservations than Guthke himself does about whether the "complete and subtle mingling of the tragic and comic,"[19] the "synthetic phenomenon of the tragicomic"[20] is really as recent a phenomenon as Guthke argues: more attention than Guthke permits himself might be paid to such works as Euripides' *The Bacchae,* Shakespeare's *Troilus and Cressida* and, in fiction, Cervantes' *Don Quixote.* One may also share Bernard Dukore's doubts about the validity of the eight specific types of modern tragicomedy than Guthke defines (though Dukore's insistence on a single type of Ibsenian tragicomedy—one moving from clearly comic beginnings towards sardonically ambivalent endings lacking any indication of moral order—is equally suspect).[21] But it is undeniably true that once the grip of neoclassical categorization—its objection, among others, to the "mingling of kings and clowns," of "hornpipes and funerals" (in Sir Philip Sidney's conveniently concise phrases)—was loosened, a workable theory of tragicomedy, new at least in modern European drama, was free to develop.[22] Such tragicomedy is not mere mingling of modes in the manner of the Greek satyr play as exemplified by Euripides' *Cyclops* and denounced with reference to early Elizabethan drama by Sidney. Nor is it merely the irreverent intermingling of characters—gods, kings, and slaves—which had been achieved as early as Plautus'*Amphitryon*. It is not simply the tragic play with the happy ending to which, as Guthke points out, the Jesuit Pontanus (Jacobus Spanmüller) and Donatus referred in the sixteenth and seventeenth centuries respectively. Nor is it the play which turns from happiness and light-hearted ridicule to grief, which the German Jesuit, Jacob Masen, felicitously termed "comitragedy" (*'comicotragoedia'*). The whole area of tragicomedy dealt with in detail by Marvin T. Herrick in *Tragicomedy: Its Origins and Development in Italy, France and England*[23] precedes that of Guthke's concerns. According to Guthke, modern tragicomedy is foreseen, rather, by such German theorists as F. W. J. Schelling, one of whose professorial dicta in the *Philosophy of Art* (1802–3) Guthke quotes: "the mingling of opposites, that is, above all of the tragic and the comic itself, is the basic principle of modern drama."[24] Other German contributors to tragicomic theory include E. T. A. Hoffmann, Heinrich Heine, the Schlegel brothers, and, in his later years, Goethe. In France, it is, of course, Victor Hugo who champions tragicomedy in his crusading preface to *Cromwell*. Because they foreshadow so clearly what Ibsen and others, rather than what Hugo's plays themselves, achieve, Hugo's well-known but still exciting phrases are relevant here: "and the drama," Hugo proclaims, inspired by recent Shakespearian productions in Paris, "which, in the same breath, molds the grotesque and the sublime, the terrible and the absurd, tragedy and comedy—the drama is the distinguishing characteristic of the third epoch of poetry, of the literature of the present day."[25]

Guthke's essential historical point in reviewing this material is that while German and French romantics elaborated the theory of tragicomedy (very largely in response to Shakespeare), it was left to others, notably the great naturalists and expressionists, to explore its many mansions and to query the nature and existence of its deity, one of whose manifestations is undoubtedly that "savage god" whom Yeats saw as presiding over modern literature since the appearance of Jarry's *Ubu Roi*.[26] There is room in it for Strindberg's indignant anguish, for Chekhov's keenly ironic sympathies, for O'Casey's more brusquely comic humanitarianism, for Shaw's paradoxes and unrepentant didacticism, for Brecht's subtly poised doctrinal ambiguities and Pirandello's living and contradictory abstractions. But, for the nihilism expressed by Jarry himself – and by all who have, more recently, contributed to absurdism – there is room in this modern genre only to the extent that it does not destroy hope.

Guthke convincingly demonstrates that Ibsen opened the door to modern tragicomedy on the stage. And it should be added that Ibsen's contributions to the genre (which are only now beginning to be fully appreciated), though made with far fewer of the flourishes which characterize Strindberg's self-proclaiming experiments, are ultimately just as radical as those of his great Swedish contemporary. Even the most wary critic must concede that Ibsen's fondness for a portrait of the wild-eyed Strindberg (which Ibsen kept in his study) is of more than biographical importance. And surely there is a splendid joke in the fact that Ibsen's projection of himself as the careful, respectable, bourgeois gentleman, frock-coated and, on occasion, be-medalled, has pulled the wool so successfully over so many earnest critical eyes. If in Strindberg as tragicomedian the man and the author are a spectacle of disturbed inseparability, Ibsen as tragicomedian is, in one sense, like Shaw, who invented a persona to display his wares to the world. But whereas G.B.S. cavorts before us to advertise the central concerns of Shaw's plays, through rhetorical exaggeration and distortion, Ibsen's solemn Scandinavian gentleman, Herr Doktor Ibsen, is a persona devised to keep critics and audiences guessing until they have plunged sufficiently deeply into the realities and illusions of self-understanding to recognize the consummate humour of Ibsen's humanity and the inexhaustible inventiveness of his dramatic imagination.

Guthke is one of the critics whom Dr Ibsen has bamboozled much less successfully than many others (including one recent commentator who, despite a marked consciousness of Ibsen's humour, interprets his twelve last plays as dramatic renditions of the second section of Hegel's *The Phenomenology of the Mind*—a play for each successive phase of Hegel's thought, after p.258 in the definitive German edition, and all in chronological order).[27] I would like, therefore, to draw attention to particular statements by Guthke which may be taken as defining some of the critical bases of the present study. I shall attempt to show that in Ibsen's work as a whole there exist tragic and comic elements which are capable of being distinct at one level and integrated at another. As Guthke puts it: "This fusion, far from weakening the tragic and comic, strengthened each in a precarious, though thinkable union which, while preserving the identity of each, made each identical with the other."[28] A useful caveat that needs to be entered here is one of which Guthke's general theory takes account, namely, such tragicomedy neither necessitates nor requires that the tragic and comic elements be constantly integrated, or that, as distinct or fused forces, they be sustained at a constant degree of intensity. An awareness of complete duality of vision ebbs and flows both in the tragicomedies themselves and in the minds of those responding to them.

One of Guthke's statements about the nature of the tragicomic vision,

as distinct from form or forms, is also most appropriate to a consideration of Ibsen. If, like Peer Gynt, one were looking for a signpost showing
the "Master's intention," this statement points as directly as is possible
towards the heart of Ibsen's work:

> ... the tragicomedian ... lacks ... ultimate reassurance. When he
> views the comic as tragic and the tragic as comic, he is face to face with
> the questionability of the smaller or greater scheme of things and
> denies himself the firm footing that more fortunate writers have. Or
> rather: if there is one thing he is sure of, it is that this firm footing can
> only be gained temporarily and precariously, for it is constantly
> threatened. Thus, the tragicomedian, more often than not, is exposed
> to the challenge of ultimate and total meaninglessness, without, how-
> ever, necessarily falling prey to it.[29]

Critical appreciation of both tragicomic form and vision in Ibsen is
dominated, naturally but far too exclusively, by discussion of *The Wild
Duck*. A consideration of this unideal state of affairs probably provides,
therefore, a reasonable way both to point out the weaknesses in existing
theories and to make some suggestions for improvement. Ibsen, as we
have seen, refers to the play as a "tragicomedy," and Shaw, in one of his
insights into Ibsen not confined by ideological theories, asks:

> Where shall I find an epithet magnificent enough for *The Wild Duck*!
> To sit there getting deeper and deeper into your own life all the time;
> until you forget you are in a theatre; to look on with horror and pity at
> a profound tragedy, shaking with laughter all the time at an irresist-
> ible comedy; to go out, not from a diversion, but from an experience
> deeper than real life ever brings to most men, or often brings to any
> man: that is what *The Wild Duck* was like last Monday at the Globe.[30]

Fifty years later, Muriel Bradbrook comments succinctly, "One day
[*The Wild Duck*] will read as a tragedy, the next as the harshest irony."[31] In
general, however, the critical assessment of the play is surprisingly disappointing. Despite cogent, but often partial, statements of general
tragicomic theory in relation to the work, actual analysis of it tends to
concentrate too much on the interaction of its more obvious elements of
comedy and pathos. Eric Bentley's comment, made in 1947, that "in this
play the farce takes its life from the pathos, the pathos from the farce"[32]
has some basic truth (except that the term "farce" has a number of
unwanted connotations, which Ibsen himself warned against with reference to the role of Hjalmar Ekdal), but it also detracts from the importance of the ideological and genuinely tragic dimensions which co-exist
with the play's ironic comedy and pathos. Guthke observes that "pro-
claiming tragicomedy as the truly 'modern' genre is one thing; writing
one is quite another."[33] One might add that writing about tragicomedy is
also not undemanding.

11

Guthke's own analysis of the play[34] (it is the only work by Ibsen which he treats fully in his study) falls prey to the fundamental error of regarding Hjalmar as the central figure and interpreting the entire range of emotional experience in the work as embodied in Hjalmar's "mental anguish." Hjalmar's horribly mistaken and self-aggrandizing statement to Gregers Werle, shortly before Hedvig's death, of his belief that Hedvig has never loved him may, as Guthke observes, evoke "that kind of sympathy . . . [one] usually feels in great tragedy" and, simultaneously, a sense of the ludicrous. But, as I shall attempt to demonstrate, the tragicomic vision of *The Wild Duck* is not centered in the irony and pathos of Hjalmar's usually false epiphanies. Hjalmar *is* "in the center of the play," but only as part of a structure relating him and all the other major characters to basic thematic concerns. The total extent of tragicomedy in the play must be perceived in more basic association with the inconclusive ideological and spiritual battle fought by Gregers Werle and Dr. Relling in response to the kind of world-view with which Haakon Werle is most fully identified.

J. L. Styan in *The Dark Comedy* (1962) also overloads Hjalmar's feeble shoulders with a greater weight of tragicomic significance than they can bear, and he quotes Bentley's remark about farce and pathos twice in making his point. The presence of genuine and at least partially supported ideological values in the play is substantially ignored, and predictably, therefore, Styan sees *The Wild Duck* as part of a general historical process which replaces the glories of tragedy with the different and lesser virtues of a supposedly illegitimate kind of tragicomedy. In the context of his comments on the play, Styan concludes that "tragedy, 'in the full sense of the word' is missing today. Our present-day mongrel conventions, interbred with the spirit of naturalism, can better do other things . . ."[35] Tragicomedy, as discussed by Styan, is characterized by "the uncertainty and the whimper of the ending of Jean Cocteau's Oedipus story, *The Infernal Machine*".[36] A spirit of "moral indifference" supposedly submerges established tragic values, which are viewed, all too simply, as arising from "a world which is religious in its affirmation of human greatness."[37] These assumptions about tragedy now sound as weary as Styan's notions about naturalism and tragicomedy. Suspension of moral judgement is usually more apparent than real in naturalistic work, and undoubted moral indifference is hard to find even in the work of many absurdists, whose attacks on all forms of conventional ethics are themselves an expression of moral energy. Expressionistic tragicomedy such as Strindberg's *The Ghost Sonata* or O'Casey's *Cock-a-Doodle-Dandy* is written out of moral and spiritual passion which is not rendered ridiculous by comparisons with the works of antiquity. In *The Wild Duck* itself, which, like the plays just mentioned, has a strange bird at its centre, Ibsen is not less concerned with moral values than elsewhere, though his concern expresses itself in a degree of ambivalence found only in his greatest work.

Styan's disdainful image of naturalism as a stray dog siring artistic modes of who knows what lack of pedigree, invites some statement on my own use of the term, because an understanding of its positive connotations is a *sine qua non* for the interpretation of much of Ibsen's tragicomedy.

No one, unfortunately, has done more harm to the reputation of naturalism than Zola, who yet attempted the most outspoken statement of its theory. What the literary world has tended to remember most clearly about Zola's theorizing in *Le Roman expérimental* and *Le Naturalisme au théâtre* is his insistence on verisimilitude and analogues such as that between the author and a note-taker busily recording "reality" without regard for form. But Zola confuses matters by implying, on the one hand, that naturalistic art has no form in a conventional sense and, on the other, that it somehow manages to derive form from the very accuracy of its records of the author's perspectives of life itself. As one might expect, this stance invites and has received a thoroughly hostile reception from those who consider realism of any kind suspect. T. S. Eliot, who feared that since "Kyd, since *Arden of Faversham,* since *The Yorkshire Tragedy,*" there had been "no form to arrest, so to speak, the flow of spirit" in English drama,[38] and who declared that "realistic drama . . . is drama striving steadily to escape the conditions of art,"[39] has influenced numerous critics of Ibsen to think of his "realism" and his "naturalism" as kinds of anti-art. Raymond Williams, in a book owing much to Eliot, puts the matter succinctly when he declares: "Ibsen was a great artist, working in a tradition which was acutely inimical to art,"[40] and "lack of a mature form . . . was Ibsen's greatest weakness."[41]

What I mean by the term "naturalism" is not a form of writing nor a denial of form: I mean a set of attitudes which, taken together, do much to distinguish the non-theistic, non-metaphysical writing which appeared in the nineteenth century. It is distinct in its very expression of these secular attitudes from much of the writing which preceded it, was contemporaneous with it, or has succeeded it. The attitudes to which I refer combine their secularity with an interest in psychology (whether of individuals—in which case the mythopoeic capacity of characters may well be emphasized—or of social groups) and in aspects of physiology which have a determining influence on psychology (the physiology of adolescence and of ageing, for example). An ironic perspective is likely to define itself in relation to established character types (conventional kinds of hero, for instance). And, though not necessarily amoral, such naturalistic attitudes preclude the acceptance of all kinds of fixed or facile ethics, and thus move the works in which they are expressed closer to moral relativism.

13

In his naturalism Ibsen is close to Chekhov, who wrote to his brother, Alexander, that though the stereotyped villains and angels of contemporary drama were repugnant to him, he continued to cherish a fondness for its clowns.[42] Ibsen's mature naturalism is, in fact, invested with kinds of irony and pathos which were perhaps to some extent shaped by knowledge (derived possibly through Georg Brandes's study of the great French novelist) of Flaubert[43] and which are certainly close to the similar achievements in all Chekhov's major plays. The pity for humanity and the fierce indignation which together distinguish Strindberg's naturalistic plays—especially *Miss Julie* and *The Father*—are also present in Ibsen's naturalism. I am therefore writing of naturalism not as a set of techniques, or an absence of technique, but essentially as an approach to life combining such certainties as empirical science can offer and much of what might be termed "the courage to doubt" in other areas of experience. As will be demonstrated, such naturalism, far from being inimical to poetry, is associated with the expression, in fiction as well as in drama, of modern tragicomic perspectives.

Clearly these views are at odds with those of critics who see naturalism (in terms of both vision and technique) at one end of a continuum and poetry, complexity and sublimity at the other. Perhaps the best recent example of this in Ibsen criticism is Orley Holtan's *Mythic Patterns in Ibsen's Last Plays* (1970), where an enduring and endorsed metaphysic is seen as operating in all of Ibsen's plays (though "displaced" in the realistic works) and as totally inseparable from Ibsen's poetry.[44] Such opinions, in my view, make a full appreciation of the dramatic poetry in *The Wild Duck, Rosmersholm* and *Hedda Gabler*, for instance, impossible. In these plays the assertion of naturalism is more complete than elsewhere in Ibsen, though even in them its triumph is not absolute—possibilities for the victory of the will in its conflict with "scientific" determinism remain and preserve the ultimate openness of Ibsen's vision. This is true of all the plays written during the most obviously non-metaphysical phase of Ibsen's writing, which includes most of the works written after *Emperor and Galilean* (1873) and before *The Master Builder* (1892).

Cyrus Hoy's analysis of *The Wild Duck* in *The Hyacinth Room* (1964), though fundamentally influenced by the bogey of anti-naturalistic critical theory, is an important contribution to the interpretation of Ibsen's tragicomedy.[45] Hoy rightly finds "the clue to . . . the tragicomic quality [of *The Wild Duck*] . . . in the character of Gregers Werle" and forcefully demonstrates from the play both "tragedy that involves more than the usual amount of waste" and the tragicomedy of "illusions and delusions." Hoy's analysis suffers from its acknowledged biases, however. Since in *The Hyacinth Room* Hoy sets out to demonstrate how a comedy of serene reconciliation, invested with the sublimity of some medieval expressions of the comic spirit, emerges in works as far apart in time as Shakespeare's

The Winter's Tale and *The Tempest*, on the one hand, and Strindberg's *Easter* and *To Damascus*, on the other, he regards the moral and spiritual dimensions of *The Wild Duck* as too certainly partial and unfulfilling. Hoy rightly observes that "comedy, tragedy and tragicomedy are concerned with deviations from the ideal—any ideal" and certainly "when the ideal is fulfilled and the human aspirations to it are found to square at last with the grand conception, then the protagonist of drama has entered the kingdom of heaven." But Hoy's belief that "worldly truth" is bound to be inferior, lacking the "blessing" which accompanies "truth of a supramundane sort" is, however attractive to some, open to contention by agnostics and denial by atheists, both of whom, for better or worse, share the modern world with Hoy and his fellow metaphysicians. Ibsen would surely agree with Hoy that knowledge of truth which has no necessary reference to a transcendental order "may or may not compensate for the loss of cherished illusions." But the certain lack of any endorsed metaphysic in *The Wild Duck* does not so definitely preclude the attainment of lasting and significantly redemptive truths as Hoy argues.

The importance of Hoy's commentary on the play as tragicomedy lies ultimately in the scope he defines for its themes. He reminds us that its range of human concern is vast. There is much more here than a nice balance of limited ironies and pathos, and more than a dramatic rendition of Dr Relling's theories about "life-lies" brought off with Scribean finesse. *The Wild Duck* is closer to *King Lear* than to Scribe's *A Glass of Water,* as is implicit in Hoy's judgement that "[Gregers] might say with Shakespeare's Cordelia, another truth-teller . . . 'We are not the first/ Who with best intentions have incurr'd the worst.' " Ibsen's tragicomedy whether charged with metaphysical significance, as in *Peer Gynt* or *When We Dead Awaken*, or apparently bereft of it, as in *Rosmersholm* and *Hedda Gabler*, nearly always has expansive horizons and depth below depth of meaning.

If the full implications of the tragicomic form and vision of *The Wild Duck* still invite further interpretation, it is also noticeable that only a fraction of Ibsen's other work has been more than marginally considered as tragicomedy in terms similar to Guthke's. Irony, if not fully fledged tragicomedy, has been detected in *Love's Comedy, Emperor and Galilean, An Enemy of the People, Hedda Gabler,* and *Little Eyolf*, but both these and other plays tend to be regarded finally in other, non-ironic ways, as though Ibsen's humour, even where it undeniably exists, is a detachable commodity which may be referred to and shelved while other matters are discussed. Such attitudes seem to underlie, for instance, G. Wilson Knight's insistence that Ibsen never wrote the comedy of which some isolated characters give evidence of his ability to do so,[46] and John Northam's surprising affirmation that "Ibsen's humour, though genuine, is never very complicated."[47] And while Guthke, for instance,

15

mentions (without elaboration) *Emperor and Galilean* and *Little Eyolf* as being tragicomic, he regards *Hedda Gabler* as tragicomic "only in a minor key,"[48] and he includes *The Master Builder* in a list of "bona fide tragedies."[49] Styan detects a balance of tragic and comic impulses in *An Enemy of the People*,[50] though he finds in the work neither true tragedy nor true comedy (the preoccupation with pedigree is again apparent in Styan's thinking), but *The Master Builder* "is wholly tragic."[51] Like other critics, Styan is doubtful about the value of the humour he detects in Ibsen. Describing him as "the most sober of modern dramatists in many ways," Styan writes, for instance, that in *Pillars of Society, A Doll's House, Ghosts*, and *An Enemy of the People*, "the subjects are presented in terms of a simple conflict between an individualist on the one hand, and the community with its codes of behaviour on the other."[52] He comments that there is a "degree of satire" in these works, but regards it as unrelated to Ibsen's central concerns: it is the psychology of the "grimmer side of the problems" with which Ibsen is supposedly concerned, and though Pastor Manders, for instance, is a "comic butt," the laughter which Manders may provoke in performance is essentially "unwanted", not in keeping with the "vital and tragic slant of the play."[53] Hoy perceptively, though without elaboration, mentions *When We Dead Awaken* as an indication of the "tragicomic nature of human experience . . . most poignantly defined in *The Great Highway*."[54] But he emphasizes the tragic element in his brief references to *Rosmersholm, The Master Builder*, and *John Gabriel Borkman*, and he mentions *Little Eyolf* as an example of the sublime comedy of "rebirth . . . deliverance from past sin and error," of the "comedy that lies beyond tragedy."[55]

Perhaps it would not be an exaggeration to suggest that Ibsen criticism has been adversely affected by uncertain responses to Ibsen's humour in the theatre. Most productions of *The Master Builder*, for example, continue to be generally solemn; not even the Norwegian theatre itself is free from this exaggerated solemnity, as Otto Homlung's production of *Byggmester Solness* demonstrated in Bergen in 1975. In Regina, in 1965, an interesting production of *Rosmersholm*, directed by Eric Salmon, was fascinatingly infected by the ironic humour generated by an excellent portrayal of Ulrik Brendel. But the director did not actually regard Brendel's humour as the clue to the entire relationship of Rosmer and Rebecca, and the tragicomic spirit of the work emerged substantially in defiance of unambiguously romantic portrayals of Rosmer and Rebecca. It is only quite recently that in both England and North America some of the supposed heavyweights among the later plays—such as *Rosmersholm, The Master Builder*, and *John Gabriel Borkman*—have begun to appear in repertoire with, or (by at least apparent design) during the same theatrical seasons as, the works of Beckett, Albee, and Pinter. As a result, the lines of comic and tragicomic connection between Ibsen and these playwrights are beginning, as in the right circumstances they inevitably will, to emerge. The sound of an audience laughing, in the right places and without embarrassment, during Peter Hall's National Theatre production of *John Gabriel Borkman* in 1975 (when Ralph Richardson was, almost miraculously, playing Borkman and Hirst in Pinter's *No Man's Land* in the Theatre's current repertory), was music which the real Ibsen, as distinct from his staid persona, would surely have appreciated.

The time seems to have arrived when both criticism and the international theatre are ready to discover Ibsen the tragicomedian. The fundamental truth of Ibsen's remark in the preface to the second edition of *Catiline*—that life itself is tragedy and comedy at the same time ("tragedie og comedie på engang")[56]—is becoming more clear and is no longer treated as merely an interesting statement for academic contemplation. And it is basically important that the National Theatre production of *John Gabriel Borkman* arose from one of those rare partnerships between a scholar and a director who share the knowledge and expertise to bring on to the stage a dramatic work as subtle in literary as in theatrical terms.[57] If ever there has been a dramatist the successful interpretation of whose work demands the particular skills of the literary critic and those of the expert in theatrical techniques, that dramatist is Ibsen.

Whenever the dramatic poetry of his work is fully revealed, it is evident that in Ibsen's tragicomic world there are certain constants and at least an equal number of variables. The constants are an element of ethical or spiritual appraisal, kinds of dramatic tension which are rooted in that appraisal, and the juxtaposition of a heroic with an equally powerful mock-heroic vision. Variables include the presence or absence of a metaphysical dimension, a dominating or comparatively minor concern with social issues, and realistic or anti-realistic techniques.

The crucial importance of ethical appraisal in Ibsen's work was, of course, recognized by a number of contemporaneous critics. And, in writing about it, Georg Brandes and Bernard Shaw, for instance, were much less narrow in their interpretations of Ibsen's moral concerns than are many subsequent critics. Brandes, writing in 1882,[58] comments, "Ibsen is by nature a polemic," and "His mode of apprehension is not the purely scientific one of the observer: it is that of the moralist." Referring to the ethical bases of Ibsen's approach (and it must be remembered that he was writing when *Ghosts* was Ibsen's latest work), Brandes writes of "a whole group of topics and ideals that revolve about distinctions between the two sexes, about the mutual erotic and social relation of man and woman, especially about woman's economical, moral and spiritual emancipation." But Brandes notes also, in a comparison of Ibsen and Kierkegaard, that "there [is] in [Ibsen's] nature a dual tendency, which must necessarily expose him to inner tumults: a native propensity to mysticism and an equally inbred inclination to sharp, dry common sense." Shaw, in his much slighted *The Quintessence of Ibsenism* (1913), emphasizes Ibsen's moral responsibility.[59] He informs us, with reference to Ibsen's ethical values, that "the whole point to be settled is Guilty or Not Guilty." But Shaw also speaks forcefully about Ibsen's "vigilant open-mindedness," pointing out, for instance, the unlikelihood that "the cases of Nora and Mrs. Elvsted are meant to establish a golden rule for women who wish to be 'emancipated,' the said golden rule being simply, Run away from your husband." And he observes, with regard to Ibsen's ethical preoccupations that "the quintessence is that there is no formula."

Both Brandes and Shaw are as aware of one kind of poetry which springs from Ibsen's struggle with ethics as they are of the "duality" or "open-mindedness" of the expression of that struggle itself. Brandes writes that "Ibsen shares with Kierkegaard the conviction that in every single human being there slumbers the soul of a warrior." Brandes overstates the case here, for though he wrote before Ibsen demonstrated how little of the Viking spirit slumbers in the souls of Hjalmar Ekdal or Rosmer, for example, he could have contemplated its ironic absence in the characters of Julian Poulsen, in *Saint John's Night*, or in those of Hilmar Tönnesen or Jacob Engstrand. But Brandes's general claim about the ethical basis of Ibsen's poetry is, despite its too confident optimism, generally correct:

> To extricate the race from "Böjgen's" [sic] stifling embrace, to capture the spirit of compromise, force it into a casket and hurl it into the deepest part of the sea,—this is the goal at which Ibsen, as a poet, has aimed.

Quoting Ibsen's letter to himself (of 20 December 1870), which contains the famous battle-cry "What is needed is a revolution of the human spirit," Brandes observes, "I have never been able to forget these words; for they contain, in a measure, Ibsen's entire poetic programme." Similarly Shaw sees Ibsen as a visionary engaged in the dramatization of spiritual struggles which reveal not one but many evolving truths: "He is on the side of the prophets in having devoted himself to showing that the spirit of Man is constantly outgrowing ideals." Halvdan Koht's definitive biography quotes Ibsen's famous epigrammatic verse:

> *Life*—a war with demons
> waged in the caverns of our hearts and minds.
> *Poetry*—that is to hold
> doomsday judgement over ourselves.[60]

And continues with the comment: "[Ibsen's] inner struggle forged drama out of poetic insights. The conflicts and contradictions he felt took shape as the characters he sent into battle, actually on his own behalf."

These views are now, very properly, firmly entrenched in Ibsen criticism, despite the jaded attempts of H. L. Mencken and Mary McCarthy, for instance, to prove that Ibsen's ideas are either dead as doornails[61] or as disagreeable as a "confessional closet-smell" to those who prefer not to think of sin,[62] and the reluctance of some critics to conceive of moral issues in literature as in any way central to its appreciation. If, largely owing to the pioneering efforts of John Northam, we now know that Ibsen's remark that "to be a poet is to see" refers in part at least to "poetry of the theatre,"[63] Ibsen scholarship is also realizing that Ibsen's "poetry *in* the theatre" is inevitably related to the enduring ethical and spiritual values in his work. He doubted—or questioned—everything in order perhaps that others might eventually affirm, and the courage of his humane doubting is the ultimate source of all his poetry. And if Brandes and Shaw were sometimes too eager to interpret Ibsen's vision in over-simplified ways, at least they recognized its poetic intensity and its final openness.

What I have referred to as a third constant in Ibsen's work—the juxtaposition of heroic and mock-heroic visions—will not be surprising in view of what has already been said about tragicomedy and naturalism, but it is essential to stress that there is a crucial difference between Ibsen's mock-heroism and the more obvious anti-heroism of the naturalistic and post-naturalistic traditions. It seems almost certain, as I have observed earlier, that Ibsen knew of Georg Brandes's account of Flaubert as an outstanding nineteenth-century depicter of the anti-hero,[64] but in Ibsen's works themselves, the anti-hero occurs only rarely, and the two best examples of the type (Julian Poulsen of *Saint John's Night* and Bishop Nicholas of *The Pretenders*) occur long before Brandes's description of Flaubert's achievements in this line. It is possible that Brandes's theories influenced Ibsen's conception of characters in *The Wild Duck,* but even in that work, as almost everywhere else, Ibsen is concerned primarily, at least, not with the anti-hero (as, for instance, Weigand and Thompson would have it) but with the possible mock-hero: the figure who half convinces himself (or herself) and us that it is possible for him to carry through some mighty endeavour and who appears to fail lamentably in its execution. The fundamental point is that the causes which these would-be heroes espouse are themselves rarely discredited by those who lose or seem to lose so ignominiously. Writing to Georg Brandes in 1871, Ibsen pictures the aspiring heroes of the past and present as having succumbed to the histrionic delights of role-playing: they lack the humility of the true workman, who would dedicate himself unremittingly to tasks which seem inglorious, even prosaic:

> All of human history reminds me of a cobbler who doesn't stick to his last but goes on the stage to act. And we have made a fiasco in both the roles of hero and lover. The only part in which we have shown a little talent is that of the naive comic; and with our more highly developed self-consciousness we shall no longer be fitted even for that.[65]

19

The territory of Ibsen's juxtaposed heroism and mock-heroism lies between that of a devoted shoemaker and that of the young artist who, with frightful egotism and inhumanity, contemplates the possibility of supposed spiritual freedom in the early poem *On the Heights*. The range of significances to which the mock-heroic aspects of Ibsen's aspiring figures may be related is immense, but the causes defined in their careers are rarely finally discredited, just as it is very difficult, if not impossible, to decide whether numerous Ibsen protagonists are, in fact, ultimately heroic or mock-heroic. And in this Ibsen's fully tragicomic figures differ fundamentally from that whole line of anti-heroes from Stendhal's Julien Sorel to Ionesco's Bérenger, from Flaubert's Madame Bovary to Mrozek's Arthur or Stomil. Ibsen presents us with only one or two figures (Haakon in *The Pretenders* and Borghejm in *Little Eyolf*) who actually achieve the wondrously delicate balance between the lofty detachment of the artist in "On the Heights" and the down-to-earth humanity of a cobbler who would stick to his last. Like the tramps in *Waiting for Godot*, Ibsen's would-be heroes very often wear shoes they could not have made for themselves and which are several sizes too large, but they stumble, only half ridiculously, towards dizzy heights where their feet may find some uncertain purchase. Even when they are most like Vladimir and Estragon, they are not altogether unlike Oedipus (the ironic image of whose wounded feet the myth and Sophocles exploit) or Hamlet.

The choice of plays for this study is intended to illustrate clearly the principal features of Ibsen's tragicomic world. I hope to show that Peer Gynt is the most comprehensively contradictory of Ibsen's tragicomic figures: he goes out to do real or imaginary battle in worlds shaped by, for instance, Ibsen's knowledge of Kierkegaard, Lutheran pietism and Goethe on the one hand and by, for example, Ibsen's response to Taine and Darwin and contemporary archeological theory on the other. The play's changes of mood and technique, which are astounding and abrupt, will be discussed as foreshadowing the realism, expressionism and romantic sublimity of Ibsen's later work. In dealing, in the second chapter, with *Ghosts* as the most profound but least technically unified of the plays from *Pillars of Society* to *An Enemy of the People*, my emphasis will be upon Ibsen's exploration of the credibility of some contemporary ideological theories through the presentation of tragicomic figures perceived in a not entirely successful realistic manner. The third chapter will discuss *The Wild Duck* as Ibsen's consummate naturalistic tragicomedy. In the final chapter, *The Master Builder* will be considered as representative of the spirit and methods of the last four plays, each of which works, in its particular way, to accomplish Ibsen's late reassessment of the hero (man and superman) in the light of renewed though diffuse metaphysical concerns. This selection of plays also, and for my purposes, most illuminatingly, illustrates the principal modes of Ibsen's "vigilant open-mindedness": in large things as in small, in terms of theme, technique, and every meaningful detail of his work, these plays show Ibsen's remarkable and possibly unique capacity to look life in the face, to listen to its many plausible explanations of itself with humour and humanity, but ultimately to say neither yea nor nay to even the question whether life or art themselves have ultimate meaning.

It is probably evident, from what has been said so far, that in this study Ibsen's plays will be considered not only as isolated units capable, as indeed most of them are, of standing alone, free of any dependence on external factors—such as those which emerge from the treatment of the same or similar motifs in numerous Ibsen plays. Ibsen himself was conscious of having created an entire body of work of which all the individual plays are constituent parts. He stressed this towards the end of his active life when, in 1898, he advised his readers, in a prefatory note to Danish and German editions of his collected works, as follows:

> Only by grasping and comprehending my entire production as a continuous and coherent whole will the reader be able to receive the precise impression I sought to convey in the individual parts of it.[66]

Quite apart from what has become known as the "intentionalist fallacy", such an injunction may be unwelcome to the critic who prefers, on perfectly respectable academic grounds, to judge plays solely as independent units: unwelcome or not, however, a statement such as this from Ibsen himself about his own plays is neglected only with considerable loss. To take an instance of the kind of loss I refer to, one might single out the light thrown on the significance of the "castle" motif in *The Master Builder* by the names "Lövborg" ("Leafcastle") in *Hedda Gabler* (which immediately precedes *The Master Builder*) and "Borghejm" ("Castlehome") in *Little Eyolf* (which immediately follows *The Master Builder*). Lövborg does not establish his Dionysian ideal, though the play implies that the fault is society's (and Hedda's) at least as much as his, so the implication of the "castle" element of his name and nature remain positive. Borghejm, at the end of *Little Eyolf*, seems set fair to establish a home on a castle-like foundation of love and integrity. When we discover that Solness and Hilde are committed to "castles in the air"—and that *The Master Builder*, as a whole, centers on the motifs of "home", "foundations", and "Dionysian dreams"—the connections begin to make themselves, whether we wish them to do so or not. In theory, the argument against the investigation of such cross-references is strong; in practice, however, knowing how Ibsen went to work—and feeling, as one does after long acquaintance with the plays, how extensively they really do interpenetrate and illuminate each other—I have decided to take Ibsen's advice. Any loss, if it is more than theoretical, of critical focus is susceptible, I would suggest, to analytical readjustment and is, I believe, more than made up for by the sense gained of closeness to a great imagination at work.

2

Peer Gynt: Journeys into Uncertainty

Not surprisingly, in the case of a play of such immense complexity, it is not difficult to assemble widely divergent interpretations of *Peer Gynt*. On the one hand, the play has been positively interpreted—by Philip H. Wicksteed[1] and Trevor H. Davies,[2] for example, as a Christian morality; by Muriel Bradbrook,[3] G. Wilson Knight,[4] and F. L. Lucas,[5] among others, as a celebration of romantic love; and by Horst Bien[6] as a hymn to social revolution. On the other hand, Peer is seen negatively by Georg Brandes, who views him as the central figure in a world characterized by "contempt for humanity and self-hatred,"[7] an opinion close to the revulsion felt by another and notorious early critic, Clemens Petersen.[8] Recently, James McFarlane has seen Peer as one who, in terms of the Hebbelian "life process' (*Lebensprozess*) fails to find his true self and is damned by his own illusions.[9] Rolf Fjelde, in one of the most important recent analyses of the play, sees Peer, finally, in a Kierkegaardian light: "Here [in Act V] certainly is one of the earliest and most arresting images of the new existential picture of man as simply the history of his acts, an inventory of roles abandoned, of selves outlived and discarded."[10] None of these representative interpretations is unsupported by the play or untrue to aspects of its spirit: they are, rather, valid commentaries on parts of a whole, on elements of the network of contradictions which lies at the heart of the play and defies all unilinear interpretations, however subtle. The play will respond, for instance, to Christian, Marxist, Freudian, and existentialist theories, but it is not fully comprehensible within the terms of any univocal theory. As one of the most comprehensive expressions of Ibsen's "vigilant open-mindedness,"[11] which includes, of course, an openness of emotion and spirit, the play begins and continues as an evocation of a tragicomic enigma: what value does life have once traditional beliefs have become questionable and attempts to find alternatives seem at least as likely to increase as to remove confusion? It asks Ibsen's fundamental questions about the value of the individual, about his social, moral, and spiritual commitments, and about his capacity to perceive and evaluate many kinds of possible truth. Though its satire disposes of a world of hypocrisies, the play concentrates ever more emphatically on its central psychological and metaphysical preoccupations, yet always without providing certain answers. Peer achieves no clear triumph; neither is he irredeemably condemned. His final value is as much subject to doubt as that of all those about him—the people, trolls, birds, beasts and supernatural personages who share his world and attempt to shape it with their own versions of reality. Peer himself is no mere aesthete, as is sometimes claimed: he is the greatest doubter of all, not in the sense of a Hamlet paralysed by scrupulous indecision or a Macbeth unable to reconcile his conscience to a dreadful deed (as Henri Logeman suggests[12]), but in the sense of one who explores almost every possibility for heroic achievement which his world provides, and finds them or himself wanting. He is also a considerable ironist in his own right, who may be finally heroic precisely because his philosophic explorations are sufficiently wide-ranging and profound to demonstrate that life itself may (but only may) lack any ultimate meaning. His humour may, in the end, be the greatest redemptive force in the work. As he examines, through one tragicomic experience after another, many plausible interpretations of life, Peer, unlike so many of Ibsen's other protagonists, is only too eager not to take himself too seriously, to laugh at his own real or apparent ridiculousness as well as at that of the world around him. He is a liar, a self-deceiver, and, at times, a conscious hypocrite, but he is also, and above all, a poet who cannot deny his vocation, however hard he tries. His imagination, specifically Norwegian but also representative of modern humanity in general, encompasses many of the most intractable difficulties of modern experience. Unwillingly possessed by a kind of typical nineteenth-century high seriousness and a complementary obsession to mock everything it represents, Peer drives himself on from one seemingly abortive quest for truth to another until finally the most terrifying invention of his own imagination, the Button-Moulder, awaits him like a parody of the Wordsworthian child's world come to haunt the man, with a summons of doubtful authority at a crossroads the whereabouts of which are unknown and which lead to unknowable destinations.

It is, of course, no accident that the play opens with a verbal duel between a son and his mother. Like the relationships between parent and child in, for instance, *Lady Inger of Ostraat, Ghosts,* and *Little Eyolf,* that of Åse and Peer is a central human and dramatic reality, and from it everything else in the play, including the apparently sublime love of Peer and Solveig, derives its origin and thematic meaning. The first great lyrical outburst in the work, Peer's wonderfully exhilarating account to his mother of his reindeer ride along Gendin Edge, both establishes the psychological dimensions of this particular parent–child attachment and surveys, in dramatic and poetic terms, the wider horizons of psychological, social, and metaphysical perceptions with which the play is also concerned.

Peer has been away in the mountains for more than a month "in the busiest season." Like the young man in "On the Heights", or Alfred Allmers in *Little Eyolf*, he has experienced, or says he has experienced, a wondrous epiphany, and, real or imaginary, it will determine his life and attitudes for the rest of the time that we are to see him, poised at indeterminate points between reality, mundane or mystical, and fantasy, delusive or illuminating. But while he has been rapt in visions, Åse has endured an agony of anxiety about him and everything for which he is responsible—a once splendid house falling ever more certainly into ruins (just as, figuratively, Rosmersholm does), earth untilled and clogged with salt (one thinks of Rosenvold before Helene Alving assumed the management of the estate), and marriage prospects seemingly laid waste. She demands to know by what right he dreams his life away when starvation stares them in the face and hostile neighbours exult in their humiliation. She confronts him with his duties:

> Don't you blush before your mother?
> First, you skulk among the mountains
> Monthlong in the busiest season,
> Stalking reindeer in the snows;
> Home you come then, torn and tattered,
> Gun a-missing, likewise game;—
> And at last, with open eyes,
> Think to get me to believe
> All the wildest hunters' lies!—

But, despite herself, she is caught up by Peer's excitement—"Well, where did you find the buck, then?"

In launching into his account, Peer begins in a factual manner. He found the buck "west near Gendin"; he was downwind of it, hidden in a clump of alders, and saw it scraping the snow, looking for moss. He heard the "crunching of his hoof" and observed "the branches of one antler." He stalked it on his belly and admired the sleekness of his prey with a hunter's appraising eye. He fired and wounded the buck, and when he leapt astride the creature to kill it, the marvellous ride began:

> I sat firm astride his back,
> Gripped him by the left ear tightly,
> And had almost sunk my knife-blade
> In his neck, behind his skull—
> When, behold! The brute screamed wildly,
> Sprang upon his feet like lightning,
> With a back-cast of his head
> From my fist made knife and sheath fly,
> Pinned me tightly by the thigh,

Jammed his horns against my legs,
Clenched me like a pair of tongs;—
Then forthwith away he flew
Right along the Gendin-Edge!

Åse's interruption, "Jesus save us" ("Jesu navn da") is, at the level of
immediate effect, simply a realistic expletive; but mentions of God, like
references to trolls, are never ultimately simple in *Peer Gynt*. Åse, unlike
many other characters, has a residual Christian faith. It is natural for her
both to call idiomatically on God and to turn to Him when in distress. It is
uncertain, however, whether Åse, Peer, or any one else may be saved by
Him and equally uncertain whether He or any other deity hears or cares
about the play's many prayers, oaths, and blasphemies.
  Peer is now caught up in his own vision:

Have you ever
Chanced to see the Gendin-Edge?
Nigh on four miles long it stretches
Sharp before you like a scythe.

It is a world of "glaciers, landslips, screes." As in *Brand* and *When We Dead
Awaken*, the landscape itself is dominated by frightening transitions, the
wonder of mighty and unthinkable forces. The whole account is full of
that "frightfully thrilling" spiritual agitation to which that other young
mountain climber and dangerous visionary, Hilde Wangel of *The Master
Builder*, responds. The buck carries Peer along the knife-edge ridge
where reflected suns glitter blindingly and from which "brown-backed
eagles" are fleetingly seen "sailing/In the wide and dizzy void." Giant
ice-floes crash on shores far below but cannot be heard as "sprites of
dizziness" (Ibsen himself assisted Archer with the translation of this
phrase[13]) envelop both rider and mount. A "great cock-ptarmigan" is
started up by the buck's hectic feet, and then, having faltered, the buck
leaps "sky high" before he and Peer plunge down towards the only
apparent permanence in this fabulous world:

Mountain walls behind us, black,
And below a void unfathomed!
  First we clove through banks of mist,
Then we clove a flock of sea-gulls,
So that they, in mid-air startled,
Flew in all directions, screaming.
  Downward rushed we, ever downward.
But beneath us something shimmered,
Whitish, like a reindeer's belly.—
Mother, 'twas our own reflection
In the glass-smooth mountain tarn,
Shooting up towards the surface
With the same wild rush of speed
Wherewith we were shooting downwards.

. . .

> Buck from over, buck from under,
> In a moment clashed together,
> Scattering foam-flecks all around.

But the outcome, like those of the deaths of Brand and of Rubek and Irene, or that of Solness's dreadful death plunge, is in doubt. Peer, seen here as the poet he is, is seemingly incapable of differentiating between truth and falsehood in both life and the creations of his imagination:

> . . . at last we made our way
> Somehow to the northern shore;
> Swam the buck, I clung behind him:—
> I ran homewards—

Man and beast are physically separated, but just as the buck may be "there still" for anything that Peer knows, Peer himself will never again be free from the dizzy inspiration of his real or supposed fall.

When he talks with his mother, Peer's feet are apparently on firmer ground. He is shortly to begin attempting to solve his domestic problems, to drive towards solutions of the economic and social difficulties with which Åse is obsessed. He concedes that all that he has said about the reindeer ride has been foreshadowed in one of the folk-tales—that concerning Gudbrand Glesne—which everyone in Gudbrandsdal has known for years;[14] it is similar to other stories in which he and Åse have long taken refuge from reality. But Peer's response to his mother's outraged taunts is not shame or contrition; instead he attempts to console her with another heroic tale (this one rooted in an actual and recent experience)—that of his fight with Aslak the Smith. He is content to be either winner or loser to suit Åse's mood, but finds that neither of his versions of the fight is acceptable. Before laughing, he tells Åse

> Though I hammer or am hammered,—
> Still we must have lamentations.

The social and psychological implications of this scene are plain: they constitute the obvious dramaturgical reasons for its existence and place in the play. Åse cannot forget her degradation, and she still hopes that Peer, "devil's story-teller" as he is, will restore the Gynt family name to the glory that Peer's grandfather and father knew. It is true, as Åse herself later admits, that she and Peer have willingly occupied a dream world, like that of Soria Moria Castle, to which Åse rides in death, but she cannot quite abandon hope that Peer will acquire "so much sense/One day, as to do the darning/Of [his] breeches" and confront, like the devoted shoemaker Ibsen seems to have in mind in a letter to Brandes,[15] the struggle for survival on its own terms.

Broader contexts of perception are, however, just as clearly defined in this opening scene. They are especially emphatic in Peer's account of the reindeer ride. Every detail of this fantastic excursion beyond everyday reality foreshadows what is to come. The play is structured upon a series of long or brief rides and journeys, explorations, and sudden encounters. Many of these voyages of discovery contain fantastic animals or personages drawn from Nordic or Germanic folklore and literature, ancient myth, and Biblical legend. They all take place in situations deeply imbued with spiritual significance and eschatological judgement. Peer again rides the knife-edge between reality and delusion with, for instance, Granë, the legendary horse that pulls Åse's sleigh to an eternity of material comfort and respectability. Together with the Woman in Green he mounts a pig to ride into the Troll King's palace, bragging that the great may be known by their riding-gear. With Anitra, in an ecstasy of lustful yearnings, he mounts the "milk-white charger" of an Arabic sheik, while his encounters with the Boyg, the Statue of Memnon, the Sphinx, the Thin Man, and the Button-Moulder are all expressions of the motif of the spiritual journey. And, though the analogue presents itself gradually, it is eventually apparent that Peer's journey, like the Stranger's in Strindberg's *To Damascus*, has its stations on the way to some kind of Crucifixion.

Like the Gendin-Edge mountainscape, the entire spiritual topography of *Peer Gynt* is permeated with impermanence, with transitions from one uncertainty to another, with real or apparent approaches to seemingly unknowable truths. The separation of Peer and the buck (both of whose identities are in doubt) is associated through iterated imagery with the final separation of "the sheep from the goats" to which Peer refers in Act V, and the most basic thematic concern throughout the work is with the worth of Peer in relation to that of his various travelling companions or of the characters he encounters. As Peer himself puts it with ironic understatement in the auction scene, when he meets the living dead of his own past, "One meets with acquaintances" ("En træffer nok kjendinger"). In the description of the reindeer ride, as everywhere else in the play, we must decide whether Peer is in fact "troll-taken", and what that may mean. We are obliged to wonder whether he is merely a liar or a poet. He is called the former frequently and the latter, albeit ironically, occasionally, and the Norwegian word *digter*, which is applied to him at certain climactic moments, means both. We are invited to wonder whether the buck is merely a malignant troll or Satan himself carrying out the promise made to Christ (and which, for instance, Professor Rubek makes to a woman he does not love in *When We Dead Awaken*) to take him up into high places the better to contemplate the glory of the earth. The white ptarmigan which starts up at the buck's feet is associated with a later reference (by Peer) to a ptarmigan representing the soul in anguish. The "brown-backed eagles" of the Gendin-Edge ride reappear in one of Peer's imagined flights over the romantic land of Engelland, in which he expresses a wish for a sacramental baptism in the pure waters of a mountain lake—before deciding that it might be more fun to descend to earth to dally with the young maidens who await him on the ground. Over and over again, Peer ascends to some height from which he appears to discern some great truth, but comes down, often ludicrously, to make an indecisive retreat towards "home" and a woman, Åse or Solveig (apparent opposites) or some parodic manifestation of one of them, who seems to wait and to guard for Peer some kind of questionable identity. It is the "women behind him" who apparently save Peer from the trolls, the Boyg, the Cairo madhouse, and the wreck of the ship taking him back to Norway; but always, as in Peer's initial return home to Åse, doubts surround almost everything about him. Even if he is a poet rather than a "devil's story-teller," what value are we to place on his artistic vision? To echo one of the homely images repeated in the play, we are made to ponder whether all the shoe-leather that Peer expends on his journeys is, in any ultimate sense, worth its cost. And, if it is, in the rest of the play as in the reindeer ride, the truths offered are the strange truths of a tragicomic traveller's tale, close perhaps to those of, for instance, Oehlenschläger's *Aladdin,* Heiberg's *A Soul After Death,* and Paludan-Müller's *Adam Homo,* by which Ibsen is known to have been influenced.

Peer Gynt is, of course, a vast and complex work. Its meaning struck many early critics as "misty," to use the term that Peer himself applies to the Troll King's riddle about the meaning of being oneself. William Archer endeavours to demonstrate that the play is a "phantasmagoria" and argues against precise and sustained allegorical interpretations.[16] Clemens Petersen, outraged at the work's negation of contemporary Danish poetic idealism, rashly accuses Ibsen of intellectual deceit.[17] Modern critics, wisely undeterred by Archer's hesitations and Petersen's insensitivity, have, as we have seen, interpreted the themes of the play in many distinct ways, but the most successful criticism is surely that which views the play as a poetic enigma built upon the motif of the spiritual journey. Significantly this approach relates *Peer Gynt* (which might appropriately have been called *Peer Gynt's Travels*—recalling Strindberg's early work *Lucky Peter's Travels*) to the European fictional traditions of the picaresque novel and the *bildungsroman.* As in *Gulliver's Travels, Tom Jones,* or *Wilhelm Meister,* every stage on the way of Peer's life has its own particular revelations as well as integral associations with every other stage; a chronological treatment of the action is therefore even more appropriate to the interpretation of this play than it is to that of some of the more tightly organized plays which follow, and which often employ a markedly retrospective technique. In *Peer Gynt* the movement, though interrupted by moments of retrospection, is generally forward in time, however "roundabout" (to use the Boyg's term) philosophically. The cumulative effects of Peer's precipitate excursions can be more easily appreciated if the critic adopts Ibsen's own chronological principle. And the links which bind the realistic with the expressionistic episodes also become more apparent in such an approach: the fictive reality of Peer's world, in which psychological realities, folklore, myth, ancient history, and contemporary social and political events are related, almost demands that the idea of forward movement in time (whether positive or negative in its effects) should not be violated by the critic. Philosophically Peer may discover, to quote his words to the Boyg, that "Forward or back, and it's just as far;/Out or in, and it's just as strait": he is heroic or mock-heroic, liar or *digter*, aesthete or visionary by turns or simultaneously. And both philosophically and psychologically his journeys seem to form a great circle—from Åse's womb to Solveig's lap. Appropriately enough, some see Solveig's lap, Peer's last resting place in the play, as another womb, from which Peer may be reborn to fulfil his uncertain final destiny. But whether he travels the highlands or lowlands of the spirit, Peer's movement in time is obsessively forward. An understanding of the tragicomic ironies of the work substantially depends on the appreciation of this progressive chronology juxtaposed, as it is, with possibly regressive thematic revelations.

If the ride along Gendin Edge establishes the total dimensions of Peer's world, his next encounter is with the squalid realities of social survival. Down from the heights, he listens to his mother's reproaches and, eventually, takes them to heart. The foolish Mads Moen has cut him out with Ingrid, the Hegstad heiress, so Åse must accompany him to Hegstad and negotiate the marriage she wants between Peer and Ingrid before the latter is married to Moen. In the heat of the moment it does not seem to matter that he does not love the girl; like many another of Ibsen's men in desperate need of money, Peer sets his sights on her wealth as surely as Alfred Allmers succumbs to the promise of Rita's "gold and green forests." There is no hesitation. Finding that Åse is too confused to arrange matters for him, he pretends to be a buck, carries her across a stream, with a significantly shelving and slippery bed, and lodges her on a mill-house roof, where she may rave to her heart's content. She is abandoned "high upon the straw"[18] of the thatched roof, as Peer is later to find himself crowned with straw after his more terrible ravings in the Cairo madhouse.

> Stepping out by himself, Peer begins to have second thoughts:
> Yonder lies Hegstad. Soon I'll have reached it.
>> [Puts one leg over the fence; then hesitates.]
> Wonder if Ingrid's alone in the house now?
>> [Shades his eyes with his hand, and looks out.]
> No; to the farm guests are swarming like midges.—
> H'm, to turn back now perhaps would be wisest.

Memories of the taunts he has already endured from the valley people make him wish he had "a good strong dram" to comfort him, "for the laughter don't bite then." But, out of sight though not earshot, he hears the wedding guests deriding him on their way to Hegstad. Typically his first response is a marvellous day-dream. High in the clouds he becomes an emperor on horseback pursued by Åse, "an old crone on a broomstick." His mount is magnificent, "gold-shod and crested with silver," and a splendid company of courtiers surrounds him, none of whom sits the saddle as firmly as he. Like Jon and Rasmus Gynt, he scatters money along the highway for peasants to scramble for, and all Engelland's maidens and nobles await him as does its emperor.

This fantasy, the play's third example of the ride motif, is shattered by Aslak the Smith, whose gibes re-establish Peer's determination to go to Hegstad. At the feast, he is the butt of more malicious peasant humour, as Ibsen satirizes the nationalistic preoccupation with a supposedly good-hearted, heroically quick-fisted Norwegian peasantry. Ostracized and insulted, Peer drinks heavily and tells a story about his supposed imprisonment of the Devil in a nut and the humiliating consequences to Peer's most implacable human enemy, Aslak. But Peer is not too drunk (his inebriation is, of course, here as elsewhere, a figurative equivalent of a journey—a "trip", as some of his recent bloodbrothers and -sisters would call it) to guess at Mads Moen's impotence or to single out a family of new arrivals to the valley. They are pietists, intent upon the social niceties, and feel they must pay their respects to "the good people," their host and hostess, before joining the company of guests. Solveig belongs to this family, and Peer, turned down by all the other girls, at once, like an "ashlad" asking for the hand of a princess at a fairytale ball,[19] entreats her to dance with him. But his rudeness and dirty appearance (not a bit like that of his imaginary emperor) is too much for Solveig. After much hesitation, during which Peer badly frightens her with wildly disgusting troll-talk, she declines his invitation. In desperation (as he so often is), Peer sees his chance to triumph: he manages to get into the storehouse where Ingrid has taken refuge from Moen (who, significantly, in both sexual and social terms, cannot find the key). Then, becoming once more a buck or a goat, Peer astonishes everyone, especially Åse, newly arrived to curse him, by carrying the bride herself off up a mountain. In the first draft of the play, Solveig's father delivers a solemn address at this point. But in the final version, he is content to enquire what is happening and to defer his personal pronouncement upon what he perceives as Peer's certain and deserved death and damnation until a little later.

What Peer says to Ingrid before the "bride-rape" (itself reminiscent of the grand old Viking and general pagan custom of marriage by capture) is not known, but it has been pointed out (by Logeman) that, despite his forced entry into the storehouse, Peer's visit to Ingrid before he carries her off might have been enough, according to country custom, to constitute a binding promise of marriage.[20] Ingrid may look like "a pig", as Mads Moen imagines, when she is being carried by her drunken buck up the mountainside, and as Åse warns him to "take care of [his] footing," but there is hope that, in Åse's terms at least, all may yet be well. Ingrid, like Maja in *When We Dead Awaken*, cannot resist a Viking-like male, and, enamoured of Peer, she tells him as much, offering him "Hegstad Farm and more besides." But recollections of Solveig, her prayer book, her golden hair, and her modest glances "adown [her] apron" have stuck in Peer's memory, and, for better or worse, he unceremoniously abandons Ingrid on the mountain. "Each alone must go his own way," he remarks, even after the night he has just spent with his well-disposed heiress.

The episodes with Ingrid are an excellent example of sustained tragicomedy. Peer plays the hero—several heroic roles at once, in fact: those of Viking warrior, demon lover, and young man anxious to please his mother. He is also drunk, full of lust, and at his wits' end. His struggles—undeniably strenuous—to make some sense of his predicament evoke exactly that mixture of emotions to which Shaw refers in describing his reaction to *The Wild Duck*.[21] And the immediate outcome of this particular conflict is not unrelated to similar moments when Falk, Brand, and Rubek have to make up their minds about a woman's claims and significance before starting or continuing a mountain climb. The tragic note which sounds throughout the comedy here is evident in Peer's decision to leave Ingrid. Unlike Julian Poulsen in *Saint John's Night*, who runs away from his Juliane in terror of the trolls, Peer argues with Ingrid his need for freedom even though she is the woman he has abused (at least to the extent that he has deliberately deceived her). Then, believing the whole parish is pursuing him, he chooses to stand—or rather run—alone. He and Ingrid could have returned like sheep to the valley fold and to the forgiveness of the father Ingrid dominates ("where she leads," Åse remarks, "step by step/Stumps the gaffer, grumbling, after"). But the fold, as Peer seems to realize, is enmired and not free from such proverbial wolves in sheep's clothing as Solveig's father appears to be. Even as Peer makes his decision to abandon Ingrid, this man, who is to become to Peer a kind of father-in-law, is out for his blood—"Best if you saw him on the gallows hanging," is his steely judgement of Peer's deserts. The multidimensional nature of Peer's tragicomic identity is never more apparent than at this moment. He is, symbolically, already a buck, a ram, a goat, associated with a "pig"—Ingrid (in the Biblical sense and in Goethe's of one possessed by the Devil)—and yet he is also and simultaneously, in Christian terms other than Solveig's father's, the "lost lamb" that Åse calls him.

The ironic ambivalence of the Peer-Ingrid episodes extends to Solveig as well. Her name, according to Logeman, probably means "sun-woman,"[22] but it should not be forgotten that the sun and its reflections which glittered over the Gendin Edge were blinding, and as much like the brilliant glare which reveals the monstrosities of the African desert in Act IV as like the light of truth which converted Paul on the way to Damascus. A sun-woman might not, then, in the context of such imagery, confer certain spiritual enlightenment. There is a real possibility, but no certainty, that Solveig embodies that miraculously redemptive force that Peer himself ascribes to her when he scornfully informs Ingrid that Solveig's presence can "sanctify".

Solveig is, unfortunately, however, one of the play's most negatively ambivalent characters; that is, her actual presentation, unlike Peer's or Åse's, for instance, is technically deficient. This, it seems, is the reason for James McFarlane's insistence that we should not allow the weight of the play's allegory to rest too much on Solveig.[23] William Archer seems to take a similar attitude further when he claims that it would be best not to think of allegory at all but of "phantasmagoria."[24] Despite such advice, Solveig is generally accepted as a straightforward incarnation of spiritual integrity. If the general impression of wholesomeness which she creates is accepted, it seems almost dishonourable as well as distasteful to wonder whether her maidenly heart can harbour anything but goodness.

General impressions, however, are not at all reliable in *Peer Gynt*, as Peer himself learns from the Troll King. The latter tells Peer that he cannot, as a naturalized troll, wear Christian attire because, after all, a troll is judged by his appearance and not by the spiritual condition of his heart. And part of the pain of tragicomedy, which is unavoidable, is that it forces its audiences to encounter the distasteful.

Solveig may be the most ennobled and ennobling character in all of Ibsen; she seems so, especially if she is considered in isolation from her dramatic context. She certainly appears to be Ibsen's closest approach, in a metaphysical context, to a fully supported, wholly positive female character. Her apparently unalloyed concern about Peer's spiritual well-being, her unshakable loyalty to him, and her unfailing tenderness are all strongly indicated. And the last sight we have of her, cradling Peer's head in her lap as he falls into a sleep which may be death, is deeply moving. It is, indeed, as deeply moving as the scene in which Peer renders a not dissimilar service to his undoubtedly dying mother. And in that comparison the difficulties are evident, for the play does not allow us any more certainty that Peer will awake in heaven than that his mother has already awoken in hell—although her apparent spirit in the "thread-ball scene" upbraids him for driving her into the dirt on the way to eternity.

A totally positive reading of Solveig's character would include an unquestioning acceptance of the textual intimations that all she says and does illustrates Christ's teaching, according to St. Mark (X, 14–15), about the privileged wisdom of children. Peer's early comment that she is "only a child" fresh from confirmation class would be taken to verify this interpretation. Also, her departure from home and the valley where her family lives, and her comments, in Act III, to Peer about it, may very reasonably be taken as an exact demonstration of the fulfilment of some of Christ's specific demands of those who wish to follow Him:

> If any man come to me, and hate not his father, and mother, and wife, and children, and brethren, and sisters, yea, and his own life also, he cannot be my disciple (Luke xiv, 26).

So exactly, it would be argued, does Solveig comply with these specific demands, that she fulfils the Button-Moulder's mystical imperative of, in some sense, slaying the self in order to redeem the self. And thus she becomes capable of redeeming others.

A negative appraisal of Solveig, both ideological and artistic, is not only possible, however, but is strongly and naturally impelled by the play's undeniably open ending. It must take account of the following: the disconcertingly abstract impression made by Solveig's character, which increases as the play moves on;[25] the element of sheer insistence on transcendent wisdom in childhood unsupported by any convincing dramatic observation of children's behaviour; the apparent fact that Solveig is approaching or already in puberty, a phase of life which interested Ibsen considerably and recurrently because it is characterized by its uncertainty; some aspects of Solveig's behaviour that call into question her religious status. Among the latter should be noted that there are signs that Solveig may, as an adolescent, be flesh and blood enough to leave home for reasons more complex than the vocation of religious love which she speaks about to Peer. Her pietist father, who embodies exactly the kind of religious fundamentalism that seems to have been the cause of Ibsen's own early and permanent departure from his family, is singularly disagreeable, and his righteousness is not taken in the play as unquestionable. Solveig's talk about the difficulty of turning her back on him is far from wholly convincing! Like several other female characters in Ibsen, Solveig could be conscious of and articulate about uplifting ideals, whilst being actually drawn to a male of considerable sexual energy whose physical magnetism she never mentions. She does, after all, adjust one of her garters at the conclusion of her first conversation with Peer, an action which, whatever her conscious motivation, is not the way to distract a drunken man's attentions! Undoubtedly she is shocked by Peer's trollish threats, but not too shocked to wish later to learn everything that she can persuade Åse to tell her about this obviously disreputable man. Her eagerness on that occasion—just after Peer has abducted Ingrid—can scarcely be ascribed solely to an aspiring confessor's interest in sin or to the kind of delight that Desdemona takes in hearing about Othello's exploits. Peer's sins appear too obvious to need detailed definition, and his exploits are, if only to judge from what Solveig has seen at Hegstad, not necessarily of a romantically uplifting nature.

The negative appraisal of Solveig is not easy, perhaps because Ibsen is not yet candid about the physiology and psychology of imperilled adolescents. Her virtues, however, are not wholly convincing, and the intimations of her possible weaknesses, though perfunctory, are intriguing and thematically important. Unless one is prepared to defend the position that in this work the treatment of Solveig (and Solveig alone) is based solely on Biblical allegory (enhanced by suggestions of the Eternal Feminine), the play raises such questions as whether Solveig, in coming to the outlawed Peer and claiming to have been summoned by the man she loves, has, like Hilde Wangel, for instance, some not wholly appealing carnal as well as spiritual desires.

This, of course, is a question, not an affirmation. Since questions in Ibsen are frequently contradictory, it is possible, ultimately, to find oneself wondering whether Solveig may be finally inadequate in the role of Spiritual Integrity — in human or artistic terms or both — not because of disagreeable sexual urges but because of inability to love Peer in the body as well as the spirit. From what we see of Solveig when Peer leaves her, there appears to be, for her, an element of ironic good luck that Peer asks no more of her than to dream of him in her maidenly imagination.

Some of the uncertainties that surround Solveig in *Peer Gynt* also centre upon Svanhild in the earlier *Love's Comedy*, but the intenser ambiguities of the entire dramatic context of *Peer Gynt* suggest that in this play there is a greater awareness of how some of the more glorious aspirations of loving relationships may be interwoven with and defeated by inglorious inadequacies. Awareness of the apparent failure of a whole culture, as Ibsen saw it in *Emperor and Galilean*, for example, to recognize its Dionysian impulses, or to retain effectual Christian values, may inform the strange and, as some see it, strained relationship of Peer and Solveig. And not the least of the parallels between Åse's death scene and what may be her son's is that we do not and cannot know whether these "sleepers" will wake to a glorious new beginning. If they are to awake at all, which again we do not know, we can only hope that it will not be to nothingness or nightmare.

Peer's next three journeys of exploration, all still in Act II, take him deeper into the heart of sexual and metaphysical realities than he ever ventured, it seems, while living with his mother (though she is never forgotten by him). His experiences, in both the real and dream worlds, are punctuated by phases of reflection (by Peer or others) when the vast contours of his spiritual world are poetically suggested.

Having left Ingrid to make her way home, Peer thinks he discovers that "the parish is all at [his] heels in a pack!" Actually, as we subsequently learn from Åse, Peer is wrong, for when the shouting about the bride-rape is over, only three people are prepared to look for Peer. Peer's image of "the pack" is ironic because it is self-aggrandizing; it also indicates, by the contrast of Peer's imagined crowd with the reality, the spiritual poverty of the villagers (the parallel with those who would not follow Brand springs to mind). And, irony of ironies, there are senses in which the actual "pack" — Åse, Solveig, and her father — seem to prey upon Peer while seeking to save him. The first pursuer to speak is Åse (who had earlier presented herself to Peer's imagination as a witch on a broomstick). She is shortly to admit her complicity in Peer's "sin" of taking refuge from life in the fantasy world of fairy-tales. The second to speak is the Father, whose harshness suggests gloating over Peer's assumed damnation at least as much as valid spiritual appraisal. "His heart is hardened: his soul is lost," says the Father, condemning Peer to the hangman. The third to speak is Solveig, anxious to hear all there is to be told about a disreputable man's adventures. It is not too unkind to see in Solveig's, "Say on, tell me more" or "Tell everything" or "Sooner will you tire of the telling than I of the hearing" some of that dangerous curiosity and insatiable appetite for vicarious experience which causes Hedda, another young woman dominated by a strict father, to interro-gate Lövborg about his exploits. Hedda does so in her father's presence, but, like Solveig, it seems, out of his earshot. It is comforting to believe that Åse is wise to respond with an open heart to Solveig, and the play invites us to do that and to accept that Solveig ultimately, half a lifetime later, grants Peer a credible absolution. It also, though more tentatively, invites us to consider Solveig as one of Ibsen's many pitiably deficient idealists. The irony — the essential tragicomedy — goes further, how-ever, for, at this stage, this girl who means so well is, like many other adolescents in Ibsen, herself extremely vulnerable. If her big sisters may be Hedda Gabler and the Hilde Wangel of *The Master Builder*, her little sisters are Hedvig Ekdal and the Hilde Wangel of *The Lady from the Sea*, and her young brothers are Peter in *The Pretenders*, Oswald as a boy in *Ghosts*, and Gregers as a boy in *The Wild Duck*.

Before Peer's orgy with the Sæter-Girls there occurs what might be called Åse's epiphany. After it, and before the troll episodes of Act II, Peer experiences a similar moment of apparent insight. And after the hideous encounter with the Boyg, some moments of what seems like genuine spiritual serenity occur as Peer converses with Helga, and, somewhat awkwardly, also with Solveig, who modestly refuses to come out of hiding, having sent her actual younger sister to Peer with a basket of food.

Emotionally it is almost impossible to detach these times of reflection from the bewildering rush of the ever more tragicomic occurrences which accompany them. As was the case in the Norwegian National Theatre's production of *Peer Gynt* in 1975 directed by Edith Roger, the dramatic mood, now more than ever, is one of worlds on the move: a parish (in Peer's imagination at least) pursuing its quarry; their prey himself cavorting like a three-headed troll to the fleshpots of a Norwegian rustic Saturday night or rushing away on a pig into a folklore palace to negotiate a marriage contract with the Troll King's daughter, only to stumble upon an invisible tormentor, the Boyg, more dreadful still — because more incomprehensible — than any of the frightful creatures he has already encountered. But critically, the separation must be made.

Åse begins the explicit talk about spiritual realities in the act, and she is calm only at certain moments. She begins in a frenzy, "tossing . . . her arms and tearing her hair," suggesting many another literary character about to unburden herself of great truths. Consciously, perhaps, she echoes Peer's description of his Gendin-Edge ride:

> All things are against me with wrathful might!
> Heaven, and the waters, and the grisly-mountains!
> Fog-scuds from heaven roll down to bewilder him!
> The treacherous waters are lurking to murder him!
> The mountains would crush him with landslip and rift!—

She blames the Devil for tempting him, and then more calmly, "turning to Solveig," she recounts, as she so often does, her family's woes before admitting how she and her "Peerkin" ("Vesle-Peer") sat and told tales to avoid looking reality in the eyes:

> The best we could do was to try to forget;
> For ever I've found it so hard to bear up.
> It's a terrible thing to look fate in the eyes;
> And of course one is glad to be quit of one's cares,
> And try all one can to hold thinking aloof.
> Some take to brandy, and others to lies;
> And we—why we took to fairy-tales
> Of princes and trolls and of all sorts of beasts;
> And of bride-rapes as well. Ah, but who could have dreamt
> That those devil's yarns would have stuck in his head?

Åse and Peer diagnosed their own inadequacy, and in the absence of a Dr. Relling, took folktales as their "life-lies." Now, still only half able to distinguish between reality and fantasy, Åse entreats "our Lord" to be less harsh than Solveig's father and sets out to rescue Peer body and soul, not necessarily because, as, the Father says, in anticipation of many of Ibsen's seemingly dead souls, "It's a Christian's duty," but because she loves him and needs him. While the Father ponders the direction of a "sheep-path," anxious to be about his Lord's work, Åse (not Solveig) more compassionately cries out, "If he's taken by trolls, we must ring the bells for him."

Here is surely one of the cruxes of tragicomic ambivalence in the play. It seems clear that the Father is a negative figure, though it might be possible to justify him as some kind of positive endorsement of Old Testament wrath whose stern desire for vengeance is complemented by his daughter's loving-kindness. But, as we have seen, Solveig's religious credentials are not necessarily as resplendent as they seem, and Åse's compassion, which appears to distil from residual Christianity and Norwegian folklore a quintessential humanity, never, even in this scene, admits of Peer's damnation as a real possibility. We are left to wonder what, if any, kind of reality she is ultimately capable of offering. Just as there is no more than a possibility that the Father and Solveig are in any way invested with endorsed scriptural truths, so Åse's humanitarianism is finally of questionable worth; her love may equally well be a kind of smothering maternalism similar to that expressed in Helene Alving's desperate half-wish to clutch her lost and mindless boy to her breast as the sun rises to blast, as some see it, all her hopes.

After his night of abandon with the Sæter-Girls, Peer enters, "dizzy and bewildered," to contemplate his situation. It seems that another moment of truth is about to dawn for him, though the sun is actually setting among the "shining snowpeaks all around." He begins with a lyrical account of the landscape, but finds that nothing will stand still. In the throes of sexual exhaustion and doubtless also drunkenness, Peer sees the mountain peaks as towers with a "glittering gate." Though all is "drifting," he sees a weather-cock (reminiscent of the cock-ptarmigan in the Gendin-Edge ride) arching his wings for flight. The trunks and roots of trees growing in the clefts of ridges become "warriors heron-footed," but rainbow colours shoot through his brain as the throbbing in his head mingles with the actual sound of bells ringing far away. He "sinks down" and reproaches himself for all his dreams and self-deception:

> Flight o'er the Edge of Gendin—
> Stuff and accursed lies!
> Up o'er the steepest hill-wall
> With the bride,—and a whole day drunk;
> Hunted by hawks and falcons,
> Threatened by trolls and such,
> Sporting with crazy wenches;—
> Lies and accursed stuff!

Then, glancing upwards, he sees "two brown eagles" and migrating geese, and is filled with a sense of waste and sin:

> Yonder sail two brown eagles.
> Southward the wild geese fly.
> And here I must splash and stumble
> In quagmire and filth knee-deep.

Leaping up, he determines on a baptism:

> I'll fly too! I will wash myself clean in
> The bath of the keenest winds!
> I'll fly high! I will plunge myself fair in
> The glorious christening-font!

But at once the idea of flying betrays his imagination, and his fantasy of riding through the skies to Engelland as an emperor recurs. Again he will be the envy of "Engelland's prince"; eager maidens again await him, and, significantly, the real brown eagles disappear—"They've vanished, the devil knows where!" For the rest of the speech Peer exults in a vision of his grandfather's house restored to its original grandeur. Recalling that he is descended from a family considered great and convinced, like Rosmer, that he is himself destined to greatness, Peer leaps forward, strikes his head against a rock, and falls unconscious.

It is important that all the troll scenes of Act II and the episode with the Boyg occur, as Brian Downs,[26] for instance, observes, in Peer's unconscious mind (and in Act IV, Peer himself confirms this interpretation). The rest of the act, with the exception of the scene with Helga and Solveig, is presented as the direct product of Peer's own deeply poetic imagination. Affected by the promptings of an impulse for self-evaluation which sometimes suggests egomania, Peer now reviews his experiences since the reindeer ride with all the freedom of a genuine artist and all the terrifying self-condemnation which never deserts him even during the most mock-heroic and magniloquent posturings in which the conscious Peer later indulges. If the orgy with the Sæter-Girls is an exuberantly ridiculous piece of self-indulgence occurring in the "real" world, the troll and Boyg episodes have the reality of expressionist nightmares. Peer perceives the Woman in Green in a mock-pastoral landscape: "Stars are gleaming through the leaves; birds are signing in the tree-tops." He performs "all sorts of lover-like antics." He boasts to this apparition about his wealth and status, and she replies in kind; he lusts for her money as he did for Ingrid's and he longs to possess her as though she were a fourth Sæter-Girl. He replies to her boast that her father is King Brose (Logeman shows a connection between the name and a Norwegian word for a buck[27]) with the claim that his mother is Queen Åse, who "can ride through the rapidest river." He is dressed in rags—again like an "ashlad"—she in "tow and straws." But what are rags and straw when higher truths are in the offing (one is reminded of the conversation of the vagabond, Brendel, and Rosmer)? It is part of our humanity, Ibsen implies, to see what we wish to see, and Peer and the Woman in Green ride off to be reminded, as ex-President Carter reminded us, of Christ's teaching about the perils of lusting in the heart, and to learn the real or apparent differences between men and trolls.

The trolls are gigantic creatures, as Logeman makes clear[28] and a 1973 BBC television production emphasized.[29] In the first draft of the play, the ceremonies in the Dovrë Palace commence with the singing of the Norwegian national anthem, and perhaps in production it would be useful to have the trolls sing it (or any other national anthem) as a reminder of Ibsen's detestation of nationalistic complacencies and the distorting effects of apparent spiritual self-sufficiency. But we should not forget that this condemnation is as much part of Peer's response to life—an example of his integrity perhaps—as of Ibsen's polemics.

Peer is fully aware of the loathsome sensuality of the troll world. In the Act I he has threatened to come as a troll, at dead of night, to Solveig, to drain her blood into a cup and to "bite [her] all over the loins and back." As a three-headed troll for the Sæter-Girls he had sparkled and glistened "like white-heated iron." (Christopher Fry, in a moment of poetic licence, is even more explicit in using "a white-hot poker" as a translation of Ibsen's original phrase).[30] But now he is to discuss with the Troll King the meanings of being oneself while hordes of young trolls anxiously wait to tear him to pieces, and an operation on his eyes is impending.

Much of the scene is given over to nationalistic satire; here in Rondë oafish behaviour and everything local is best by virtue of being itself (Stockmann's "compact majority," are it seems, the arbiters of taste and consciousness). And Peer, whether in Rome or Rondë, determines, as Ballestad puts it in *The Lady from the Sea*, to "ac-acclimatize" himself. He will wear a tail, with a ribbon, learn to admire grotesque dances, and eat ordure, insisting that good taste must be acquired. Ironically, he finds, however, that he will not be required to abandon Christian doctrine, for in the troll world that "goes free: upon that there's no duty." Here, as at Rosenvold or Rosmersholm, for example, appearances matter most, and Peer is obliged only to put off his "Christian garb."

It is in this way that the ironic contrasts between being and seeming, extending from such homely things as cakes and ale to the complexities of aesthetic theory, are established in the troll scenes. Another climax of ambivalence is reached. The Troll King's oracular pronouncements about being oneself—men strive to be themselves, trolls to be self-sufficient—have achieved wide critical acknowledgement as thematic truths. They are so, but in an enigmatic and tragicomic sense. Peer, in what may be another of his genuinely heroic moments, declares that the Troll King's riddle is "misty." Like the poet he is, he doubts the entire groundwork of heroic vocation in modern life. At this point he seems, as Guthke might put it, to gain an uncertain footing on the way to truth, and we are invited to wonder whether, in a world where every living creature must reach an accommodation with the inimical conditions of life, clear-sighted heroism is possible at all. Ibsen was furious with A. O. Vinje's suggestion that Brand was a mock-heroic figure comparable to Bayes in

The Dunciad; he responded by representing Vinje, conveniently a language reformer (*målstræver*), as Huhu in the Cairo madhouse of Act IV.[31] But it is true that Brand, despite his undoubtedly heroic efforts, cannot understand that people living in a subsistence economy must catch their herring before they can climb visionary mountains. Comparisons of the two works show that the unfortunate Vinje may have impelled Ibsen himself further into an understanding of tragicomedy between the composition of *Brand* and that of *Peer Gynt*. It may be that splendid deeds of heroism are still possible in Ibsen's world (though the age of Christian or any other kind of miracles, at times, seems dead), but in *Peer Gynt* and all subsequent plays, Ibsen regards the idea with all of Kierkegaard's scepticism. Most ironically of all, as Peer is to discover, those who struggle most ambitiously to be their heroic selves may end, like the inhabitants of Professor Begriffendfeldt's asylum, as monsters of egotism. The Troll King, in his vision of human potentiality, is only one of many dreamers in *Peer Gynt* who envisage a Hegelian world of heroically expanding consciousness, and, naturally enough, he is professionally biased against giving Peer any specific advice about a heroic quest. In any case, like the Button-Moulder and the Thin Man, he himself belongs in the realms of the high and mighty and is not temperamentally inclined to view, as Ibsen appears to do in the crucial letter to Georg Brandes, an industrious shoemaker as a hero, so he is unlikely to give Peer any wholesome advice about pride.

In tragicomic terms, however, the entire play demonstrates the ambivalence of the Troll King's pontifical utterances. In the Oxford *Peer Gynt*, Christopher Fry ingeniously puts Polonius's words "to thine own self be true" into the Troll King's mouth, appropriately emphasizing that this old Ibsen wiseacre, like Polonius, offers, in a kingdom that has been much less glorious lately, doubtful advice to a young man who may be about to lose his way. And when, at the end of the scene, Peer seems to be saved from the trolls by invoking Åse's aid—"Mother, help me, I die"—aspects of Christianity continue to be exposed to ambivalent irony even as the possibility of grace is intimated: the "bells in the mountains" frighten off the ravening young trolls, but the latter quit with the cry that the bells are the "Black-Frock's cows." In doing so, their words recall, for instance, Ibsen's treatment of Bishop Nicholas in *The Pretenders* and foreshadow the black-clad Sister of Mercy in *When We Dead Awaken*. In Ibsen the black clothes of the clergy often have implications that go further than a denial of mortal vanity. And nearly always (though Pastor Straamand in *Love's Comedy* is a probable exception) the benign appearance of clergymen is treated with scepticism. As Peer, who admits in Act IV that he may still be a hill-troll, seems to realize in the final act, not only may trolls and humanity be indistinguishable, but all those claiming metaphysical authority to make judgements about spiritual value may

41

also be destined for their own casting ladles, butterfly nets, and pathological laboratories.

As is predictable, critics have offered many "definitive" interpretations of the Boyg (the name means literally "Bender"). He has been viewed as the spirit of compromise in general, its social or religious manifestations in particular, and as the embodiment of Peer's psyche.[32] Obligingly, the Boyg lends himself to theological, psychological, political, and existential interpretations, accommodating all theories and, like the play, discrediting them all in so far as they insist on exclusiveness. There is a tragicomic warning for Ibsen critics in the fact that the Boyg threatens the destruction of nearly all Peer's ideas of the heroic without ever striking a blow.

But if the Boyg is an enigma—perhaps as much God as Godot, as much the soul of naturalistic determinism as the dark god Yeats detected in *Ubu Roi*—the literary origins at least are fairly certain. The Boyg is, as Logeman puts it, "an invisible but apparently enormous troll, related it would seem to the Giants of ancient and old Norse mythology . . . intimately connected with the Midgardsorm of Edda-fame: the world-serpent which like Okeanos was supposed to be coiled round the world." Associations in literary tradition with Milton's Leviathan and with Grendel also have been observed. Like other supernatural personages, including the god Thor, the Boyg perishes only to rise again; but unlike the phoenix or the owls of Zeus (to which Peer later refers) or Christ himself, there is nothing beautiful about the Boyg. Although he may not be simply or only a negative force, he is, among his many identities, a grotesque parody of spiritual renewal or continuity, rightly associated by Peer with his perceptions of the Troll King, the Statue of Memnon, and the Sphinx. The Boyg is the embodiment of all the fundamental doubts of the modern world, a Nordic manifestation of the disturbing denunciations to which the world's religions, its irreligion, and its secular philosophies have been exposed since the Victorian era. Like all great devils, however, he is also indispensable to any metaphysical or moral system that is more than arbitrary. In striking out at him, Peer is like a modern Luther or John Knox attacking the anti-Christ. But the Boyg is also, like Lucifer, the assertion of the possibility of all faiths, even in his hideous parody of the regenerative principle. He is also, through his literary and spiritual kinship with the fabulously evil beasts of literature both preceding and following *Peer Gynt*, one of the play's most forceful reminders that Ibsen is concerned with the whole history and destiny of man: Peer's battle with the Boyg is universal, just as in Acts IV and V Peer himself is obviously a cosmopolitan and an Everyman. There is a compliment, albeit a singularly sardonic one, in the fact that Peer encounters this monster in the recesses of Norwegian mountains. It was in the Boyg rather than in the niceties of dialect that Ibsen located the integrity of the Norwegian folk imagination.

There are as many dimensions to Peer's attack upon the Boyg as there are to the Boyg himself. Sword in hand, Peer is a Viking, a knight of the Faith counting on Solveig's psalm book to save him, and a slayer of the negative aspects of his doubts and compromises. But he is also attacking the spiritual agitation which sustains his poetic imagination—the positive aspects of his doubts and compromises. Later we are to see him entranced by a priest's funeral oration for the peasant who amputates a finger to avoid military service. Then, as in his battle with the Boyg, there is the possibility of destructive negation about Peer's wish to do away with doubts for good and accept the solace of the Church. Peer is never more utterly tragicomic than he is with the Boyg, and the whole problem of selfhood is never more dramatically evoked.

If the troll and Boyg scenes offer no clear spiritual direction, the final scene of Act II is no certain resting place for the spirit. Ultimately the cool, peaceful mountain place where Peer speaks with Solveig and Helga may resemble the black tarn into which Peer and his reindeer fell, as much as the christening font where the eagles circled. Solveig, from her hiding place, assures Peer that he was rescued by the bells (the interpenetration of realistic and expressionistic elements is absolute here), and he is provided with apparently wholesome food from the valley, the spirit of which, however, is decidedly not immaculate. Peer, in a beautiful gesture, (it has much of the miraculous pathos of Peer and Solveig's final encounter) sends to Solveig, through Helga, their go-between, a "silver button." It is initially Peer, or the poet in him (and not Solveig), who articulates the idea that she shall be the guardian of his soul. But like other Ibsen protagonists who entrust what they regard as their innermost being to the care of the women they love, Peer is to discover, horrifically and pathetically, that there is no more than a possibility that his "silver button" has been kept whole and untarnished.

If, for much of Act II, Peer is either troll-taken or possessed by poetic frenzy, in Act III he encounters human beings again vividly and realistically, but not straightforwardly. His tendency to compromise has been reinforced by his experience with the Boyg, and he "goes roundabout" with a vengeance. Act III is also the last part of the play set in a relatively actual Norway. Act IV takes place beyond the seas, and Act V is set in a Norway as fantastic as Peer's Engelland and, ultimately, perhaps, as romantic. In Act III most of the characters, but especially Peer and Åse, have the flesh-and-blood, body-and-soul reality which is one of the signs of Ibsen's kinship with Shakespeare and the Greek tragedians.

When the act opens, Peer is in his shirt-sleeves, felling timber for a hut. An outlaw, he tries to face mundane realities. But though he swings his axe with a will, he does not make a promising beginning: he cannot resist the temptation to address the tree as an old knight in "a chain-mail shirt." He just has time to reproach himself for his deluding fantasies before launching into a fresh one about his hut (not yet built) as a resplendent palace, admired by all passing strangers. The tree, once more an old knight, then "topples and measures his length on the ground." Shortly afterwards, the peasant who amputates his finger appears and astonishes Peer by his determination:

> Ay, think of it—wish it done—will it to boot,—
> But do it—! No, that's past my understanding!

For the time being, this incident is merely recorded in Peer's memory—an instance of unflinching will driving towards an apparently achieved end. Its ironic evaluation is postponed until the final act.

Next, in one of those rapid changes of scene which seem to foreshadow the cinema, we see Åse talking with Kari, a neighbour. She finds among the few things accidentally left to her by the officers of the law the casting ladle with which Jon and Peer Gynt used to play. The scene ends with a reference by Åse to the clergy, and the promise of divine forgiveness. Cinematographically the scene again changes to Peer finishing his hut, the reindeer antlers over the door of which seem an ironic comment on his vows that the hut shall be a refuge from troll thoughts.

As though summoned, and claiming that she has set herself free, Solveig appears. She comes to a man in great need and believes she has relinquished all ties with her former life (thus apparently fulfilling Christ's demands of his followers according to St. Luke[33]):

> In all of God's wide earth
> I have none I can call either father or mother.
> I have loosed me from all of them.

Peer, in an access of possibly misguided chivalry, or of real Christian feeling, treats her as a woman whom physical love (especially his) would defile:

> Solveig, you fair one—
> And to come to me?

Like Solness, he speaks of having drawn a wonderful woman to him, of how he has longed for her "daylong and nightlong." Her welcome to his hut is as dignified as she seems to wish, but, fairy-tale-like, it also resembles Solness's invitation to Hilde to take possession of Orangia:

> My king's daughter! Now I have found her and won her!
> Hei! Now the palace shall rise, deeply founded!

Poised as he is, again like Solness, between sanity and madness, Peer, having closed the door behind Solveig, sees the Woman in Green in broad daylight. His consciousness of sin, real or imaginary, is now so great that he feels unfit to keep company with Solveig even with "outstretched arms"— and he leaves her, pathetically expressing a hope that she will wait. Explicitly metaphysical in its orientation, this scene establishes Solveig's claims as a representative of the Eternal Feminine who may also be the agent of Peer's possible ultimate redemption, but its ironic implications are equally strong. Although the essence of the scene is not evaluated until the final act, it is clear that Peer's failure to embrace Solveig, "lovely and warm one" as she is, may be significant of more than his conviction of sin: it suggests that no full marriage of flesh as well as spirit is possible between them. And Solveig's repeated insistence that she has left for ever "the paths all [her] dear ones tread," though presumably spoken with the utmost sincerity, in Act III, is shown ultimately, in Act V, to be literally untrue. Solveig replaces Åse as a mother of invention, but the promise of a radical improvement in Peer's spiritual fortunes is no more certain than that which Hilde Wangel offers Solness on her dispossession of Aline.

On the stage, at least, Åse's death can silence all rational considerations. The tragicomic mode of the play is, however, now so firmly established that further intimations of its nature from within the play itself are superfluous. Having made innumerable suggestions about connections between the ludicrous and the pathetic, the heroic and the mock-heroic, and the metaphysical and the naturalistic interpretations of life, Ibsen seems to pause and find the perfect "objective correlative" for all that he has so far implied: an old woman—destitute, terrified, and alone—lies dying. Her son has the choice of telling her the "truth" or of inventing yet another comforting fantasy to ease her passage from life to death. In the circumstances, even Gregers Werle, though not Brand, might have resorted to the beautiful and amusing ride to Soria Moria Castle, a fictitious monument, based on Arabic folklore,[34] where God has supposedly established residence.

The tragicomic ambivalence of Åse's death can communicate itself more directly to an audience than perhaps any other single incident in Ibsen. Every detail is right: Åse mentions a prayer book (Kari has earlier spoken of the need for a priest), but Peer enquires about an old cat (most famous familiar of witches) and is told that "She makes such a noise o'nights now." Peer, however, with infinite compassion, urges Åse to "Forget what's awry and crooked," and easing his mother's dying discomforts—

Åse.   My back aches,
         Because of the hard, bare boards.

Peer.   Stretch yourself; I'll support you.
         There now, you're lying soft.

—the ride to Soria Moria begins—"Peer, I'd be moving." The destination of the sleigh ride is, of course, the Pearly Gates, where, in a delightful variant of a folktale according to which a peasant woman managed to get her worthless husband into Paradise by tricking St. Peter and other worthies on extraordinary gate-duty that day,[35] Peer—known in Act IV as Peter—braves it out with his namesake (himself famous for having thrice denied Christ) to ensure Åse's wished salvation.

The scene fundamentally questions—in terms of perceived dramatic emotion, not of rational analysis—the whole nature of divine judgement. It pits humanitarianism, heroic legend (the horse that pulls the sleigh is Granë), and peasant cunning against theological implications. Peer seems to know that he is, in a sense, driving his mother to hell—"broad is the way," he assures her—but it is hard to challenge the emotional integrity of his assertion that "There comes not a soul to beat her/From the parishes nowadays." Peer, telling his mother what she wishes to hear, speaks of a deceased wife of a dean who is handing round coffee and cakes for newly arrived souls. And, in the original draft, the gracious hostess is not merely the wife of a comparatively lowly clergyman, but the Virgin Mary herself! Blasphemously, but with irresistible humour, Peer is laughing at what some would see as the tragicomedy of all doomsday legends, though neither here nor later does the play endorse his imaginings. Åse's death is tragic in that it is the consummation of a life wasted in terms of both Christian and humanitarian principles, comic in that it shows one "saved" by a ridiculous parody of Christian belief, and tragicomic in that it reveals the desperate means by which humanity seems forced to snatch some comfort in an age when the tides of faith were receding on every European shore. Suitably, however, God is blamed no more certainly than man for the tides' retreat.

Fittingly Åse's death releases Peer to journey to African climes where colonial and imperial theories may be assessed in all their probable ingloriousness and compared with equally suspect manifestations of indigenous heroic culture ancient and modern.

In Act IV the physical and explicitly intellectual scope of the play is suddenly broadened. Peer, now an ex-cotton-plantation owner, slave-trader, and supplier of idols and missionaries' requisites to China, is surrounded first by a set of loud-mouthed cosmopolitan adventurers, then by human or monumental embodiments of Middle Eastern attitudes, and finally by a collection of the world's madmen presided over by a keeper whose name, Begriffenfeldt, suggests the mass of intellectual ideas— and their satirical treatment—with which the entire act is concerned. There is no diminution of dramatic power in the act, but it is of a different kind from that in, for instance, Åse's death scene. Here the struggle to preserve the integrity of the self, and the terrors of death and madness are just as real, but, as in the earlier troll and Boyg scenes, they are conveyed through explicitly expressionistic means, this time without any use of a "natural" explanation such as that provided by Peer's unconsciousness in Act III. Together with Act V, Act IV is Ibsen's boldest experiment in non-realistic drama, bringing together much that Ibsen had learned, in terms of ideas, from Scandinavian literary sources, Egyptian myth, and contemporary events with what he may have learned, in terms of freedom of technique, from the *Walpurgisnacht* sequence of Goethe's *Faust.*

The act is dominated by imagery associated with the head, appropriately in one of Ibsen's most complete dramatizations of the battle between trolls and the human consciousness which takes place "in the depths of heart and mind." If Begriffenfeldt is the lord of misrule in this terrifying kingdom, Peer is its willing hero and unwilling mock-hero:

> The Gyntish Self—it is the host
> Of wishes, appetites, desires,—
> The Gyntish Self, it is the sea
> Of fancies, exigencies, claims,
> All that, in short, makes my breast heave,
> And whereby I, as I, exist.

Every one of the names of the cosmopolitans refers, in one way or another to the head: Eberkopf ("boar's head") Trumpeterstråle ("trumpet blast"), Ballon ("windbag," mouthing ridiculous notions,) Cotton (whose head appears to be stuffed with the cotton balls, themselves heads, from which, presumably in Manchester, his fortune has been derived). Peer's head is constantly in peril, like those of all the Cairo madmen, one of whom goes to hang himself and another of whom slits his throat in efforts to set their heads to rights just before Peer himself goes, perhaps permanently, out of his mind. There is some question whether Anitra's cranium is large enough to contain a soul; Peer measures it to find out. Peer mock-heroically claims to have wounded the Boyg's "skull," and the Receiver wonders whether his head will roll (and Ibsen makes him use the word *Knappen*, which means "button" as well as, colloquially, "head"). In a crucial image, a toad, symbolic in Norwegian folklore of the soul, is found imprisoned in a petrified rock with only his head visible.[36]

With the genius of the tragicomedian, Ibsen also uses foot and shoe imagery throughout the act. Peer wishes to stand "with choice-free foot" ("med valgfri Fod") among "the treacherous snares of life." He likes to "stand on his own feet" ("står på egen Fod") in the matter of marriage arrangements. To Anitra he expresses his desire to be "wafted/Dryshod down the stream of time" ("å svæve/tørrskodd nedad Tidens Elv"). As he sets out on his journey as a peripatetic cultural historian, he declares that the present "is not worth so much as a shoe-sole" ("er ei en skosåle verd"). Even those who fail to catch the thief who stole the Emperor of Morocco's horse will receive a "hundred stripes upon the footsoles" ("Hundred Slag . . . under Saalen")—a particularly ironic punishment for those whose journeys are in vain. The images of the act, like the characters Peer meets, survey him from head to foot, and ultimately link Peer's Biblical recollection of the forfeit of one's soul for worldly goods—in the image of a "garland on a cloven skull"—with the dreadfully ludicrous sight of Peer sprawling in the dust of the madhouse with a crown of straw on his head.

Frequent changes of clothing and the assumption of one heroic posture after another reinforce the verbal imagery with Ibsen's distinctive poetry of the theatre. Peer is now like an ironic Pilgrim or a Gulliver travelling in the worlds of ancient and modern imperialism, Yahoo sensuality, and distraught academia.

The entire act is eschatological in conception. In the first scene Peer tells his cosmopolitan companions that he has been preparing for the hour of judgement when

The jury verdict [will] be delivered
That parts the sheep and goats asunder.

The Norwegian phrase "Bukkene fra Faarene" conjures up, in the very vocabulary of the original,[37] memories of the reindeer of the Gendin-Edge ride and of all the male animals that have already rushed through the action preparing us imaginatively for the specific doomsday judgements of the final act. Peer has previously been accused many times of irresponsibility, but in this act he is to be arbitrarily chosen by Begriffenfeldt to stand in for "The Absolute Reason/[which] Departed this life at eleven last night." As an only partially aware poet of final judgement, Peer becomes, in the madhouse, what Eberkopf called him in jest—a *digter*—a master poet of the sublimely ridiculous. In Act IV, as in Act V, Peer sets himself up to play God (who seems Himself to participate in the tragicomedy). And he is to reach, among other hideously ludicrous interpretations of the human condition, the conclusion which may be Peer's truest epiphany, that it is "one and the same misprint to be either mad or sane!"

But the act, for all its expressionism, proceeds in an orderly manner from episode to episode, journey to journey. In so doing it is not, like Shaw's plays, a "celebration of cerebration," to use Eric Salmon's amusing phrase;[38] it is, rather, a nimble-witted mockery of cerebration. If there is some truth in Ezra Pound's image of Shaw as a cheese-mite astonished at its own ability to surface from its burrowings in the great cheese of world thoughts,[39] Ibsen seems to have submitted to such temptations only once (in the turgid lucubrations of *Emperor and Galilean*). And then he seems to have been responding to Georg Brandes's admiration of philosophical literature. In *Peer Gynt*, Ibsen slices through the philosophical world's cheese with the accuracy of a cutting wire, exposing to view many crawling creatures with apparently mouldy answers to Begriffenfeldt's *Lebensfrage*. Among such answers exposed and implicitly queried in Act IV are Christianity, aspects of which are usually contrasted with determinism, Mohammedanism, the Eternal Feminine—and the "Higher Love" in general—pantheism, heroic imperialism, capitalistic free enterprise, Darwinism, atheism, and democratic idealism.

As the act opens, Peer's cosmopolitan guests pay fulsome compliments to his bounty (foreshadowing the tragicomic feasts in *An Enemy of the People* and *The Wild Duck*). Each of these men of the world (Oswald Alving meets their kindred in Paris) is an embodiment of a particular nationalistic approach to life; they are international trolls, and Peer is their Troll King. Eberkopf is anxious to spread his nation's culture (culture is equated with political power, as in numerous regions aspiring to nationhood in the 1970s and 1980s) over the entire globe. He is prepared to "grab the whole concern," as he does Peer's yacht, if necessary. (The reference is, of course, to Prussia's conduct during the Dano-Prussian War.) Ballon—an unsubtle but not untruthful caricature of Gallic attitudes—is an embodiment of "la politesse," "la gloire," and "l'amour." Trumpeterstråle is rapt in memories of military chauvinism. (Ibsen might be gratified with the social progress made by the Scandinavian nations in twentieth-century Europe; they appear to have learned more than have other nations from *Peer Gynt*.) Cotton (Ibsen inaccurately gave him the English title "Master" to emphasize his kinship with John Bull), anxious to keep the wheels of trade in motion, is preoccupied with thoughts of "solid cash" and contracts—particularly for armaments. (Master Cotton, revisiting the England of the 1980s, would also find many changes, not all unwelcome, in terms of Ibsen's political consciousness, though he would soon find British Bernicks and Aunes sniping across familiar barricades.) Peer, the prosperous American immigrant, is only too willing to acknowledge what he has gained and learned from the advanced nations:

> For fortune such as I've enjoyed
> I have to thank America.
> My amply-furnished library
> I owe to Germany's later schools.
> From France, again, I get my waistcoats,
> My manners and my spice of wit,—
> From England an industrious hand,
> And keen sense for my own advantage.
> The Jew has taught me how to wait.
> Some taste for *dolce far niente*
> I have received from Italy,—
> And one time, in a perilous pass,
> To eke out the measure of my days,
> I had recourse to Swedish steel.

Of the more deserving targets, in twentieth-century experience, only Russia, at the time of the composition of *Peer Gynt* still in the Chekhovian dream preceding its supposedly glorious revolution, is omitted from this satirical catalogue.

It is on these terms that Peer confronts the ancient culture and the economic potentialities of part of the "third world." Aiming to be its emperor, "so unlike the foreign policy of our own dear Queen" as Cotton or Lytton Strachey might put it, his will to power expresses itself, like that of Shaw's Undershaft, in a commitment to money and arms deals. But for the rest of the act and the action, Peer emphasizes the truth of his claim that

> Even as a boy, I swept in dreams
> Far o'er the ocean on a cloud.
> I soared with train and golden scabbard—
> And flopped down on all fours again.

The last phrase is an indication of the Darwinism which is later to emerge more explicitly. For the moment, Peer wittily encapsulates the work's tragicomic themes by defining the Gyntish Self as

> The world behind my forehead's arch,
> In force of which I'm no one else
> Than I, no more than God's the Devil.

When the cosmopolitans' romantic idealism is outraged at the revelation that Sir Peter Gynt intends to support the Turks against the Greeks in the Greeks' struggle for democratic nationhood (they are all under the sway of Europe's fascination with Byron), Peer is, with the suddenness of tragicomedy and life, divested of all, or nearly all, his worldly goods. But the idealists, who are also Darwinian contenders for survival, "brute beasts of friends" as Peer calls them, are blown to some undetermined place by the explosion aboard the yacht they steal. And Peer impiously ascribes the destruction to God's intervention. Blasphemously (and recollecting the subject matter of Osborne's *A Subject of Scandal and Concern*, one admires Ibsen's courage), Peer equates himself with a sparrow that God could not allow to perish and, more dreadfully, compares himself with Christ in the Garden of Gethsemane:

> He knows well what share
> Of the chalice of need I can bear to drain.

God is not "economical," but "He takes fatherly thought for [Peer's] personal weal." As is often the case in Ibsen, it is difficult to know whether Providence or the attitudes of one who mocks it are being satirized.

Shortly after this, with that marvellously cryptic humour which characterizes Ibsen's expressionism, Peer is given the opportunity to compare the Darwinian with the Biblical version of creation. Surrounded, in another echo of the Rondë happenings, by apes who pelt him with their ordure, Peer concedes that it might be preferable, in the circumstances, to admit the human kinship with these repellent beasts, for Bus (Peer's name for the "grandfather ape") and he are "kinsfolk, you see." As the "whole cargo" of filth is dropped upon him, Peer, recalling the troll banquet, tries to re-convince himself that taste is a matter of habit, but finds that this reasonable theory will not stand. Peer concludes the scene with this tragicomic juxtaposition of Biblical and Darwinian themes:

> It's really too bad
> That man, who by rights is the lord of creation,
> Should find himself forced to—O murder! murder!
> The old one was bad, but the youngsters are worse!

If, for some, the legends of the Creation and Fall seem hardly adequate to explain the ludicrous obscenities of life, for others Darwin's picture of a mindless struggle for survival among the "fittest" is equally unacceptable. In thirty-five lines of brilliantly theatrical writing, Ibsen achieves a perfect expressionistic embodiment of the seemingly endless arguments about the origins, nature and destiny of man.

Just as Jehovah's ordering of matters is taken to task in the ape scene, in the scenes immediately preceding and that immediately following it, parodic hay is made with Allah's not dissimilar attempts. In the first of these two very brief scenes, two Slaves and an Officer disturb the peace of a Moroccan military camp to declare the dreadful fate awaiting all those who do not catch the thief of the Emperor's "milk-white charger." One Slave is seen "tearing his hair"; the other "rending his garments"; and the Officer appears distracted: the possibilities of honesty or justice seem remote here. The Thief and Receiver, in the second brief scene, discuss their supposed vocations in terms of an ironically willed Fate. These scenes prepare the ground for the Peer–Anitra episodes in which Mohammedanism—or at least a widespread conception of it—is satirized.

For the moment, however, before chance or Allah provides him with the horse to ride off to his destiny with Anitra, Peer has time to extol, in a pathetic, blasphemous, and irresistibly funny mock-lyric, the glory of his Creator's handiwork. It perfectly foreshadows Peer's daring pronouncement, made just before Hussein cuts his throat,

> A pity for the world which, like other self-made things,
> Was reckoned by the Lord to be so excellently good.

Like any shepherd swain, Peer cuts himself a "reed whistle" and eulogizes the "delectable morning-tide" as particular instances of its charms catch his eye:

> The dung-beetle's rolling his ball in the dust;
> The snail creeps out of his dwelling-house.

And

> the lizards are whisking about,
> Snapping, and thinking of nothing at all.

Like a Wordsworth removed too precipitately from Rydal Mount to Morocco, he is moved to unsure mystic utterance:

> What innocence ev'n in the life of the beasts!
> Each fulfils the Creator's behest unimpeachably,
> Preserving its own special stamp undefaced.

And, distilling the Troll King's wisdom from this pantheistic vision, Peer spies the toad in his petrified prison "sitting and gazing as though through a window/At the world . . . to himself enough."

As distinct from the trolls, however, Peer dreams of an ideal colony. It is unlikely that Ibsen had heard of the "pantisocracy" of Wordsworth, Coleridge, and Southey, but, as a good Norwegian, he was very familiar with Ole Bull's Oleana, a short-lived socialist colony actually established in America in 1852. Peer's plans to flood the desert and populate the islands thus created with a hybrid race—the result of crossing an Arab people with Norwegian dalesmen (the breeding stock was Norwegian and English in the draft)—anticipate fascism and Hitler's revolting "experiments" in the breeding of a "master-race" rather than Ole Bull's utopian socialism. But, interestingly, the play's satirical recollection of Oleana's failure and the conception of Gyntiana as a place where a super-race will be bred foreshadow Dr. Stockmann's disillusionment with democratic attempts to build a new society and his wilder speculations on eugenics as the answer to political intransigence. With a sense of humour which the good doctor lacks, however, Peer, perhaps unconsciously, ridicules the whole idea when he declares that

> Like the ass in the ark, I will send forth a cry
> O'er the world, and will baptize to liberty
> The beautiful, thrall-bounden coasts that shall be.

And, in a carefully modified echo of the most famous utterance of Shakespeare's most theatrically subtle villain, Peer begins his quest for capital with the cry,

> My kingdom—well half of it, say—for a horse!

The Moroccan Emperor's horse neighs, and, christening his mount "Granë," Peer rides off to yet another group of anxiously awaiting maidens, who, this time, actually sing and dance to welcome him.

Peer's imposture as a prophet (Anitra takes him for Mohammed himself) is his most outrageous piece of charlatanism. Certainly, as he has admitted earlier, his familiarity with academic learning is superficial, but Ibsen himself is concerned only with some of the more widely known and contentious aspects of Islam. As has been observed, Anitra also is badly informed about Mohammed, believing, as she does, that Kaaba, a holy building at Mecca, was the dwelling of Mohammed (Ibsen substituted "Kaaba" here for the historically accurate "grave in Medina," apparently to emphasize Anitra's ignorance[40]). But some of the teachings of Islam are undeniably derided in these scenes, and Peer's practical studies in comparative religion drive towards the conclusions that one faith may be no better than another and that the Troll King would charge no more duty on Peer's pretended Mohammedanism than on his supposed Christianity.

Until the moment of her escape from Peer, Anitra is true to the conception of women enunciated by Mohammed. As this subject is dealt with in the Koran:

> Ye people! Ye have rights demandable of your wives, and they have rights demandable of you. Upon them it is incumbent not to violate their conjugal faith nor commit any act of open impropriety; which things if they do, ye have authority to shut them up in separate apartments and to beat them with stripes, yet not severely. But if they refrain therefrom, clothe them and feed them suitably. And treat your women well, for they are with you as captives and prisoners; they have not power over anything as regards themselves. And ye have verily taken them on the security of God, and have made their persons lawful unto you by the words of God.[41]

And, as H. G. Wells points out: "Allah also had to speak very plainly about the general craving among [Mohammed's] household of women for 'this world's life and its ornature' and for 'finery.' "[42]

Peer tries to make himself totally responsible for the welfare of Anitra, though, troll-like, he has to refashion his notions of beauty in order to appreciate the allurements of this particular Moroccan maiden's generous contours and grubby limbs. But if lust is his dominant motive, both pathos and ludicrousness are present in this middle-aged man's attempt to strut like a gamecock and dance like a buck before his would-be conquest. His yearnings are matched in their comic implications by Anitra's appetite for jewels and gold. Like a parody of Brachiano's presentation of his precious jewel to Vittoria Corombona—itself a highly salacious episode—Peer's willingness to offer his misbegotten horde to Anitra, piece by piece, in return for her favours, represents a tragicomic trading in bodies and souls. Anitra may be provided with the soul she says she lacks and, like Åse, be assured of a place in Paradise if, in return, Peer may

> reign,
> As a sultan, whole and fiery,—
> Not on Gyntiana's shores,
> Under trellized vines and palm-leaves,—
> But enthronèd in the freshness
> Of a woman's virgin thoughts.—

The Peer and Anitra sequences are perhaps the most unrestrainedly comical scenes in the entire work. In an image which recalls his departure from Solveig, Peer, "sitting beneath a tree with an Arabian lute in his hands," sings outside Anitra's tent:

> I double-locked my Paradise,
> And took its key with me.

To the hill-troll in Peer, the snoring which punctuates Anitra's slumbers seems like "love sighs": it is a "dulcet strain" which puts the nightingales to shame. But Peer is still not too far sunk in lust to draw an unflattering analogue between animals and prophets:

> Child, from passion's standpoint viewed,
> May a tom-cat and prophet
> Come to very much the same.

We are, of course, well prepared for Anitra's sudden escape—

> 051Speak, O Master! When thou speakest,
> I see gleams, as though of opals!

Ironically dutiful to her lord, she fulfils Peer's entreaty to provide him with a "vehement sorrow" (which recalls, for instance, Falk's similar request to Svanhild in *Love's Comedy*) by absconding on the "milk-white charger" with all of Peer's African treasure. Having, it seems, wisely refused to gratify Peer sexually, she can and does provide instant kismet, demonstrating unromantic aspects of the Eternal Feminine. Peer's quotation from Goethe about *das Ewig-Weibliche* is ironically modified to suggest that men may as easily be led on as led upwards by it.

The comedy of this parody of a May–September love is splendid. Peer is as funny in a straightforward way as Gilbert's "highly susceptible Chancellor," but, appropriately, there are darker notes here too, suggestions of the ageing man's pathetic defiance of reality which informs Zola's *Le Docteur Pascal* as well as *The Master Builder*, the latter written when Ibsen knew more about May–September love from personal experience.

As the sound of the white charger's hooves die away, and before Peer's next journey as a "travelling scientist" begins, there is another of those points of stillness when, as so often, it is impossible to tell whether Peer is closer to the black tarn of the Gendin-Edge ride or to the christening font of the brown-eagles soliloquy. He sheds his Turkish costume and puts on a "little travelling-cap" which was still in his coat pocket. Humorously, but presumably falsely, congratulating himself on not being a troll, he comments

> It's lucky 'twas only a matter of clothes,
> And not, as the saying goes, bred in the bone.—

He laughs at his fate:

> H'm to think of it now!
> To try to make time stop by jigging and dancing,
> And to cope with the current by capering and prancing!
> To thrum on the lute-strings, to fondle and sigh,
> And end, like a rooster—by getting well plucked!

With an irony he may not fully comprehend, Peer comments that such conduct is really prophetic frenzy, but, like Falstaff, he is preoccupied with thoughts of patching up his soul for heaven. He considers the advisability of living like a Christian, not necessarily of being one, and, like the judges who, according to King Lear, lust for the whores they sentence, he is a firm supporter of law and order. He reviews his whole life and career humorously and, with his own kind of ambivalent integrity, decides that if contemporary humanity is not worth a shoe-sole and women are "a worthless crew", he will concern himself with the study of the rise and fall of civilizations; he will become a Norwegian Becker (not to be confused with Baedecker[43]) or Hegel, searching with the safety of the academic specialist (one thinks of Jörgen Tesman) for the "arcana of truth" in the past. Of course Peer is unfitted for such a task, but in the context of the play the question is also asked whether the task itself has ultimate validity. As in *Hedda Gabler*, where Tesman and Lövborg represent opposed aspects of Peer's personality, in *Peer Gynt* the hero's lengthy soliloquies often bring us face to face with the horror that we may understand as little of our past as we do of our present and future.

On this occasion, Peer's musings are succeeded by Solveig's song. Reminding us of Penelope's patience but also of Omphale's emasculating enchantment, she sits spinning as she dreams of the man she loves. Her song is an expression of beautiful ideals:

> God strengthen thee, whereso thou goest
>   in the world!
> God gladden thee, if at his footstool
>   thou stand!

Interestingly, however, in terms of poetry of the theatre, the reindeer horns above the door of the mountain hut are plain to see, and a "flock of goats [stands] by the wall of the hut." Solveig interrupts her song to call the goats, just as the song is addressed to an absent satyr who seems a doubtful candidate for the role of the lost lamb. The symbolic importance of this incident should be seen in relation to Peer's comments about the doomsday separation of sheep and goats.

Then, with cinematographic appropriateness, we return to Peer, standing before the Statue of Memnon, which squats "amid the sands" not unlike Shelley's shattered Ozymandias. Peer, with amusing mock-modesty, declares that he is not competent to look "into [the] seams" of Bible history; he is before long to hear the Strange Passenger's brazen assertion of competence to examine the "seams" of Peer's own corpse. Despite his superficial knowledge of academic matters, however, he knows that the Statue is supposed to sing at dawn and plans his itinerary while he is waiting. He combines safety—clearly, war-torn Greece is out of the question for the moment—with sensationalism—in Babylon he will look for the harlots as well as the hanging gardens. The Statue obliges with its song, precisely on cue, and Peer makes the note in his book that the "whole thing . . . was hallucination," ironically attesting to the power of his own poetic imagination.

Surprisingly, in a study full of revealing information, Brian Downs speaks slightingly of the African scenes, conceding that "something . . . must be said about them," but mentioning the Statue of Memnon only in connection with its "not over-illuminating resemblances" (noted by Peer) to the Troll King.[44] But other critics have commented more appreciatively on the Statue, which, unlike a number of the work's other supernatural characters (the Boyg, the Strange Passenger, the Button-Moulder, and the Thin Man) is present in Ibsen's draft list of characters. It seems that Ibsen had a sound knowledge of contrasting interpretations of the Statue's song (as Logeman demonstrates[45]), and in the dramatic context of *Peer Gynt*, as elsewhere, he used it for telling satirical effects. He knew both the traditional heroic interpretation of the song—as a tribute paid by her son to Eos, the goddess of the Dawn—and the anti-heroic one—as the effects of wind and changes in temperature on the remnants of a pillar erected to King Amenoph III of Egypt. Ibsen, in a 17 May Prologue for the Bergen Theatre, had spoken of the Statue's dreams as meaningless mumblings and later he compared the Statue, in a "balloon letter," to Bismarck: both were old men who sat like dirty stumps in a spiritual wasteland, useless occupants of dead heroes' thrones, with no song to offer the sunrise.

Christian Collin is surely correct to see in the Statue's song *Peer Gynt's* "innermost secret"—or at least, one of them.[46] The wonders of which the Statue sings are (alas for Peer!) phoenix-like and youth-renewing. Its "Birds ever singing" traditionally signify the omnipotence of Zeus. Collin rightly detects in the Statue's riddle the essence of the impermanent state and an inevitable need for social revolution. Ibsen speaks elsewhere of the state as an ark which must be torpedoed;[47] here Peer is once more the "ass in the ark." Probably unknowingly, and in his customarily ridiculous fashion, he seems to intimate the unavoidable mortality of myths which seek to bestow permanence on human dreams of glory. As one whose Nordic and Germanic ancestors foresaw a twilight of the gods, which, to modern sensibilities, is likely to seem tragicomic, Peer is better equipped than he knows to examine the ridiculous splendour of the Statue. Also, as Daniel Haakonsen explains, Ibsen may be implying through the Statue's song an injunction to Norwegians. It was not enough to study the heroic past at Christiania University, as symbolized by the wise owls; heroism needs practice in battle such as the ones the Norwegians ought, according to Ibsen's passionate conviction, to have helped Denmark to fight against Prussia in 1864.[48]

But Peer, having contemplated, as any scholar might, theories of change, is now brought face to face with more immediate and potentially soul-destroying embodiments of psychological change. As Peer approaches, in the next scene, the great Sphinx (which fired Flaubert's imagination as much as Ibsen's and Sophocles's), he is the epitome of the Kierkegaardian aesthete, viewing the monument "now through his eyeglass" and then, like the young artist in "On the Heights", "through his hollowed hand." Quickly, he associates it with Memnon, the Troll King, and the Boyg, and he prepares to assail this now visible manifestation of the latter with a mighty metaphysical question, "Hei, Boyg, who are you?" The answer is itself a question—"Ach, Sphinx wer bist du?"—spoken by Begriffenfeldt with an impeccable Berlin accent, as Peer observes in his notebook. And, with exact theatrical timing, the latter has his *Lebensfrage* to demand of Peer himself.

From this point on the act is driven by sheer terror, which culminates in Peer's utter collapse. But Peer, Begriffenfeldt, and all the inhabitants of his asylum are mad to some purpose. A thematic climax is reached in Peer's insistence to Begriffenfeldt that the Sphinx is "himself," that is, presumably, an unintentional monument both to human vanity and the injustice of slave societies, and to historical and economic determinism. Begriffenfeldt's insistence that the name "Peer Gynt" is allegorical sounds like, and is, the ravings of a madman, but it is also the absurd truth. Though Ibsen found the name, like the Boyg, in Norwegian folklore, he extracts from it every possible shade of allegorical meaning. Peer is a common Norwegian name (the Norwegian equivalent of the English idiom "Tom, Dick, and Harry" is "Per og Pål"), but, as we have seen, Peer (or Sir Peter) Gynt is also on familiar terms with St. Peter. The latter tried to evade the anguish of bearing Christian truths to the people, and Peer, in Act IV, states his reluctance to be "a sumpter-mule/For others' woe and others' weal." The name "Gynt" has, according to Logeman, connotations of sourness and sensitivity.[49] They are entirely appropriate to Peer's desperate attempts to hang on to his selfhood in the face of the play's naturalistic determinism. He is forced by Begriffenfeldt to bear the whole worlds of woe of the Cairo madmen. These hideously demented creatures are symbols of universal anguish, and not at all the mere topical caprices as which they were once dismissed. As Begriffenfeldt forces Peer into the madhouse, locking the door behind them and ordering the lunatics back into their cages, the reality of Peer as the "Interpreters' Kaiser" is revealed. Begriffenfeldt throws his key into a well, recalling the observation by Democritus the Derider that truth lies at the bottom of a well, and is therefore, presumably, as astonishing when beheld by mankind as it is difficult to find. The authors of the Septuagint are apparently assembled in the madhouse, together with the contemporaneous critics of *Brand*,[50] all, like Peer and Begriffenfeldt themselves, the apparent victims of deterministic deceptions. As with the Boyg and the trolls, Peer struggles manfully, and as wittily as any Odysseus, to preserve his scrap of integrity from extinction. Mock-heroically, the immediate consequences of his trickery are loathsome. Unlike Dr. Relling, he has time to manufacture only one "life-lie"—for Huhu, the language reformer—who is sent off to record the "Malibarish" dialects of orang-utangs in the Moroccan desert. Peer's counsel to the Fellah and Hussein precipitates their grisly deaths and brings his own perceptibly closer. Like the "Absolute Reason" whose place, supposedly, he has unwillingly usurped, Peer is "beside himself" rather than spiritually dead in this scene. Every important character in the madhouse scenes is an embodiment of pedantry, cultural chauvinism, and political delusion; they are as universal as the Emperor Julian, on the one hand, and Tesman and Lövborg, on the other. The facts that Huhu is based on Vinje, the Norwegian language reformer, and Hussein on Count Manderström, the Swedish diplomat who prided himself on the elegance of his ineffective notes during the Dano-Prussian war, are merely the Scandinavian starting points for a satire on pedantry or self-absorption in high places that Swift and Pope might envy.

Denmark's humiliation by Prussia demonstrated that pan-Scandinavianism was no more than a dream of students, politicians, and academics; it demonstrated Ibsen's rather than Petersen's understanding of "intellectual deceit."[51] Peer also seems to lose his battle with the fighting forces of Begriffenfeldt—another Prussian commander. In a moment of direst need, he discovers that there may be no one to whom he can call for aid. With telling irony, he forgets the name of God. It seems, as he has said to Hussein, that it is indeed "one and the same misprint to be mad or sane." He can no longer believe that he is still "in a woman's keeping a silver-clasped book," though he may still be there, despite his lack of faith, and, still in conversation with Hussein, he suddenly leaps into the air, recalling for himself and us his Gendin-Edge ride:

> Just fancy, for a reindeer to leap from on high—
> To fall and fall—and never feel the ground beneath
> your hoofs.

Pathetically, and like a man drowning, he recalls, after Hussein's suicide, all his delusions and identities. He speaks of the "Turk," the "sinner," and the "hill-troll" before "something" in his head bursts, and, vainly trying (like the Cook he is soon to murder) to invoke God, he collapses for

his horrific coronation when he is "in the mire enthronëd."
The tragicomic ambivalence of this climax is immense. Comically,
Peer's attempts to understand the fundamental processes of history have
been, in one sense, demolished; tragically, they have been, in another,
vindicated. Peer's frenzy and fall in the madhouse are the clearest possible foreshadowing of Solness's final climb and the crushing of his skull in
a pit. It is as though the key which Begriffenfeldt threw into the well has
been returned to Peer's trembling hands, and a dreadful revelation,
which could be true or a hideous illusion, has been granted to him alone:
either life really is utterly futile, or Peer has been driven out of his senses
by the delusion that it is so.

The last act of *Peer Gynt* is a succession of doomsday judgements in
which Peer's assessors are, as much as himself, satirized and derided. If,
like him, they attain to moments of tragic elevation, they are also, often
simultaneously, just as ludicrous and inept as they struggle to retain their
doubtful authority as arbiters of spiritual worth. Long ago it was suggested by a pioneer of Ibsen productions in England, Miss Pagan, in a
judgement echoed by Shaw,[52] that Peer, despite the Strange Passenger's
assurances to the contrary, actually dies in the middle of Act V. But there
is also the distinct possibility that in some real sense Peer is already dead
when the act commences—or that, at the very least, he perishes in the
shipwreck in the second scene. After his encounter with the Thin Man,
which is followed by one of his nihilistic soliloquies, and the Churchgoers'
song, Peer comments, "I fear I was dead long before I died." The act
opens in what may be a deliberately unreal though poetically evocative
seascape (Logeman, for instance, explains that the mountains which Peer
and the Captain discuss are geographically distant and could scarcely be
seen from any ship in actual Norwegian waters[53]). And the entire action
of the remainder of the play contains nothing which is not or could not be
a dream or afterlife extension of Peer's previous experience.

In this expressionistic context, however, it is appropriate that whether
Peer is actually alive or dead should remain an open question, for the
fictive reality of, for instance, the shipwreck and Peer's conversations
with the Button-Moulder, the Thin Man, and Solveig lies in their validity
as indices of what Peer's previous experience means. The central thematic concern is with what Peer has lost or gained in terms of human and
divine love as it is interpreted from an assortment of doctrinal view-
points. In this act also, actual theories of tragicomedy, in both life and
literature, emerge more clearly than anywhere else in Ibsen and confer
on Peer his status as Ibsen's most fully rounded and comprehensively
conceived tragicomic figure.

Predictably, the act opens with a journey. Peer, now "a vigorous old
man, with grizzled hair and beard" is returning to Norway on board ship.
No explanation is offered of his history after his collapse in the mad-

house, and though reasons for this might be found in the nature of the play's composition, it is hard to imagine that Ibsen, who was attentive to other details in the revision of the manuscript, omitted such a link with everyday reality by accident! We are free to wonder whether the entire act is the dream of a dying madman or whether the Norwegian ship is itself crossing the bar. The dramatic value of such speculation is clear: Peer would never until the moment of physical and spiritual extinction cease to be both "devil's story-teller" and *digter*. Unlike those Ibsen characters who seem dead in ordinary life itself, Peer—as his conversations with the Button-Moulder show—would struggle no matter how many graves had been dug, casting ladles prepared and consoling motherly lyrics rehearsed for him.

Peer is still very much "himself" as the act opens. He sees the great mountains, Hallinskarv and "Jökel, his brother" as "granite knobs" which find it difficult to stand still and to keep their minds off "The Folgefånn . . . /Lying there like a maiden in spotless white." As a young man, besotted with sex and drink, he had seen mountains on the move; now, an old one beyond lust except in the mind, he finds that mountains can keep their footing, but only by an effort of conscious restraint!

Having discussed the landscape with the Captain, Peer begins to think of final judgements—"the dregs, says the proverb, hang in to the last." Most of Peer's remarks to the Captain and crew make sense in terms of an ordinary journey, but they also have a psychological dimension which emphasizes Peer's spiritual peril in the most down-to-earth way. Hearing of the poverty of the crew, he offers to tip them generously on disembarkation. But he is filled with envy when he learns that they all have wives and families who are joyously awaiting them "in poor people's fashion." Peer's undoubted failure in these terms—he never begins to discover whether he could succeed as a husband and father—motivates his spiteful resolve to do what he can to ruin the homecomings. He will send the crew home drunk to dispel the visions of simple domestic happiness that torment him. The sight of a wreck and the cries of three drowning men, however, make him think of divine judgement. When his attempts to buy their rescue fail, Peer, shocked at the earthy reality in the Boatswain's comment "There are three new-baked widows even now in the world," goes through a familiar pattern of thought: he reviews the advantages of being a Christian, cynically concludes that, in moments of peril, "One counts but as a sausage in slaughtering time," and dreams yet again of the Gynt farm restored to glory.

Because Peer is so obviously at his most hypocritical and superficial at this point, it is appropriate that the Strange Passenger, the embodiment of Kierkegaardian dread (*angst*) should appear. He is seen by no one but Peer and, like Goethe's Mephistopheles, is able to transform himself into a dog. With Peer, he discusses the value of corpses and the absurdity of their apparent good humour:

> The corpses all laugh. But their laughter is forced;
> And the most part are found to have bitten their tongues.

He terrifies Peer by boasting an ability to probe "the centre of dreams" when dissecting corpses. Whether the anguish that the Strange Passenger produces in Peer is spiritually revealing is an open question. Action suddenly replaces talk as Peer's theories about the human condition are put to the test. After the ship on which he is sailing founders, Peer commits murder, deliberate and in cold blood (colder than usual in those icy waters): the upturned jolly boat will not float two, as Peer and the Cook agree. The choice is between the life of an old man, gifted but an apparent spendthrift of all his talents, and that of a young man, uncomplicated, accomplished only in the performance of essential but homely tasks (one thinks again of the possibly heroic shoemaker), and determined to provide for his wife and children if he can save his skin. Peer first disables one of the Cook's hands and then allows him to utter whatever brief section of the Lord's Prayer he considers appropriate before being drowned. The Cook perishes trying to ask that humanity should be provided with its daily bread. Peer, forgetting the miracle of the loaves and fishes, finds the Cook's demise extremely amusing. But he is shortly to discover that something more conducive to good digestion than wild onions is essential for anyone contemplating the value of his soul. The Cook, ironically enough, may have been himself to the last in a positive sense that is only doubtfully applicable to Peer.

Peer, like the supernatural characters in Act V, has a very high opinion of himself. He thinks about repenting for the murder only when it is convenient, and the Thin Man considers such deeds "spiritless rubbish." To judge by the lack of comment on the Cook's death, it seems that some critics agree with him. Manifestly the Cook is not heroic by conventional literary tests of value, but he is close to the humble, the poor in spirit, and the pure in heart about whom Christ spoke in the beatitudes. Also, like Aune in *Pillars of Society*, Gina Ekdal, and Little Eyolf's playmates, he is one of those specifically working-class characters in whom Ibsen seems to detect unpretentious virtues. The Cook may have been wiser than Peer in not treating his wife as an embodiment of abstract metaphysical virtues—not keeping her, that is, as Peer keeps Solveig, at arm's length for the sake of a dream of spiritual purity—but the "maybe" is a large one, and the homecoming of which the Cook is deprived might itself have been a sentimental commonplace compared with the possible spiritual triumph of Peer's return to Solveig. A consciousness of Peer's lack of experience in those domestic areas of life which basically test the humanity of most of us is evoked as another and fundamental measure of Peer's worth. But the Cook's immersion in them is no guarantee of anything either. Ambiguities and doubts such as these invest Peer's later pronouncement about Solveig—"here was my kaiserdom"—with its contradictory intimations of deepest irony and possible straightforward truth.

Peer's conversations with the Strange Passenger (whom he encounters again just after the Cook's death) conclude with the final act's first explicit reference to the theatre in relation to life. There is much to be said for discussing these theatrical allusions together, for although their dramatic effect (of disorientation) is achieved by scattering them throughout the act, they have an interesting thematic unity. As well as the Strange Passenger's cryptic comment to Peer that heroes do not die half-way through the fifth act and his remarks on Thespian entertainments in the hereafter, they include Peer's account, at the end of the auction scene, of the Devil's performance at San Francisco, the Troll King's resolve to contribute to the national drama, and Peer's own decision, if he "can but get free," to write a "farce . . . a mad and profound one" to be entitled, grandiloquently, "Sic transit gloria mundi."

In his comment on the dramatic modes appreciated on the other side, the Strange Passenger remarks,

> Where I come from . . . smiles are prized
> As highly as pathetic style.

Whatever tragedies the souls of the dead perform to uplift themselves at the weekends, during the week they entertain themselves with comedy:

> The host whose dust inurned has slumbered
> Treads not on week-days the cothurnus.

Peer decides that the Strange Passenger is a "sorry moralist," but it is notable that Ibsen's souls of the dead, a mature and select audience, find that the human condition is best understood by juxtaposing tragedy and comedy. P. L. Stavnem recalls, in connection with this passage, that God Himself is said to laugh and that both Heiberg and Welhaven may have influenced the Strange Passenger's remarks.[54] But though Stavnem appropriately cites Biblical parallels, it is clear that the God who laughs through the Strange Passenger is as likely to be the dark deity that Yeats detected behind *Ubu Roi* as the righteous Lord who is on the side of the just and will have their enemies and the heathen in derision.

Peer's account of the Devil's performance at San Francisco is as literary in origin as the Strange Passenger's comments on drama. It is a direct borrowing from Phaedrus.[55] But its function, in context, is very much Ibsen's own. A peculiar anecdote, recounted by Peer after "a look of strangeness comes over him," it suggests, as H. Eitrem observes, Peer's own witty consciousness that his audience (at the auction) cannot begin to understand either his anguish or his humour. It may be a reply to the criticism of Ibsen's earlier work, as A. M. Sturtevant suggests. Again, as Roman Woerner has seen, the anecdote seems to indicate the way in which Ibsen believed *Peer Gynt* itself would be received.[56] It is a short step from this to seeing the anecdote's ultimate significance as an indication of the incomprehension with which the tragicomic mode itself would be perceived in the modern theatre. The Devil, the master story-teller and illusionist, performs a skilful trick disguised in a cloak and concealing a pig which grunts when pinched at the requisite moment. The act is represented as "a fantasia/On the porcine existence both free and in bonds." If "human" is substituted for "porcine" (not the most difficult substitution, as the Devil knows), there could hardly be a clearer statement of the subject matter of *Peer Gynt*. "And all ended," says Peer, recalling, irresistibly, his own wish to bray like the ass in the ark, "with a real slaughter-house squeal." The audience is bewildered. They discuss the Devil's acting, the "tone" of the performance, and the Devil's lack of vocal projection. But they all agree that "*qua* grunt/The performance was grossly exaggerated." Its actual and fictive reality are too much for them. The fact that Ibsen the tragicomedian is still a relatively shadowy figure speaks for itself in relation to the San Francisco anecdote. Life may be, as Peer says, a "queer enough business" which always has some "cards up its sleeve" (literally "a fox behind its ear"), and, in such a world, a poet may well be indistinguishable from a "devil's story-teller"—and the Norwegian phrase "en vederstyggelig Digter" applied in the auction scene to Peer by the Bailiff contains both these ideas. Peer's declared wish to write a tragic farce on the transience of life is an extension of this duality, as is the Troll King's resolve to devote himself to the theatre in Norway as, it seems, both an actor and an author.[57] If the Troll King were to keep his promise—or threat—one wonders how his work for the theatre would relate to reality both mundane and metaphysical.

The thematic range of Act V is immense, but the nature of humanity is always considered in relation to the nature of divinity, with no certain palms awarded to either. Finding himself on land (the details of his getting ashore are left vague, just as in *The Lady from the Sea* we never know for sure whether the Stranger physically survives the shipwreck), Peer arrives at a churchyard, for which the English word, despite manifold sinister associations in literature and folklore, lacks at least one sardonic connotation of the Norwegian term. In Norwegian the first word of this scene (in the stage directions) is *kirkegaard*. The hint is delightful in the context of a scene in which both Kierkegaardian and pietist interpretations of Christianity are treated half sympathetically, half satirically.

The indication that the Pastor's eulogy at the Peasant's funeral may be taken at its face value is strong and certainly not discredited. This is the man whom Peer saw slicing off his finger to avoid military service, and admired so much. The Peasant had subsequently married the woman who was carrying his child at the time Peer saw him and accepted responsibilities similar to those which Peer abandons in his relationships with Ingrid and the Woman in Green. Ironically, in view of his becoming a father many months before marriage, the Peasant has spent a lifetime trying to make barren plots of earth fertile. The Priest reviews all the duties the Peasant accepted, and comes to the following apparently charitable and inspired conclusions:

> Both for church and state
> A fruitless tree. But there, on the upland ridge,
> In the small circle where he saw his calling,
> There he was great, because he was himself.
> His inborn note rang true unto the end.
> His days were as a lute with muted strings.
> And therefore, peace be with thee, silent warrior,
> That fought the peasant's little fight, and fell.

Peer, of course, seizes upon this as true Christianity:

> Now that is what I call Christianity!
> Nothing to seize on one's mind unpleasantly.—
> And the topic—immovably being oneself,—
> That the pastor's homily turned upon,—
> Is full, in its essence of edification.

He wishes for and, with unconscious irony, considers he will deserve a similar panegyric himself, for, "the Church, after all, is the true consoler." This may indeed be so, but, on the other hand, the authority of institutionalized religion is always tenuous in *Peer Gynt*.

The ironies concealed in the Pastor's eulogy are potentially withering. The Peasant had performed all kinds of laborious tasks (just as Aline Solness does) out of a sense of duty, but, despite his flight from the valley and his apparent rejection of convention, he had, to the end of his days, "sidled into church," as the Pastor observes. The graveside rhetoric is possibly thanks due to one who wore only the garb of the non-conformer (as Peer wears Christian attire without being truly Christian). The Peasant is just as possibly a man damned by unthinking allegiance to the conventional—attendance at church—as Peer is a troll. The arms of the Church are long, not necessarily loving, and they lose their grip no more easily than the Troll King's. In all the fulsome praise of the Peasant's virtues there is not one indication that his family loved him or that he loved them. The Pastor claims that

> In the small circle where he saw his calling,
> There he was great, because he was himself.
> His inborn note rang true unto the end.

But his three sons grew up to emigrate to America and forget him. The attitude of his wife, who had much to endure, is not mentioned. There is no indication whatever that the Peasant, like the Cook, whom Peer envies and despises, was rewarded with affection by his family, nothing to show that he was ever welcomed home as the crew of the foundered Norwegian ship would have been. Possibly we are meant to admire him for his sheer devotion to forgetful and ungrateful children, but there is no certainty about that.

Though the text permits a positive reading, its ambivalence is important. The Pastor, like Manders in *Ghosts*, seems prepared to draw an attractive veil over the apparent waywardness of an erring soul in order to magnify, for the greater glory of the Church, the Peasant's fundamental loyalty to convention. It may be no wonder that Peer, who murdered the Cook, admires the Peasant.

In the auction scene, which immediately follows, Peer's unimpressive efforts to scale the heights of religious contemplation give way to unwholesome realities he left behind him in Gudbrandsdal. Shadowy figures of Peer's youth ironically examine the rubbish of his life as well as that of their own (the motif is introduced in the second act where Åse searches through the odds and ends left her by the law officers). Aslak the Smith and Mads Moen taunt each other about their associations with Ingrid, now dead and buried. There is the suggestion that Aslak may be the father of Ingrid's twenty-year-old son, just as Peer might once have fathered a child by her. The scene is full of recriminations, envy, and bitter memories of sensuality and despair. As Peer justly comments, the deeper one digs in some soils, the fouler the smell. A casting ladle, a reindeer skull, and Peer's supposed cloak of invisibility have all been held up for the crowd to jeer at before Peer himself offers to sell his "palace . . . in the Rondë," "Granë [his] steed," his "dream of a silver-clasped book," and the straw crown from his empire of the mad. His behaviour justifies what the Bailiff calls him—an "abominable dreamer" ("vederstyggelig Digter"). At this point the frightfulness of his poetic vision—uninformed by any moral or metaphysical ideal—matches exactly that of the apparently irredeemable Gudbrandsdal.

The fifth scene, containing one of the most famous passages in Ibsen, the onion soliloquy, appears to move through nihilism towards faith, for if each layer of the onion corresponds to a stage of Peer's life, its emptiness may be only apparent. "Nature is witty," and so is the soliloquy, renewing yet again and in a wonderfully fresh way, Peer's entire life. But the "kernel" of truth which will not come to light for Peer by his own efforts is soon to be presented to him triumphantly, and apparently void of all odour, by Solveig. Only she, it seems, can save him now, reaching out for him with her song for Whitsun Eve.

More existentially, however, the onion may represent not simply

Peer's soul but the souls of all humanity. Its emptiness may be that of life itself. Peer is possibly a poet of the horrendous inconsequentiality of the universe when he comments ("scratching his head"):

> A queer enough business, the whole concern!
> Life, as they say, plays with cards up its sleeve;
> But when one snatches at them, they've disappeared
> And one grips something else,—or else nothing at all.

Solveig's song is suggestive of all the powers of wondrous succour that Christ offers to wounded humanity:

> Now all is ready for Whitsun Eve.
> Dearest boy of mine, far away,
> Comest thou soon?
>   Is thy burden heavy,
> Take time, take time;—
> I will await thee;
> I promised of old.

But the humble hut she inhabits is decorated with reindeer antlers, and in one phase of Peer's imaginings, at least, a "mermaid, shaped like a fish from the navel." (One thinks of Rebecca West at her most dangerous—she is specifically compared, by Brendel, with a mermaid—or Ellida Wangel at the height of her sea-changes.) Solveig, whose presence, Peer has said, "sanctifies", may herself be a victim of the very deceptive illusions which the nails and planks of her home were intended by Peer to keep at bay. That Solveig should have fallen prey to a beautiful but destructive illusion—as Peer and Åse do in their absorption in folktales—does not seem probable, but the play does not grant the certainty that Solveig's love is redemptive. The best we can do, like Peer when he can resist no longer, is to hope.

The threadball scene, occurring in a charred wasteland wrapped in mists, now follows with its concerted attacks on Peer's apparently misspent life. The threadballs, withered leaves, broken straws, and Åse's voice (Ibsen originally contemplated bringing Åse's spirit on to the stage as an old hen—reminiscent of a description Ibsen supplies of Pastor Straamand in *Love's Comedy*) all have valid complaints about Peer's spiritual negligence and his betrayal of himself and others. But Peer's retorts are not without good sense in relation to the play's determinism. There is some justice in Peer's claim that in a world such as his and ours, it is hard enough to bear one's own sins without being blamed for the Devil's as well. At the very time when Peer may be unwittingly moving towards a Christian salvation through the pure thoughts of a chaste woman, he is also, not without validity for those who are not Christians or committed metaphysicians of any kind, refusing in an obdurately un-Christian manner to be "a sumpter-mule/For others' woe and others' weal."

The remaining scenes, in which Peer encounters the Button-Moulder, the Troll King, and the Thin Man, appear to reinforce the idea that only divine love can redeem Peer's soul and the belief that he is guilty of having "set at defiance" his Master's design. According to this interpretation, he is a silver button the loop of which gave way, making him fit to be only spiritual raw material in the Button-Moulder's ladle, unless Solveig has kept her youthful promise. His verbal duel with the Thin Man is hilariously funny because Peer takes the Devil for an ordinary parish priest and, thinking himself very astute, opens the encounter with all the mock-modesty and servility which he considers necessary to achieve his ends. He is as ridiculously obsequious as Engstrand in conversation with Pastor Manders. A serious issue, however, underlies the fun; namely, the Kierkegaardian idea that the grand sinner is reserved for some special fate in the hereafter. But again doubts rush in.

The Button-Moulder, the second of the supernatural doomsday judges whom Peer meets in Act V, looks like an honest old workman (he carries "a box of tools" as well as his casting ladle). But he is afflicted with myopia ("My sight's not very good"). He seems unable to understand the force of Peer's argument that "One is born only once/And one's self, as created, one fain would stick to." And the humour of Peer's statement that there must be some bureaucratic mistake about the requirement that Peer should be melted down in the casting ladle is lost on him. All the same, he appears not quite certain that Peer is wrong. More like a confused magistrate (Justice Shallow, for instance) than an agent of an omniscient Almighty, he agrees to give Peer more time to make a case.

The Troll King terrifies Peer with the insult that Peer has always been a hill-troll, but Peer has accused himself of the same thing earlier and, as we have seen, one of the play's basic thematic suggestions is that all humanity are inhabitants of the same troll kingdom.

The Thin Man, none other than Satan himself, is an equally doubtful arbiter of doom. He ponders a dreadfully amusing redemption of magnificent sinners. But though he has information—from sources which ought to be incontestable—about "Peter Gynt" as a salvable "negative," he does not recognize Peer when he sees him and is easily deceived into hurrying off to the Cape of Good Hope (the name is hilariously ironic), which he is nevertheless reluctant to visit because it is crowded, he claims, with missionaries from Stavanger! The bureaucrats of whatever deathless regions the Thin Man inhabits seem strangely confused and have obviously forfeited all claims to omniscience (one feels that had the play been written in the 1980s, Ibsen would have had the Thin Man issued with orders from a badly programmed computer). But the Thin Man carries on with business as usual, equipped with documents and pictures such as a sleuth might use to track down his man.

In such a context it is hardly surprising that Solveig's final appearance is not necessarily as reassuring as it might otherwise be. Peer comes to her pleading for proof of sins major enough to satisfy the Thin Man, and Someone ought to know that his claims have merit. He is told, however, that he is without sin. And there is the possibility that whatever she represents to Peer, he, the poet, has fashioned her in his own skilful imagination. It would, in fact, be odd if the man who made his mother's death acceptable through lies could not, under the pressure of annihilation, perform the same office for himself. The miraculous vision of a man saved through the "faith," "hope," and "love" of an innocent woman presents itself. To deny that this vision has any validity is to deny utterly and incorrectly the effective indications of possible redemption in the play. Whether Solveig is "real" or an emanation from Peer's imagination, she is the incarnation of the possibility of divine forgiveness and atonement, but also, and quite equally, she is a dream woman possibly as unreal (lacking, that is, all metaphysical support) as some would say she is undeserved by Peer.

In a forceful demonstration of the openness of Ibsen's dramatic world, ironic ambivalence continues to insinuate itself into the final scenes with Solveig. It is surely ironic that Solveig is associated with psalm-singers from the very community she claimed to have left for ever for Peer's sake. When Peer meets her for the last time, she is "dressed for church, with a psalm book wrapped in a kerchief, and a staff in her hands." Evidently Solveig never truly severed her ties with the valley, and unlike the Peasant, she is prepared to walk boldly into the church. In a play in which the agents of the Almighty and, dreadfully, even that Ineffable Being Himself, seem to be unsure of themselves, it is tragicomic that Solveig should, in complete disregard of part of her early vows to Peer, be about to join a community of conformists in their worship. In the valley where so much is seen as unwholesome, it may be that the psalm-singers on their way to church sing too confidently of the

> . . . morning thrice blest,
> When the tongues of God's kingdom
> Struck the earth like to flaming steel!

If this Pentecostal hymn were undoubtedly true, *Peer Gynt* would be a fine example of Cyrus Hoy's delineation of modern divine comedy.[58] Significantly, only a minority appear able to see the play in that way.

The most sceptical critic of *Peer Gynt* surely cannot deny that Peer must be allowed to cradle his head in Solveig's lap, there to sleep and dream—only Brand would struggle to pull him away. But Peer cried, when he heard the Churchgoers' song

> Never look there! There's all desert and waste.—
> I fear I was dead long before I died.

Heroic, in more ways than one, and simultaneously mock-heroic to the end, Peer tells Solveig, explicitly, that she is the mother of his inventions. And this claim may be an implicit indication that he is literally a drowning man (one who never did reach land after the shipwreck), inventing the image of Solveig as he dies. When Solveig speaks of his spiritual preservation in her faith, hope, and love, Peer tells her, in an agony of what may be lingering integrity:

> These are juggling words.
> Thou art mother thyself to the man that's there.

Against the miraculous hope that Solveig may be the way, the truth, and the life is set the chaotic vision of life as a curse which assails Peer (no less than Job, Oedipus, and Hardy's Jude) in the terrifying soliloquy culminating in the spectre of a tomb with the inscription "Here No One lies buried." Peer has applied Odysseus's famous riddling answer to the Cyclops to both himself and his Maker. All the soulful humour and pathos of these realizations is present in Peer's final encounter with Solveig no less than in Peer's inextinguishable cry to a (significantly) falling star, "Greet all friends from Peer Gynt, Brother Starry-Flash."

Images of shoes—wearing out or pinching—are frequent in the last act, as are references to crossroads. The play ends with the possibility of some final crossroads to which Peer may yet be compelled to stumble, unaided by Solveig. Like the age which produced him, we do not know what Peer may find there, what his ultimate fate or who his final judge may be. He may or may not have been "himself" to the last, and his worth remains an infinitely ponderable enigma. Like other great Scandinavian dramatic poets who set out on journeys in self-imposed exile, Peer arrives at no certain destination. Whether he arrives, in terms of both art and life, at "the arcana of truth" is an open question—unlike the power of his imagination.

Peer Gynt begins with a possible moment of truth in the mountains—like that of the young artist in "On the Heights". Ultimately the blessed human endowment which may save Peer is something which the artist (and Brand and Rosmer, for instance) lack; namely, his inexhaustable humour. Peer and the play which contains him laugh, sometimes joyously, sometimes in great pain, at everything on the earth and in the heavens. Something possibly divine laughs in him, at him, and through him. But if a god, potentially more benign that the deity of Absurdity, laughs in the play, the sanity of Norwegian peasant humour is also present. As Peer lies enfolded in Solveig's mothering arms, he may be a shining silver button in an expressionistic *pietà*, a credible Christ-figure to Solveig's possible representation of the Blessed Virgin. But he also may be merely a fresh corpse tossed onto land by an ocean as incomprehensible in its treatment of the dead as of the living. And in this case, Solveig has all the pathos and the lack of glory of the "new-baked widows" to whom the Boatswain refers when he sees, in Act V, the last three members of another ship's crew drowning.

3

Ghosts: The Vision Blurs

Ghosts, perhaps more than any other Ibsen play, has been interpreted in astonishingly contradictory ways. In performance, when well directed, it is still rivettingly dramatic. Yet it is a seriously flawed work, and to a disquieting extent, an illustration of the kinds of negative openness that result from loss or lack of artistic control. In numerous instances, its attitudes are not thoroughly absorbed by the creating imagination. Its ambiguities sometimes seem to issue from confusion or evasiveness, or from erratic technique. *Ghosts* is accordingly unrepresentative of Ibsen's mature work to the extent that responding fully to its widely divergent and sometimes mutually exclusive ideas and moods is likely to produce not admiration but a disquieting awareness of thematic and structural inconsistency.

A representative sampling of interpretations of *Ghosts* shows that the play is, or has been, thought of as: (1) a documentary treatment of physiological and social determinism, (2) a defense of free-thinking or existential attitudes to sex and society, (3) a study in specifically modern heroism, (4) a traditional tragedy with an intact ethic, (5) an existential tragedy with an apprehensible metaphysic, (6) a nightmarish evocation of spiritual decline in which all the pretentions to dignity of modern Western culture are seen as brutally destroyed in a process of "reification," and (7) a model illustration of fundamental Laingian theories of family relationships.

The "Second Impression" of Ibsen's work, written by Georg Brandes in 1882, is important as an early statement of the first and second of these views,[1] and intriguing in that Brandes is apparently unaware of completely contradicting himself. On the one hand, he declares that *Ghosts* is

> a poetic treatment of the question of heredity. It represents, on the basis of that determinism which is at present the last word of modern science in the matter, the general determination by the parents of the physical and mental nature of the child, and gives this fact an emotional and suggestive background by representing it in connection with the more universally acknowledged fact referred to in the title, namely, the preservation by heredity of feelings (and through them of dogmas), whose original life-conditions have died out and given place to others with which those feelings are at variance.

Clearly Brandes does not have a high opinion of determinism, as is implicit in his slighting reference to "modern science." And this is predictable enough in the author of *The Emigrant Literature*, which had been published in two editions in the 1870s, and which essentially confines its perception of evil in the human condition to the theory that destructive powers, exerted by the ignorant and the prejudiced at every level of society, isolate and condemn to heroic suffering the few—mostly courageous authors—whom Brandes perceives as champions of the liberty in thought and love which should be the guiding star of European civilisation.

But he congratulates Ibsen, as much more recently John Northam has done,[2] on placing the heroic figures in *Ghosts* in a well understood, contemporary social environment. And in doing so, he supports the idea that social and biological determinism cannot be disregarded:

> he [Ibsen] has become thoroughly aware of the fact that no amount of "courage" can enable us to disregard [social convention], but that we all, by the destiny of our birth, are bound up with persons, environed by conditions, that we cannot control.

Earlier, Brandes, who also implies in the "Second Impression" that, under his tutelage, Ibsen's intellectual development is coming along very well, sees *Ghosts* in a much rosier light, as just the ticket, in fact, that contemporary Europe—and especially contemporary Norway—needed for its journey to a Brandean Utopia. Ibsen is "sceptical" in *Ghosts*, Brandes concedes, but "he does not actually doubt the possibility of happiness." Warming to his topic, Brandes goes on:

> Even Mrs. Alving, who has been so sorely wronged by circumstances, believes that under other conditions she might have been happy, believes that her wretched husband himself might have been happy. And Ibsen is evidently of her opinion. What she says about the "half-grown town" that has "no joys to offer, only dissipations, no object in life, only an official position, no real work, only business," comes from Ibsen's heart. Life itself is not an evil. Existence itself is not joyless. No, some one is to blame, or rather many are to blame, when a life is lost to the joy of life; and Norwegian society, depressing, coarse in its pleasures, enslaved to conventional ideas of duty, is pointed out as the culprit.

Clearly, according to this view, if Helene Alving's mother and aunts, when advising her on marriage, had stopped thinking about Alving's money and social position and had told her about the joys of love instead, Helene could have nurtured Alving's vocation in their connubial bed, and, from the joys shared there, they could have gone on together to other fulfilling activities—real work, of course, not just "business"—and even in Norway! Brandes, wishing to stress all that is positive in his response to Helene Alving, is unable to dismiss the play's determinism, and, in effect, he argues, inconsistently, on both sides. Quite apart from self-contradiction, however, Brandes is also one of the first who, with reference to *Ghosts*, is too confident about Ibsen's own opinions.

Others, however, have interpreted the themes in *Ghosts* as springing from determinism on the one hand, and from considerations of free will on the other, in a logically consistent manner. Sandra Saari, for example, in a revealing article, recently published,[3] having shown that early productions of *Ghosts* by August Lindberg and André Antoine made Oswald the central figure and thus overemphasized the play's physiological determinism, goes on to claim that, in Helene Alving, seen as the play's natural protagonist, we have an existentialist heroine. Helene cannot overcome the evils inherent in her situation, but she can and does make an existential decision which demonstrates her noble elevation of soul:

> The plot of the play is dramatically different with Mrs. Alving as protagonist. Stated simply it is: to confront the ghosts of the past. These take two forms, mental and physical. Manders' visit in Act I is the occasion of what Mrs. Alving believes to be her final act of ridding herself of the physical past. She has built the Orphanage with a sum equal to Alving's fortune when she married him. By giving the Orphanage to the town she will dispose of the Alving money, so Osvald will inherit only from her. But the Alving inheritance is biological as well as monetary. This aspect of the plot unfolds, as outlined earlier, to reveal Osvald's final inheritance from his father, which she is powerless to prevent.
>
> The mental ghosts are more elusive. Her free-thinking books, to which Manders so objects, represent what she asserts to be her present beliefs. Superstitions of the past, however, are not easily discarded. Manders' insistence in Act I on not insuring the Orphanage because of public opinion, echoes his insistence 29 years earlier that Mrs. Alving return to her husband because of duty and public opinion. That her mental habits have not totally altered in the intervening years, is demonstrated by her acquiescence to Manders' arguments, again against her better judgment. Though she fails this preliminary test of insuring the Orphanage, no moral issue is at stake. Her three subsequent choices are increasingly difficult tests of her freedom from the social and religious dicta of the past. Shall Osvald honor his father or shall he know the truth about his debauched progenitor? Mrs. Alving finally chooses to tell the truth rather than to conform to the Commandment by which she has lived for the past 28 years. Shall Osvald be allowed to marry his half-sister or shall the incest taboo be upheld? Mrs. Alving chooses to tell the whole truth about Captain Alving in order to forestall an incestuous marriage, though she had admitted earlier, "If only I were not such a miserable coward, I would say to him: marry her, or arrange things as you both will." Her final test is the most crucial, whether to grant Osvald the death he wishes.

Not only is the Commandment, thou shalt not kill, at issue, but also the more deeply rooted response of the mother for her child. She has made one ethical choice out of freedom from, and one choice out of obedience to, the ghosts of the past. Though she is not always able to choose freely, Mrs. Alving's capacity to exercise choice is so important to the plot that Ibsen concludes the play precisely at the moment of her greatest ethical decision. Many have argued that she will, or that she will not, administer a fatal dose; none has been able to demonstrate the logical inevitability of either choice, which is to say that Ibsen has constructed the terms of the play so that Mrs. Alving has a *real* choice.

With Mrs. Alving as protagonist, her psychological and metaphysical positions take precedence over Osvald's physical, physiological and social victimization. Her free will becomes a major consideration in the play. From this perspective, the plot concludes precisely at the moment of Mrs. Alving's greatest existential choice.

This theory is persuasive and, unlike Brandes's, is neither self-contradictory nor unwisely hyperbolical in its claims for Helene Alving. Like many other readings, however, it implies that the approach to life of the mature Mrs. Alving is entirely wholesome. Whatever the degree of her success as an exorcist, there can be no doubt, according to this view, that she is on the right side using every ounce of her energies against evil.

The reading of John Northam, supported at every stage with painstaking reference to aspects of visual and verbal imagery conducive to it, is one which rightly commands respect.[4] It is in many ways most fully representative of the positive interpretations of Mrs. Alving, and, like Saari's, concentrates on the growth of Helene's ability to exercise choice with courage. Northam, in a critical context which is humanitarian rather than metaphysical, certainly sees and stresses some limitations and inadequacies that he detects in Helene: they are, however, all contained within what he sees as her spiritually debilitating status as an educated upper-class woman living in a narrow-minded convention-ridden society. Helene is essentially an intellectual radical too inured to social expectations to defy them openly. Amusingly mimicking what Mrs. Alving may think of herself at the beginning of the play, Northam writes: "Of course one keeps one's radical ideas quiet; society expects it of one." From this starting point, the idea is developed that Mrs. Alving's integrity and heroic stature grow to an extent commensurate with her determined but faltering acquisition of humanitarian principles. The progress is slow. Indeed the very horror of Oswald's collapse, according to this view, is needed to shock Helene out of a consciousness still structured upon borrowed formulae into one of direct acceptance of reality. The famous "No; no; no.—Yes! No; no!" uttered in distraught response to Oswald's collapse into idiocy, and the indecision it reflects about whether to administer the morphine to Oswald, are seen as an inspiring triumph, for "Mrs. Alving faces the real fact and responds to it with language that has become naked."

It is tempting to accept this interpretation as wholly convincing. Certainly it makes sense of horror which is otherwise difficult for us, as well as for Mrs. Alving, to endure. Those who can convince themselves that Ibsen incontestably allows a romantic impulse to gain the upper hand in *Ghosts* will be able to find solace in the thought that, as John Northam puts it: "For all the pain and disaster, the existence, the beauty and the majesty, and the irrepressibility of truth have been affirmed." Mrs. Alving is seen, then, as one of Ibsen's "poets of living"—and though never fully articulate as we see her, her greatest epiphany comes to her as the play closes and may actually mark the acquisition of a hard-won ability to speak of reality as it is. *Ghosts* would be a more successfully artistic work if this view of Mrs. Alving as a fundamentally "splendid woman" were entirely convincing. However, there is much to indicate that Ibsen did not produce in *Ghosts* unified tragedy appropriately relieved from time to time by what have been regarded as episodes of broad and obvious comedy, but disunified tragicomedy.

Two other views which, like Saari's and Northam's, see Helene Alving as a convincing tragic heroine are those of Daniel Haakonsen[5] and Charles Leland.[6] And these, too, are persuasive but ultimately too generous to a character to whom Ibsen in fact gave, almost haphazardly, it seems, gravely negative characteristics, which go much further than concealment of life-giving convictions and hesitancy in articulating and acting upon them.

If, however, one can persuade oneself that there is an essentially unified vision in *Ghosts*, Haakonsen's theory that ethical sacrifice is the endorsed theme at the heart of *Ghosts* is entirely acceptable. Mrs. Alving certainly has the characteristics ascribed to her as a "passionate idealist." She traverses a stage of "blinded" idealism, mistakenly demanding a "purity [from] her husband" of which he is incapable—and thus precipitating the series of catastrophes which destroy Alving, her regard for him, and, much later, but inevitably, their son and with him all hope of happiness for Helene herself. And she may be seen as going on, as Haakonsen indicates, as a "doomed hero" to a second stage of passionate idealism in which she attains an *anagnorisis* ("discovery") which raises her to a level of heroic distinction comparable to those of the heroes of the metaphysical tragedy with whom Haakonsen compares her—Oedipus and Hamlet, for example. And this she may be seen as doing by learning to understand all that is positive and indicative of a creative and untainted way of life from the figure representative of a tragic type which is rightly seen as recurrent, namely that of the "innocent victim"—in this case Oswald. The "passionate idealist," who is also the "doomed hero," has sacrificial aspects, according to this theory, and though they are different from the more obvious ones of the "innocent victim," they complement them: the doomed hero demands too much of others and herself and the cost is high in terms of her own spiritual sufferings as well as others'. Ultimately, however, her reward is the recovery of "sight" and the possibility of independent action. Tragic unity, therefore, is seen as underpinning human and dramatic relationships, which, though not actually metaphysical, have reverberations which echo the profundities of the sacrifice motif in Greek and Shakespearian tragedy:

> The act of sacrificing another person to oneself, and the act of sacrificing oneself to another, are both portrayed on the stage and the final anguish experienced by Mrs. Alving exposes at one and the same time her guilt and her innocence, her greatness and her limitation.

There can be little doubt that the apprehension of the human condition in *Ghosts* penetrates at times to mysterious levels from which, to some minds, ethical and religious intimations seem to proceed, if not simultaneously and inextricably, at least almost indistinguishably.

Charles Leland's *"Ghosts* seen from an existential aspect" is a response to the suggestions of mystical profundity in the play. Leland points out that he has taken account of existential theories both theistic and atheistic, both Catholic and Protestant in formulating his conviction that Helene Alving's spiritual progress may be understood to advantage in terms of "situation ethics." Her dramatic stance is perceived in relation to the following pattern of ideas:

> Traditional norms of good and evil considered as absolutes are rejected. Human freedom itself is the only value, the source of all others. Man is "condemned to be free;" human freedom can never be abstract because it is always exercised and realized in a given concrete situation in which he must choose. Man must choose in a concrete, real world, and the choices are unique, involving unique human actions and unique human encounters. In this system, then, there are no universal moral principles or laws, no universal criteria of action. As a consequence, a person must ultimately take complete responsibility for his own acts, instead of hiding behind the protection of abstract laws which require no genuine personal commitment.

Pastor Manders is viewed as the incarnation of "essentialist" ethics, which are in the sharpest possible dramatic contrast to Helene's existential apprehension. Interestingly, Leland, in contrast with Northam, sees the initial disposition of Helene Alving's mind as being less inclined to syntheses of doubtful value and, long before the horror of Oswald's collapse, "open to the existential, the unexpected, the contingent." Rather than being most clearly distinguished by a Cartesian quality, her "mind [is] struggling towards further, unknown and mysterious dimensions of reality."

This inherently metaphysical approach culminates in the conviction that Helene's stuggle to know whether she would be right to kill Oswald is an utterly convincing, totally ingenuous echoing of the central sacrificial mysteries of the Old and New Testaments: after the "parody of the sacrificial victim," which Leland, like others, perceives in Engstrand, "comes the real sacrifice: Mrs. Alving is called upon to offer up her only son. No moral categories cover this act. One can only invoke the archetypal sacrifices: Abraham's offering of Isaac and Christ's offering himself to the Father." In considering these conclusions, it seems likely that some will again find themselves wishing that the play had as much clarity and unity of focus as the interpretation. Once more, however, Mrs. Alving's most seriously negative aspects are too kindly passed over, and even though she is associated—because of her adulterous inclinations—with sin, the association is seen as ultimately redemptive because it places her in a positive relation to "sin mysticism." The idea, a compelling one, is that sinners can be closer to God in reality than the *bien pensant*, the self-righteous, the virtuous. Mrs. Alving is therefore charitably viewed by Leland as only (but savingly) a *"sinner manqué."*

Hans Georg Meyer, in a work which seems to have met with undeserved neglect, makes a very strong case for viewing Mrs. Alving as a savage predator in a horrifyingly destructive world, one which Ibsen has created to demonstrate his "own version of the Fall," his own study of "regression into barbarism" through convincing representation of a culture bent upon the "reification of man."[7] Meyer's study is unfortunately briefer than most, but he succeeds in showing, persuasively, that the only values that may be finally recognized in *Ghosts* are those of property and money. It is widely acknowledged that Engstrand and Regine are the revolting products of what Marxists refer to as "the callous cash nexus." Rarely, however, are the indications of the negative aspects of Helene Alving's character perceived as clearly as Meyer perceives them. According to Meyer, Mrs. Alving not only sells herself into marriage on the misguided advice of her female relatives, but, having done so, and become inured to acquisitive values, she perversely excises any possibility of compassion and love from her relationship with Alving. Simultaneously, she seeks to possess Oswald no matter what he is—an incontinent cretin, for instance—or to assert total predatory control over him by destroying him if *she* pleases. Meyer expresses these not widely discussed views succinctly:

> Oswald's return to his mother . . . is the counterpart of Regina's return to her father [actually, stepfather]. While the father–daughter relationship is commercialized, the mother–son relation reverts [as another form of "reification"] to an instinctual tie, reduced to the need for food and nurture in the one and the mothering instinct in the other. A "terrible fear" announces that Oswald's disease is about to

enter the paralytic stage, a fear whose dark threat imperils his individuality. Oswald's paralysis demonstrates disintegration of personality as starkly as Regina's prostitution. Helene, whose whole life has been devoted to maneuvering Oswald back into the nursery, is grimly taken at her word. Her son is restored to her—infantile for the rest of his life. She herself is finally fixed in her maternal role. There is even the possibility that she will agree to "lend him a helping hand" and take back the life she gave. This would be a second form of degenerate love, one that negates human beings.

The last of the sample interpretations also has a deeply negative emphasis in both general and specific terms. David Thomas develops, in a Laingian discussion of the psychological aspects of *Ghosts*, interesting theories which leave him convinced that in "Ibsen's vision of life there is ultimately no remedy for the suffering inherent in human being."[8] And, in specific terms, he views as totally destructive the relations between, in ascending order of dramatic importance, Engstrand and Regine, Manders and Mrs. Alving, and Oswald and Mrs. Alving.

In presenting the evidence that "may point to a radically new view of what constitutes the tragic core in *Ghosts*," Thomas seeks to demonstrate that established readings of the work, concentrating on Mrs. Alving's supposed enlightenment and Oswald's physiologically determined insanity, make the play seem both more static and more retrospectively analytical than it is. *Ghosts* must be seen, suggests Thomas, as concentrating not on Helene's quest for truth—which naturally calls for a scrupulous re-evaluation of the past—but on what characters may be seen to be doing to each other in the present and before our eyes. Their past is important only in so far as it makes comprehensible their inability to extricate themselves from wounding past relationships and to enter into sane and sound ones in the present. Regine cannot forgive Engstrand for what she perceives as his continuous mental torture of her mother; Engstrand, deeply humiliated, Thomas suggests, by a wife who rejected his genuine love and taunted him about his physical deformity, still sees in Regine the girl who always sided with her mother against him.

Mrs. Alving is seen as a woman so scarred by Manders's rejection of her love—an experience from which her recovery is impossible—that her principal aim in all her dealings with Manders is to wound and insult him as appallingly as she was herself once hurt by Manders. She is, according to this interpretation, utterly ruthless in her pursuit of vengeance, while Manders is "psychologically if not actually physically impotent" and a coward guilty of "blatant evasion" of the truth both about himself and about social realities in general.

Mrs. Alving's intellectual commitments, humane and progressive or otherwise, are not primarily important to the comprehension of the crushing psychological defeat she is seen as inflicting upon Manders nor to an understanding of her struggle to dominate Oswald, which necessitates, among other things, the getting rid of Regine, whom she perceives as a rival in the struggle of which Oswald is the prize. This mother–son relationship Thomas interestingly perceives as so complex and devastating as to be quite beyond the reach of reason for both Helene and Oswald. They are trapped in it to the peril of their sanity. As Thomas puts it:

> Their relationship has been characterized by an avoidance of issues that might lead to conflict and this, in its turn, has forced them to suppress explosively powerful emotions. Over the years their relationship has festered on. In Mrs. Alving it has produced suppressed guilt for neglecting and, ultimately, rejecting, her son during his childhood, a guilt that turns into feverish possessiveness as Osvald grows older. In Osvald's case, his relationship with his mother has made him chronically insecure; he feels unwanted and yet emotionally imprisoned. This has gradually produced in him a sense of burning resentment.

The horrific results of the turmoil in Mrs. Alving's mind are, it is claimed, that she drives away in utter degradation the man who dared not accept her love and, in attempting to take possession of the only human being still left at the centre of her emotional life—Oswald—brings about his madness.

It is possible to set aside reservations about particulars of this interpretation—such as the supposed capacity of Engstrand for genuine love and the contentious imputation to Manders of impotence—without rejecting what is most valuable in it. Its worth lies in drawing attention to some of the attributes of the play which *are* quite different from what may be observed in *Oedipus Rex*, for instance. In the Sophoclean tragedy, truth is decreed by the gods: the present is made unendurable by discovering the truth about the past, which is fixed and essential. There is a temptation to see *Ghosts*, especially because its retrospective method is so reminiscent of *Oedipus Rex*, too exclusively in terms of a Sophoclean quest. Thomas, who understands the truth in *Ghosts* as continually defining itself within a series of psychological interactional conflicts, provides a useful counterbalance.

But there remains the element of *Ghosts* which *is* Sophoclean, which substitutes a physiologically deterministic fate for divine fate (and so makes a naturalistic vision compatible with Sophoclean attitudes and techniques) and which enables Ibsen to achieve some of his best situational ironies by juxtaposing the efforts, admirable or otherwise, of human beings to control their lives with intimations of implacable agencies beyond human control. Thomas's efforts, which enlist one of Ibsen's notes for the play, to demonstrate that the fate motif in *Ghosts* is "inorganic" are ingenious but not ultimately convincing.

The exigencies of theatrical production, to which Thomas appropriately refers, do indeed necessitate the emphasis of a clearly definable and theatrically communicable reading of the play. The Bristol Arts Centre production of *Ghosts* of 1973, which was directed by David Thomas, and which is used to demonstrate the theories expressed in his article, must have been thoroughly intelligible, but its Laingian orientation, however revealing in certain respects, ultimately has the same weakness as other univocal interpretations: it suppresses those elements of the play, some well, some poorly developed, which cannot be made to serve it. One of the casualities of Thomas's approach appears to be the play's humour: with such a profusion of psychological anguish, one wonders where the Bristol production found a place for laughter at the knowing and ridiculous disingenuousness, unscrupulousness, and hypocrisy of which Engstrand, Regine, and Manders seem so capable.

Similarly the play's embodiment of types of evil not emanating from forms of psychological maladjustment is weakened if Thomas's view is accepted unreservedly. Some will find it hard to stop thinking of Engstrand as the near Devil (whose trademark is his deformed left leg) that Ibsen at least half succeeded in making him in order to concentrate on an interpretation which sees him as the maimed survivor of a marriage in which he is definitely supposed to have suffered unrequited passion. There is, after all, evidence that he married the "fallen" Johanna for money, thus committing one of the worst and most unambiguous sins in Ibsen and one mentioned in Ibsen's notes for *Ghosts* as inviting "Nemesis."[9] It may well be that we are invited to pity him, devilish or not, since his "sin" is a cruder version, as Helene is fully aware, of her own—in marrying Alving for money. But Engstrand's claims as a sympathetic character are not impressive.

Before turning to Engstrand in the context of the play's opening episode—and beginning to test the text for unity—there is something to be said, as so often with Ibsen, for turning first to the end of the play. It is in discussion of the ending that the sharpest disagreements among the critics come most clearly into focus, and there too that, if the play is in any way characteristically Ibsenian, we are most likely to be able to gauge its tone. This is, as it happens, especially true of *Ghosts*, which seems to call out for the reworking which its predecessor, *A Doll's House*, received. Hermann J. Weigand has shown that the ending of the first draft of *A Doll's House*, marked, quite literally, a new beginning in which that play, originally conceived and expressed in earnest tragic terms, became permeated by comic ironies.[10] Given, indeed, the three facts (1) that Ibsen spoke of *Ghosts* as a natural and inevitable successor to *A Doll's House*, (2) that *A Doll's House* is a tragicomic work, and (3) that Ibsen spent only five months on the entire composition of *Ghosts* (less, that is, than one-quarter of his normal period for taking a play from initial idea to completed final draft), it is predictable that *Ghosts* might be an imperfectly structured tragicomedy, and that its ending may be the surest place available to test its essential mood (if it has one) at its most mature.

The point at which Oswald forces his mother back into the drawing room (or, more precisely, "spacious garden-room") from which she has just fled in a vain attempt to get a doctor for him, marks the beginning of the play's culminating episode. A desperate mother is literally locked in, entirely against her will, by a son who has told her in the clearest possible terms that his complete mental collapse is certain and possibly imminent. In these circumstances—that is to say, under duress and still obviously feeling a need to keep Oswald as calm as possible—she agrees to the suggestion that had precipitated her flight—to administer a fatal dose of morphine to Oswald "if it becomes necessary." She offers him her hand to seal the bargain, and for a few moments, a deceptive peace descends.

Oswald.   You will . . .?

Mrs. Alving. If it becomes necessary. But it won't *be* necessary. No, no, it's quite impossible!

Oswald.   Well, let us hope so. And let's live together as long as we can. Thank you, Mother.

[He sits in the armchair, which Mrs. Alving has moved over to the sofa. Day is dawning; the lamp is still burning on the table.]

Mrs. Alving. [approaching him cautiously]. Do you feel calmer now?

Oswald.   Yes.

Here, it seems, we have every indication of positive maternal behaviour, while Oswald seems reassured by the promise, and even quietly resigned to spending whatever period of sanity remains to him with his mother. His "Yes," however, is, quite literally, the last sane word that he utters, and in the passage which follows, certainly one of the most brilliant and the most profoundly disturbing Ibsen ever wrote, there is evidence of tragicomic unity and of control over the representation of all the conflicting responses to life which the critics discuss.

If there are still people who wish to see a dramatic representation of what, in 1881, was thought to be the exact fate which overtook victims of hereditary syphilis, they may see that—in which case, what Mrs. Alving subsequently says to Oswald is likely to have little significance, for the meaning of the play will be confined, as Sandra Saari points out, to an appalling demonstration of the power that indifferent natural forces may have over us, whatever we do or say. As George Moore said of Antoine's production at the *Théâtre Libre*, in which Oswald was played as the protagonist and his destiny was interpreted entirely in terms of psychological and mental determinism, "we learn that though there be no gods to govern us . . . nature, vast and unknown, for ever dumb to our appeal, holds us in thrall."[11]

If, in terms of Georg Brandes's preferred reading, Mrs. Alving has understood for some time the social malaise (as well as the physical one) which destroyed Alving's capacity for joy and which made her its unwilling accomplice and Oswald its hereditary victim, then what she says to Oswald, after his last sane monosyllable is uttered, may be seen as an outpouring of the purest compassion, an offering of all the love, and the only kind of love he can hope for. It is permeated with untruthful reassurances and a degree of maternal sweetness not acceptable in usual adult behaviour. However, since this is a most unusual situation for a grown man and his mother to find themselves in, its evasions and its anaesthetic phrases are appropriate and truly pathetic in the light of what Brandes tells us of the consequences of stifling the "joy of life." In this particular situation, Helene must try, out of humanity, to ease her son's suffering, or "dread" as Oswald himself, unconsciously but ironically echoing Kierkegaard, calls it, by diverting his attention from the terror of truth:

> Mrs. Alving [bent over him]. What terrible ideas they were to get into your head, Oswald. But all just imagination. All these upsets have been too much for you. But now you'll be able to have a good long rest. At home, with your mother beside you, my darling. Anything you want you shall have, just like when you were a little boy. There now. The attack's over. You see how quickly it went. Oh, I knew it would . . . See what a lovely day we're going to have, Oswald? Brilliant sunshine. Now you'll see the place properly.

Mrs. Alving, the loving mother comforting her son and distracting his mind from morbidity with talk of a delightful new beginning, is as tender as Peer, the loving son, inventing soothing fantasies about heaven and Soria Moria Castle to ease the dying mind of his frightened old mother. Her tone is that of infinite reassurance. She wants to grant his every wish and to be guardian of his happiness, just as Solveig, at her most motherly, accepts the charge of Peer's soul.

In the terms of Northam's view of Mrs. Alving as a "poet of living" who confronts reality directly, and with language stripped of all evasion, only after Oswald's mindless demand for "The sun. The sun," this last coherent speech of Helene's is presumably her final attempt to deny the full truth to herself: suspecting the worst, she goes on clinging, for as long as she can, to a more bearable vision of reality. That attempt ends, as Northam sees it, when she puts out the lamp just after this speech. She is then, first, shocked by Oswald's dementia into the horror that destroys the last vestiges of her commitment to conventional ideas and verbal formulae. Then, second, she is granted the gift of truth as the sun rises to illuminate the mountain peaks behind her mindless child. Similar thematic responses underlie the interpretation of Daniel Haakonsen: and his emphases on the motif of sacrifice and the closeness of its ethical expression in some of Ibsen's works to its metaphysical significances in Sophocles and Shakespeare place *Ghosts* very firmly where many would like to see it, namely in the great tradition of high tragedy. Charles Leland's view is acceptable to those who can perceive Mrs. Alving's final state of "speechless horror" in relation to a theistic interpretation of the sun's illumination of the glacier and mountain peaks in the background. Rightly, Leland sees in this ending the possibility of a kind of salvation that is a certainty in *Murder in the Cathedral*: "Could she have been granted some of the insight of Becket in T. S. Eliot's play—that the end of all action is passion? that the action is passion and the passion, action? 'This cannot be endured,' yes! Yet somehow in the end, It is endured!'"[12] Hans Meyer's and David Thomas's negative interpretations of Mrs. Alving's motives and behaviour see hideous spiritual perversions in the ending. In Meyer's terms, Oswald, as an unthinking object, is now what his mother has always wanted him to be—hers, hers alone, incapable of resistance, to possess and use as she pleases. In these terms, of course, the sunrise is the grimmest irony, for that mythic embodiment of godlike truth and justice, that source of life and joy with which Oswald, when sane and happy, equates all that is creative in his own life and work, rises to illumine the darkest aspects of a civilisation (that of the entire West, it seems) which has driven out genuine human as well as divine love.

In Thomas's terms, the ending is similarly bleak. The whole relationship between Mrs. Alving and Oswald is viewed as a protracted "false conflict"—one, that is, in which the opponents, avoiding open conflicts as much as possible, are incapable even of clearly identifying, let alone resolving, the issues which rob their relationship of integrity and positive growth. Mrs. Alving is, according to this reading, triumphantly possessive in her last coherent speech, a child-devouring mother who has reduced her schizophrenic son to apparent acquiescence in his loss of all power of independent action. Seen in this way, the ending of the play is a succession of unrelieved horrors: it is revolting to see one human being perversely possessed by another; revolting again to hear the quiet jubilation which may inform "At home, with your mother beside you, my darling. Anything you want you shall have, just like when you were a little boy"; horrendous, when, at Oswald's collapse into what is seen as mindless paralysis, the delusions of the mother herself are shattered, plunging *her* into hideous confusion. The sun rises, according to this interpretation, upon a son and a mother both destroyed, both irretrievably lost to hope in the sunlight which, with fearful irony, irradiates for the audience the darkest recesses of the psyche of each character only when both mother and child are completely bereft of light, trapped in the secular hell that they themselves have unwittingly helped to create. The ending may, therefore, be seen as inviting without any distortion as many negative as positive readings. Wanting to see Mrs. Alving as undoubtedly heroic is as understandable as viewing her as a kind of existential Medea, but as nearly always in Ibsen, we are offered not just what we would prefer to have emphasized but a disturbing union of antitheses. And in this instance, Ibsen supplies us with a perfect visual emblem of his vision: Helene Alving falls to her knees beside Oswald, then jumps up in anguish and "tears at her hair with both hands" (as Åse does when she believes her son is lost to her for ever) before fumbling at his breast for the morphine. The last we see of Helene is "with her hands [again] clutching her hair [and] staring at [Oswald] with speechless horror." There could be no more dramatically potent expression of the full range of the tragicomic ambivalences in the play: all that may be seen as positive about Helene Alving is concentrated on her possible ability to reappraise her entire life and so arrive at a true understanding of love and creativity; the very moment of her epiphany may, however, just as well be seen as robbing her of all she has left to love and leaving her, absurdly, like an apostle in a desert, as it may be viewed as the acquisition of truth in some sense genuinely healing. Similarly, all that may be seen as negative about her, which centers upon her possible destructive possessiveness, demands that the possession become indisputable; at the very end of the play, though, Oswald has become so repulsive (even as an object!) as to be hardly worth the possession. The distraught Helene, wondering whether to administer the morphine to Oswald, may just as well be seen as recognizing the troll she has made of him as still wishing to keep him alive at no matter what minimal level or to kill him for perverse reasons. The possession is not indisputable because Helene may not want the Oswald she has helped to form. And the context in which this horrifically many-faceted vision shapes itself is as possibly metaphysical and ethical as determinist, atheistically existential, or utterly amoral. One wishes that Ibsen had reworked *Ghosts* so that the wonder of its ending—which Shaw rightly found so overwhelming as to "prevent the meaning of the play from being [with any facility] seized and discussed"[13]—might be consistently foreshadowed in its beginning and its middle.

Unfortunately the case is otherwise, for though *Ghosts* is properly regarded as a greater work than the realistic and totally secular social plays which are its generic companions (*Pillars of Society, A Doll's House,* and *An Enemy of the People*), it is more flawed than any of these patently tragicomic works. In the theatre it is now possible to see productions of *Pillars of Society* which make the most of the streak of hypocrisy which runs within Karsten Bernick and may totally invalidate his "conversion." As Inga-Stina Ewbank remarked in a programme note for The Royal Shakespeare Company's centennial production of the play: ". . . now, exactly a hundred years since the play was written, in the wake of the Watergates, of the Poulsons and the T. Dan Smiths, the dark grin at the end of this fascinating and ambiguous play seems wider than ever."[14] That is indeed true and becoming ever more obvious as we learn still more of what bribes can do to the integrity of politicians. And it is worth noting that the ironic element is not confined to revealing the cunning of Bernick's confession—which mentions nothing of his worst crime (attempted murder) and seems calculated actually to increase and entrench his power while destroying that of his rivals. If the ending is interpreted negatively, Lona Hessel may look as foolish as Bernick appears nefarious; she above all others should understand Bernick's wiliness and his capacity for betrayal, yet, as the play ends, she is seemingly sunk in sentimental acceptance of his supposed virtue: "Old love does not rust," she declares. But Ibsen does not make decisions about the ending easy. There are positive indications—Bernick, for instance, has vowed not to impose his ambitions on his son (one of Ibsen's recurrent tests of parental wisdom). So Lona's faith may be, at least in part, justified.

Similarly, not all productions of *A Doll's House* are now as boringly unambiguous as the 1971 New York production for which Anselma Dell'Olio, in a tediously predictable note, wrote that the "feminist politics of *A Doll's House* created a sensation when it first appeared in 1879: and the anatomy of oppression it exposes is still unfortunately relevant—and shockingly so—in 1971."[15] With the solitary exception of *The League of Youth*, Ibsen is never, mercifully, "relevant" in such simple-minded terms. Hermann Weigand showed in 1925 that Nora is as much an actress delighting in role-playing as a courageous precursor of Emmeline Pankhurst, and that Torvald is not, except for those who prefer to see his character forced into a melodramatic mould, a mere common or garden chauvinist.[16] And if Nora were not so intent on hyperbolic accusation, on changing her costume for her exit, and on slamming the door in high melodramatic style, the woman in her might observe what the embarrassingly naive feminist overlooks or ignores, namely the indications that Torvald, for all his faults, is taking her at least as seriously as he can—and perhaps even as seriously as she deserves.

Productions of *An Enemy of the People* are also likely to reveal the comical hysteric in Dr. Stockmann as well as the heroic and tragically hounded individualist. He is a man who can, when under the pressure of ridicule and abuse, veer, in a matter of minutes, from faith in democracy to protofascism and to advocating the breeding of a genetically engineered super-race. Appropriately, he inspires such good theatrical jokes as the one played on him in The Stockholm Royal Theatre's production, directed by Staffan Roos for the Bergen Festival of 1975: at the very moment that Stockmann announced his last momentous discovery—that "the strongest man is he who stands alone"—his family, who had all been busily occupied sweeping broken glass from the floor while he meditated, all handed him their brooms! This is not in the text, but it is certainly in the spirit of this effectively but straightforwardly tragicomic play.

Reading, writing about, and staging *Ghosts*, therefore, is both more demanding, because of thematic confusion, and more likely to be comprehensively revealing, because of the play's profundity, than similar efforts devoted to its companion pieces. It has serious flaws arising from erratically expressed visions of life, but it is nonetheless a greater play than its nearest rival—*A Doll's House*—as the depth as well as the quantity of criticism of it suggests.

The basic structural device in *Ghosts* is the verbal pitched battle—to call them "duels" would be to suggest gentility, preoccupation with fixed codes of honour, and similar chivalrous overtones inappropriate to the bloody-mindedness that is present in all the no-holds-barred fights in *Ghosts*. Occasionally, one of the contenders will appear to win a decisive victory—as Mrs. Alving apparently does in more than one struggle with Pastor Manders—but it is essential to perceive that ultimately there are no conquests definitely endorsed by the play itself as positive. There is an abundance of evil in the work—much of it centered in Engstrand, who is usually regarded as knowingly malevolent, and Oswald, who is in many ways what Peer Gynt refuses to be—a beast of burden for the sins and woes of others—but no certain evaluation of good. And that is presumably why Ibsen insisted so vehemently in conversation with William Archer that he had not allowed *Ghosts* to become tendentious:

> He [Ibsen] said, "The people in the North are terrible. I write a play with five characters and they insist on putting in a sixth—namely Ibsen. There never was a play with less utterance of personal opinion in it."[17]

He does much the same thing in a letter to Sophus Schandorph, in which he states categorically: ". . . there is not in the whole book [*Ghosts*] a single opinion, a single utterance, that can be laid to the account of the author."[18] Of course, remarks like these invite speculation that Ibsen insists too much upon an impartiality that is doubtful. And there is certainly enough truth in that view to prompt recollection of, for instance, Ibsen's claim, made in a letter to Otto Borchsenius, that he wrote *Ghosts* with the intention of stimulating radical thought in Scandinavia.[19] There is no inevitable contradiction in Ibsen's position, however. He is claiming simply that he is asking questions that must be asked—and leaving it to others to provide the answers, if they can.

Interestingly, what seems to have angered Ibsen most is the idea that he had written a mere *pièce à thèse* rather than an open-ended work calculated to arouse controversy. And behind the anger in the letter to Schandorph is a tacit admission that the form he thought he had used well enough to communicate his impartiality has failed in that respect:

> The method in itself, the technique which determined the form of the work, entirely precluded the author's appearing in the speeches. My intention was to produce the impression in the mind of the reader that he was experiencing something real. Now, nothing would more effectively prevent such an impression than the insertion of the author's private opinions in the dialogue. Do they imagine at home that I have not enough dramatic instinct to be aware of this? Of course I was aware of it, and I acted accordingly. And in none of my other plays is the author such an outsider, so entirely absent, as in this one.[20]

If Ibsen is to be taken at his word—and the ending of the play suggests he should be—he has not written a play meant to proclaim that "joy of life" is certainly attainable for those wiser or more fortunate than the Alvings, or that evil, whether social, psychological, or metaphysical, is either comprehensible or eradicable. And neither, it seems, was *Ghosts* meant to demonstrate conclusively that a tragic and destructive conflict between the sexes is as inevitable as it appears to be in the *Oresteia*, which Ibsen seems to echo in *Ghosts*, or in the theories about matriarchy of the French sociologist Paul Lafargue, whose views *Ghosts* seems to foreshadow by a few years.[21] Obviously, therefore, all univocal interpretations of *Ghosts* including those referred to in this chapter can claim only tentative status—as revealing examinations of parts of a whole.

But because *Ghosts* is such a compelling work, there is a natural tendency to try to find some way of seeing it as consistent in both theme and structure. Nothing is more tempting than to take hold of one of its loose ends and follow it into the fabric of the play, thus losing sight of the entire fascinating but ill-woven tapestry.

The first verbal battle, which opens *Ghosts*, is the one between Jacob Engstrand and his supposed daughter, Regine. It makes for a lively and vexatiously unclear beginning.

The interests of clarity are not, in fact, well served, either, by the detailed description of the set, which precedes the Regine–Engstrand altercation. As John Northam has pointed out, the garden room, which is continued into an open and rather narrower conservatory at the back, is, despite the darkness of its wall-coverings and furniture, both "spacious" and "attractive."[22] It is mistaken, therefore, to visualize, as Francis Fergusson does, a "stuffy parlor";[23] there is no clutter, no bric-à-brac, no suggestion of a Birmingham or a Chicago manufacturer's philistine tastes. But it is too generous to see here, as Northam also does, only, or even definitely, a civilised haven where the presence of books and periodicals suggests intellectual liveliness, and assumed flowers, brightness, and vitality. It is entirely *sensible* to see this room in such terms and possible also to think, as Northam does, of the foul weather outside as suggesting the gloomy and pervasive influence of social coercion. But that is a chosen rather than an inevitable interpretation. In *Rosmersholm* and *Hedda Gabler* flowers in the house are undoubtedly used to suggest Dionysian forces. It is harder to be sure here—in fact, not even plants are specifically mentioned though their presence in a garden room must be assumed, especially as Regine is holding a water syringe. The brightness of flowers is a touch of poetic licence, however, that did not occur to Ibsen (any more than John Barton's idea, for his production of *Pillars of the Community*, to have dead houseplants about the set is in the original[24]).

In fact, the relationship between the garden room (about which Ibsen provided more details in a letter to Duke Georg von Meiningen[25]) with its apparently sombre, though dignified and spacious interior and the gloomy, rain-soaked landscape seen beyond is the first puzzle in the play. Are we, in fact, witnessing an artificial haven under seige from the forces of social coercion outside, as Northam persuasively argues (both Engstrand and Manders enter from the garden and seem thoroughly at home in the rain)? Surely it would be a little odd that Ibsen should so exclusively identify the natural phenomena of the weather with the distinctly artificial forces that shape social convention? The rain-soaked landscape could just as well be another and even more direct application of the pathetic fallacy: that the gloom outside the house reflects the benighted souls of those within it. And to confuse matters further, Engstrand, with his deformed left leg and an oversized boot, speaks of "God's rain," while Regine regards it as the Devil's.

Given Engstrand's specifically satanic deformity, we certainly cannot discount this talk of the proprietorship of weather as mere colloquial chit-chat, and before long the ambiguities present in the visual symbolism of the stage direction and in Regine and Engstrand's conversation became precisely those which characterize opposing interpretations. Some perceive God in the play, others the starkest atheism; some see the Alving home as the birthplace of enlightenment, others as a chamber of horrors whose most hideous scenes of torture still await their hour. It is tempting to equate the plants and Regine's association with them with that presumably Dionysian phenomenon "the joy of life": elsewhere the present writer has been naive enough to do so,[26] not stopping to ponder sufficiently why Dionysus should have to dwell only indoors and among the houseplants in Norway while some other deity seems to preside in the garden and among the mountaintops. While we know, from Oswald, that Parisian joyfulness does not travel well, it is absurd to think of a Norwegian Dionysus of aspidistras and potted geraniums. Tensions and conflicts *are* suggested by the first stage direction: their ambiguities would be fully acceptable if only their antithetical terms were more adequately perceptible. As it is, the reader or director must take his pick and hope for the best.

It is acceptable in *Peer Gynt* to have a host of possible identities for the Great Boyg, for example, and as many possible motives why Peer should fight to destroy him, because we understand the reasons for Peer's confusion. But it is difficult to know how to react to the quarrel between Regine and Engstrand as it must be to decide how it should be performed, because some of the ambiguities are, in the end, irritating rather than revealing. If Engstrand is malevolent, for instance, does that quality suggest a satanic force behind the action, one necessary to complement the God some see in the sacrifice of Oswald? If so, how are we to respond to those indications that Engstrand, for all his sanctimoniousness, his cunning, and his manipulative treatment of others, seems, above all, as much a product of specifically secular and social factors as Uriah Heep? If we feel inclined to be as thoroughly compassionate towards him as does David Thomas, it is hard to know what to do with the ridicule that Ibsen pours upon Engstrand—whose limp, we eventually learn, was acquired in a violent brawl when he was probably as drunk as his dockside assailants, though he claims that he had gone into the dance-hall where he was injured to preach temperance. It is possible to think of Engstrand as a poor devil made miserable and malicious by years of sexual humiliation and, at the same time, a coarser version of the clownish, drunken moralist represented in a more refined (and dramatically successful) way by Ulrik Brendel. But, as the text presents him, it is hard to feel convinced that he really is such a fully rounded character, and lack of clear focus in other characters and in the themes to which they are related does nothing to remove this difficulty. Engstrand is not alone in being like a good sketch of a tragicomic character which was never fully developed.

And in this first struggle, it is also possible to think of Regine as both a sensitive young woman doing all she can to silence Engstrand because recollections of her dead mother's suffering at his hands are unendurable *and* a pert and snobbish opportunist ashamed at Engstrand's talk because it indicates her own association with him—and so may ruin her chances of marrying Oswald. The text does indicate, though again sketchily, both sensitivity and acquisitiveness. "Poor mother! You drove her to her death the way you tormented her" may, if it is more than hyperbolic rhetoric, indicate deep wounds: it would be no wonder if Regine really could not bear the thought of going "home" with Engstrand. But later she asks him how much money he actually has saved to establish the sailors' brothel he has been describing, and, when told that the amount is eight hundred crowns, she is impressed—"Not bad." Later, in the last act, we are to learn, from Regine herself, that she had long suspected her mother of being free with sexual favours, and if this is so, one wonders why her attachment to the mother she now openly disapproves of appears so strong in Act I. Perhaps this is an instance of a hastily designed plot twisting a character to meet inconsistent requirements. The extent to which Regine is a complex character—part scheming, hard-bitten opportunist and part spirited, sensitive creature who deserves something better than the work as a servant Mrs. Alving has foisted upon her—is an open question, but it is the kind of negative openness, springing it seems from technical deficiency, that *Ghosts* would be better without. The dramatic needs of tragicomedy would be better served by a Regine as clearly schizophrenic as her half-brother, Oswald.

There are indications, however, in this opening dialogue between Engstrand and Regine that Ibsen is playing obscure literary games as well as introducing suggestive motifs which are inadequately developed later on. It is potentially tragicomic that Engstrand should have a visually satanic aspect while in his trade (that of a carpenter) calling to mind Christ—with whom, later, in offering to shoulder Manders's supposed guilt, Engstrand openly compares himself. There is tragicomic potential as well in the name "Jacob," which, appropriately, means "the supplanter." He certainly supplants Manders in the possession of the remnants of the Alving fortune. But, does Ibsen, who knew the Bible intimately and who frequently makes allusions to it, mean us to recall the Biblical Jacob, with whom God established a sacred covenant for a chosen people? If he does, and it seems likely, at least to the extent that *Ghosts* is representative of the spiritual state of Western civilisation, he makes little *dramatic* use of the motif. The name "Jacob" is not actually spoken until late in Act I, and the mere mention of the name can hardly be expected, in any performance, to evoke memories of God's promise to the patriarch Jacob, together with audience consciousness of a possible parodic reflection of it. Given the untidiness of the play, the associations of Engstrand with the Old Testament through his first name and with the New Testament through his own comparison of himself with Christ are likely to produce not a controlled tragicomic effect but mere bewilderment.

Ibsen is undoubtedly using names to some purpose in *Ghosts*. "Engstrand," for instance, means "narrow beach," and must instantly, for a Norwegian audience at least, suggest a dangerous place of refuge for Engstrand's prey—those sailors "on the high seas" whose profitable destruction he has in mind. But what Ibsen meant to convey through the use of "Jacob," is, because of the vagueness in the dramatic context, likely to remain no more than a subject of inconclusive speculation. In a perfectly controlled naturalistic tragicomedy, *The Wild Duck*, Ibsen makes admirably effective use of a Crucifixion motif, and it is possible that he had St. Hedwig in mind (as well as his own sister) in choosing the name of Gina Ekdal's daughter. One can only wonder what Ibsen might have done with "Jacob" and the idea of sublime aspiration inherent in the heavenly ladder if he had worked for more than five months on *Ghosts*.

More obscurity, and uncertainty of technique, is present in the ironic association of Engstrand with the motif, which occurs repeatedly in Ibsen, of the honest workman. Within moments of starting his altercation with Regine, Engstrand tells her that he was "up and at work at half-past five this morning." But only by taking a specifically literary approach—comparing the play with all the others by Ibsen in which the "honest workman" motif occurs with varying significances—is it possible to see that Engstrand's supposed early-morning vigilance may have some thematic connections with, for instance, the diligence of the Button-Moulder, described as carrying his "box of tools and a large casting ladle," and the labours of the Cook and the Peasant who amputates a finger in *Peer Gynt*, and with the workers and the shirkers in *Pillars of Society*—where Aune has a pathetic speech about his tool-box—and in *The Wild Duck*. Perhaps Engstrand is, in some sense, the embodiment of a sinister consciousness—like the Button-Moulder. Perhaps his willingness to exploit the hypocrisy of people wealthier and more obviously powerful than himself is a reflection of entirely secular evil—like that which, for a time, oppresses Aune and makes him an accomplice in attempted murder. Not knowing, because the motif is ill-developed, is harmful to the play: it is only one of several seeds of ambivalence that might have grown to a dramatic and theatrical flowering in *Ghosts* but which seem blasted before they have properly put down roots.

The next encounter, between Regine and Pastor Manders, is less ambivalent than what precedes it: whatever is the nature and complexity of Regine's relationship with Engstrand, her supposed father, here with Manders, she is, without any doubt whatever, a scheming liar using the bait of her sexual attraction in the hope of exploiting the Pastor. Manders himself makes a comparatively neutral impression: he is not the "big baby" that Helene is later to call him, in what may be one of the play's few moments of fun (or an instance of Helene's derision of the ineffectuality of the man she once loved); neither is he the sententious voice of authority, divine and secular who, forgetting, it would seem, the Christian injunction not to judge others, pronounces Helene's supposed "guilt" as though he were personally presiding over doomsday. Here he is merely a busy man making polite conversation with a girl he confirmed and whom he can safely patronize as "Miss Engstrand" ("jomfru Engstrand") because she is a servant and he is a clerical gentleman. His susceptibility to pretty women appears here only in a comic light: as most men would, Manders notices Regine's well-developed breasts as she solicitiously places a footstool for him—and indeed there is every indication that that is exactly what Regine intends. Unlike many men, however, Manders unwisely comments, almost immediately, "You know, Miss Engstrand, I do believe you've grown since I last saw you."

There are tensions in this duologue which are presented without confusion: they are evident in Manders's concern—which appears to be genuine, however futile—about Engstrand's spiritual welfare and Regine's categorical refusal to do her supposed "daughter's duty" and go "home" to care for her "father." In the lie Regine tells when she declares that she runs across to see Engstrand "whenever [she has] a moment," it is evident that she wishes to give the Pastor the false impression of filial concern. In a second lie, declaring that she would "hate to leave Mrs. Alving," we see at once that she will not speak the truth because it would be disastrously indiscreet to reveal her real reason for wanting to stay in the Alving household, which is to encourage Oswald to marry her. And Manders's susceptibility to Regine's attractions, which causes comic tension between them, is a good way of foreshadowing what we are to learn later about the possibility of his having once fallen deeply in love with Helene.

Regine's unscrupulous attempt to ingratiate herself with Manders is linked with central themes in the play by its phraseology: the Pastor's talk about Regine's capacity to give Engstrand "a guiding hand" reminds us of the latter's request for her help in establishing a brothel a few minutes before—though, ironically, it was not only Regine's hands that Engstrand imagined as assisting him—and the phrase foreshadows Oswald's regret in the last act that Regine cannot give him the helping hand he had hoped for, to kill him, if necessary. And by that time, we have seen both the comedy and the tragedy of Oswald's very strong physical attraction to Regine.

There are, none the less, problems here. They arise not from this episode itself but from its full relationship to its context. In the Regine–Manders duologue itself we have something akin to Shaw's treatment of the relationship between the Rev. Sam Gardner and Kitty Warren in *Mrs. Warren's Profession*: it is the comedy of manners which, as Ibsen knew from the reception of *Love's Comedy*, late-nineteenth-century middle-class audiences did not care to have written about themselves. The problems, which are generic and thematic, arise, however, when, in other contexts, Regine stops being the minx appropriate to comedy of manners and becomes, once more, Regine the victim, and Regine the martyr. Manders, equally confusingly, stops being a comical cleric and becomes, as occasion demands, a complete silly ass, a voice of common sense and of an admirable Christian ethos, and apparently also, a little Napoleon.

With Regine's departure to summon her mistress, lucidity departs from the act, and events and characters are steered on an increasingly erratic course.

The lack of focus becomes evident again when Manders, who is shortly to engage in a battle about books with Helene, examines a number of volumes lying on the work-table and expresses disapproval—"H'm. Indeed!" It would add to the play's coherence if we could be told more about the books: all we learn for certain is that Manders considers that they deal with "new trends of thought" originating in "the great world outside" which have as yet made no headway in Norway, while Mrs. Alving claims to believe that "there's nothing there but what most people think and believe already." We may well be disposed—because Mrs. Alving appears at this stage such an eminently reasonable and civilised woman—to accept her judgement as objective. If it is so, then it is reasonable to accept the implication, which arises naturally enough from the conversation at this point, that whilst most people in Norway in the 1880s were, like their fellow Europeans, inhibited by respect for conventional authority, they felt drawn towards radical thought. But this idea is later dealt a body-blow, for in Act II, Oswald's observation that life should be lived for the joy it can offer appears to take Mrs. Alving completely by surprise. Oswald explains that what he sees in Regine is a woman "filled with the joy of life." Mrs. Alving is startled, and it is not because Oswald is speaking about Regine, for he has been extolling Regine's supposed zest for innocent enjoyment for some time. The context permits only the interpretation that Helene is surprised by the idea itself, the idea that human fulfilment may lie in the joy of living. How extensive, then, or how thorough can Mrs. Alving's reading of progressive literature be if she is surprised by a romantic commonplace that was no more novel in the 1880s than Rousseau, Goethe, or Wordsworth? The context of the Manders–Mrs. Alving duologue in Act I does not suggest that Helene is deliberately describing the books in euphemistic terms in order to allay Manders's fears; it suggests, in fact, precisely the opposite—that she is spoiling for a fight, which indeed takes place. So what she has been reading remains a mystery—or, rather, an instance of vexing mystification (possibly again related to the exigencies of an ill-wrought plot) about which more will need to be said.

On Mrs. Alving's arrival in the garden room, Manders greets her with that official form of her name. And it is notable also that neither here nor anywhere else do we learn Manders's own Christian name. As far as possible, to begin with, both characters treat each other in a formal fashion, though it is, in fact, hard to decide much about the tone of their conversation before Manders mentions the books.

For instance, is Helene gently twitting Manders in a good-natured way about his methodical habits and his fear of scandal when she remarks that he need not have arranged to return to town to sleep in lodgings because "a couple of old things like [them]" may be assumed to be past amorous adventures? Or is she, as David Thomas sees it, preparing in a more malicious way, for the crushing humiliation she may be seen as progressively inflicting upon him for having, in her view, betrayed her trust and her love twenty-nine years ago? It is hard, if not impossible, to decide because, at least until the battle over her reading erupts, Helene seems to be in a good mood, far too happy with her son's return and the prospect of his staying with her for many months to be much concerned about Manders: ". . . just fancy! Isn't it marvellous! It's more than two years since he was last at home. Now he's promised to stay with me the whole winter." There are tensions: Manders clearly regards "living in Rome and Paris" as extremely perilous, but Helene, with a hint of love that may now begin to sound rather more than maternal, is enraptured at the very thought of Oswald ". . . you see here at home he has his mother. Ah, my dear, darling boy . . . he still has a soft spot for his mother!" Manders is also far from convinced that "taking up Art" is good for anybody, but Helene seems almost unconscious of Manders's negative attitudes and quite caught up in almost naively light-hearted thoughts: "It will be fun to see if you recognize him again," she assures the Pastor.

A moment of calm is introduced as Helene asked Manders to sit, and sits herself. It looks as though Manders is going to be discreet and say nothing about Helene's reading. He starts to discuss business but breaks off to ask Helene accusingly, "how did *these* books get *here?*"

We cannot, therefore, avoid the books that are enough to outrage a clergyman, and yet said to be innocuous by the woman who has read them—with no certain result. In dramatic terms Ibsen may be seen—though he is usually *not* seen—as giving both contestants more or less equal ammunition for the battle. Manders's view is that though he has not read the books, he has read enough about them to believe that they are harmful; this position, which might have seemed laughable at the time of the trial of *Lady Chatterley's Lover*, is likely to seem less so now that much effort is spent in attempting to prevent the circulation of blatantly pornographic literature and films in Western countries. Mrs. Alving's position, of course, is that he is as ridiculous to condemn what he has not actually read as he is later to accept, without personal observation, what public opinion says about her marriage. And from this general antithesis—of respect for authority, on the one hand, and of assertion of the individual conscience, on the other—grows all that we can conclusively know about the rational aspect of the conflict between Helene and Manders. It is not enough.

Ibsen's reasons for not allowing us to know just what Mrs. Alving has been reading are likely to remain obscure. But it concerns us to know not necessarily titles and authors, but at least something about the subject matter of her reading. It might seem artistically crass to have names reeled off—Darwin or Taine, Marx, John Stuart Mill, George Eliot, George Sand, or Georg Brandes, for instance—but it would be helpful if we could know as much as Strindberg lets us know about Captain Adolf's interests in *The Father* (astronomy, geology, and chemistry) or as much as Chekhov gives us to understand in *The Seagull* about Trepliov's interest in the theory of the arts. *Ghosts* is, in part at least, a play of ideas—a form not well suited to Ibsen's talents, as *Emperor and Galilean* shows—and fuzziness about the ideas in question is, to say the least, a serious impediment to dramatic and theatrical effectiveness. Tentatively, however, it is appropriate to suggest that Ibsen, whose own reading is known to have been embarrassingly limited, may, in fact, be slyly implying that Mrs. Alving has been spending her leisure hours reading the works of the only free-thinking writer that Ibsen undoubtedly not only read but wrote to repeatedly, sometimes identifying him as a poet like himself, namely Georg Brandes.

The evidence for this is admittedly sketchy, though less so than it is for some other theories about the entire action of the play that have been advanced with assurance. And if Ibsen is dealing specifically with Brandes's ideas, he has reason not to make it obvious, because there is good evidence that the play satirizes notions very close to Brandes's heart whether or not Ibsen was directly influenced by Brandes's own expression of them. It has been known for a long time that Ibsen borrowed the names "Helene" and "Oswald" from Brandes's *The Emigrant Literature*, and it may be generally known also, especially since Ibsen refers to that particular work in terms so admiring as to amount virtually to veneration, that Ibsen drew support for the notions of all that is positive about Helene and Oswald Alving's beliefs—their shared ideological commitment to the "joy of life" and the "joy of work," their support of loving relationships free from legal restraint, their faith in the supposedly blissful lives of bold bohemian artists living in Paris—directly from that book[27]. There is much to be said for this view; Brandes, after all, is never more impassioned than when inveighing against what he regarded as the perverse influence of the church (in *The Emigrant Literature*, the Roman Catholic Church), never more a champion of liberty than when holding forth about the repressive forces of the state (in *The Emigrant Literature*, the Napoleonic state). Indeed, *The Emigrant Literature* deals so extensively with the theme of struggling to be free from oppressive conventions that it could have been appropriately subtitled *Ghosts: and How They Will Be Exorcised*. What seems to be neglected, though, is that Ibsen, in life and in his works, tended to veer away from even the few ideological commitments he is known to have made. When it came to fitting characters into an ideological framework, they and not it wrought the alchemical changes that almost invariably give his work broadly human rather than abstract theoretical vitality. There is, in fact, as much in *Ghosts* to indicate that Helene and Oswald Alving are credulous fools, or worse, as to show that they are apostles of enlightenment. And there is some evidence in the text to support the belief that Ibsen went so far as to turn them into parodic figures, thus laughing up his sleeve at his brother "poet" who could translate into Danish, for the supposed enlightenment of all Scandinavia, such extravagantly naive monuments to sentimentality as the following from Mme. de Staël's *Corinne*:

> Beneath the sun and the starry heavens people feel merely the desire to love one another and to feel worthy of each other, but society, society! How hard it makes the heart, and how frivolous the mind! How it leads us to live only for what people will say about us! If human beings could one day meet each other freed from that pressure which they collectively exert upon each other, what pure air would then penetrate the soul, how many new ideas, how many genuine emotions would then refresh it![28]

Within a year of the publication of *Ghosts*, Georg Brandes was publicly congratulating himself on having converted Ibsen to an ardent belief in militant feminism. This is how he puts the matter in *Henrik Ibsen—A Second Impression (1882)*:

> I believe that Ibsen originally had an antipathy to this whole movement, attributable either to his education or to natural irritation at some of the ridiculous forms the movement assumed—an antipathy destined, however, to give way to a sympathy all the more enthusiastic. In this case Ibsen's reasoning faculty wrought the change in his feelings. Like a true poet, he is ready to be the enthusiastic champion of an idea which at first failed to interest him, as soon as it is borne in upon him that this idea is one of the great rallying-points in the battle of progress. And when, in the last scene of *A Doll's House*, we read those words that fall like sword-strokes, Helmer's—
> "No man sacrifices his honour even for one he loves,"
> and Nora's—
> "Millions of women have done so,"
> words which reveal the gulf that yawns between the husband and wife, sitting one on each side of the table—yawns more horribly than the mouth of hell in the old romantic dramas—we feel not only that Ibsen has saturated himself with the thoughts of the age, but that in passing through his artist's mind these thoughts have gained a power and intensity sufficient to drive them home even into hardened hearts. The play made a powerful and somewhat alarming impression. For centuries society, through the mouths of its priests and poets, had proclaimed marriage, based upon love and disturbed by no third person, to be a haven of bliss. Now this haven was seen to be full of rocks and shallows—and it was as though Ibsen had extinguished the beacon-lights.
> *Ghosts* followed. Here again, as in *A Doll's House*, a marriage is investigated. . . .[29]

Brandes was highly gratified therefore with his pupil's progress—even though Ibsen sometimes baulked at his mentor's advice, to read George Sand or John Stuart Mill, for instance. Brandes is therefore likely to have recognized in Helene Alving an undoubted likeness to Mme. de Staël, about whom Brandes writes with perfervid admiration in *The Emigrant Literature*. One of the literary figures for whom de Staël was the model is Eleonore in Benjamin Constant's novel *Adolphe*, about which Brandes has much to say. In its extensive comments on de Staël's *Corinne, The Emigrant Literature* also refers to an English Oswald who finds the joy of life in Italy with Corinne herself, another idealized literary likeness of de Staël. Ibsen may also be giving a clue that he is ridiculing Brandes's ideas when he makes Manders refer to the "intellectual currents" ("åndelige strømninger") circulating in nations outside Scandinavia: *The Emigrant Literature* is the first of six volumes in a comprehensive study entitled *Main Currents in Nineteenth Century Literature (Hovedstrømninger i det 19de Aarhundredes Litteratur)*. If it is true, it must be one of the best jokes in nineteenth-century literature that *Ghosts* convinced Brandes that Ibsen was a fellow champion of free-thinking emancipation and feminism, while, in fact, the play substantially satirizes both its Eleonore and its Oswald, and greatly to the discredit of Brandes's crusading views.

But if the joke is there, it *is* literary and *not* dramatic. And worse than that, it is obscurely literary: only a close reading of *The Emigrant Literature* enables one to see, for instance, that Manders, the authority figure in *Ghosts*, may, in one of his guises, be a parodic version of the sadistic tyrant that Brandes makes of Napoleon. Brandes's de Staël and Napoleon are locked into epic strife. Brandes describes his "new woman" struggling ever nobly against masculine aggression and insensitivity as follows:

> Long before Balzac, long before George Sand, then, this fight for the women's cause appeared in literature: it concerned the fight of women with the established order and with society, and Eleonore [a character in Constant's novel *Adolphe*] comes to represent this fight, for she is modelled upon the woman who fought the greatest battle which a woman has ever fought in the history of the world with purely spiritual weapons, in a word, upon Mme. de Staël. For this love affair described in *Adolphe* is the one which actually happened between Benjamin Constant and Germaine de Staël. To be sure, the outward circumstances of the latter differed from Eleonore's, but it is this great and remarkable woman, whose personal life-struggle was a fight with the very world-ruler of the age, and whom Napoleon, with petty-minded hatred and ignoble fear, persecuted, banished, censored and subjected to all the afflictions to which a brutal despot can subject the individual of genius, it is this woman who presents Constant with the new type of womanhood.[30]

When, in Act I of *Ghosts*, Manders perceives it as his duty to harangue Helene Alving about the demands of duty and the frivolity of craving happiness, about her guilt as miscreant wife and negligent mother, and all this in the name of what he claims to know as best and sanctioned by God Himself for the welfare of society, we have the kind of figure that Brandes delighted to hate and one strikingly similar to Brandes's megalomaniacal Napoleon, foe to all freedom and especially that of women, and political ally of the Church in its principle of indissoluble marriage. But, unfortunately for those who place their faith in any form of optimism similar to that of Brandes, Manders is presented as having some virtues and Helene several vices.

One of Helene Alving's vices appears to be muddle-headedness. If Mrs. Alving has really found "nothing new" in her free-thinking books, she has failed to observe that an atheistic or agnostic approach to life is in fact quite different from a theistic one, and that society really does become different (for better or worse) when people feel free to express their sexual inclinations at will and not in accordance with any generally accepted and restrictive ethical code. And one of Manders's virtues may be that he is prepared, as Charles Leland sees it, to live by his principles because for him they embody religious truth.[31] And if authorities he respects condemn certain books, his refusal to read them and his disapproval of them may be seen as an act of submission and obedience which is no more inherently ridiculous than a faithful Mohammedan's refusal to drink alcohol. Manders is not lacking intelligence when he reminds Mrs. Alving that no civilised society could survive if its members were unwilling to take on trust certain truths defined for their benefit by recognized authorities.

As the first duologue between Manders and Mrs. Alving develops, Manders makes it quite clear that he takes his public responsibilities seriously and is responsive to what other people, responsible people in positions of authority, think: this is usually taken to indicate that he is a hypocrite trimming his sails to the prevailing winds of public opinion, and there is something to be said for that view, especially since Manders admits, as is rarely noticed, that he fears the competition of a rival—and that "those who support [his] colleague" would be quick to exploit, in the newspapers and elsewhere, anything that might be construed as not totally in accordance with the proprieties. But there is also much to be said for the view that if Manders is to exercise what he believes to be appropriate moral and spiritual leadership, he cannot be lax in his own behaviour nor ignore the convictions of those he is trying to guide. As Leland observes, the question of insurance for the Orphanage does not necessarily make Manders look an ass, therefore. But it must be conceded that the fire at the Orphanage deals a blow at naive reliance on providence.

Just before the arrival of Oswald, with his gospel of Brandean joy according to the bohemians of Paris, Helene makes one of the assertions which certainly supports Thomas's view that what we are witnessing between Helene and Manders is not a reasoned discussion at all but a circling around what may have been the worst trauma in their lives: his rejection of her love when she sought refuge from Alving with him. She insists not only that Regine should not go to Engstrand—as we would expect of an enlightened woman trying to protect Oswald's half-sister—but also that "Regine is going to work in the Orphanage." Knowing, as we do, that the Orphanage represents for Helene Alving everything which she wants to be rid of, there may well be darker reasons for her insisting that Regine should be employed there as a servant in a public institution where her liberty will be severely restricted. This is the first clear indication of vengefulness which has possibly survived well into the period of enlightenment that Helene claims for herself.

Oswald's arrival causes Mrs. Alving's face, according to the stage directions, to light up with joy. And the ensuing discussion of art and artists precipitates the violent quarrel between Manders and Helene which occupies most of the rest of the act. The conflicts are indisputably exciting, but their precise terms are confusingly ambiguous.

Manders finds Oswald's resemblance to his father "astounding," and hints of physiological determinism begin to accumulate: Oswald is fond of tobacco, as his father was—indeed he enters smoking one of his father's pipes. Subsequently we are to learn, of course, that he is as fond of drink and pretty women as his father was, and we must decide whether he has inherited (in addition to syphilis) "the joy of life" or less admirable traits—those, for instance, that Oswald himself hints at when, with more irony than he realizes, he speaks of himself as "the Prodigal Son."

Oswald looks well, so well that Manders ventures the observation that even some Parisian artists may be able to "preserve some integrity of soul." Whether we should take this as genuine, if naive, pleasure at the sight of an Oswald still apparently unscathed by his life in a foreign and reputedly immoral metropolis, or ironically feigned surprise thinly disguising self-righteousness is hard to know.

Helene's response is undoubtedly lyrical, "I know one who has preserved his integrity, both of soul and of body. Just look at him, Pastor Manders." Is this the joy of a woman dreaming of a world of pure liberty "beneath," as Mme. de Staël puts it, "the sun and the starry heavens"?[32] Is it simply an expression of a mother's happiness and pride? Is Helene a woman who may be already aware of how much she lost when her husband (who once, she admits later, also radiated vitality like a sunny day) slid into profligacy? And, if so, is she responding erotically to what she sees of the once handsome and attractive Alving in his son? The questions are never answered, and nor should we anticipate certain answers in tragicomedy. The problem is that because we do not know for sure that Ibsen is exposing the values of *The Emigrant Literature* to irony, we cannot be certain of the questions either.

As has often been observed, it is Manders who first speaks of the "joys of living", and he does so in order to explain why he is sure (and he probably as yet has no reason to be otherwise) that Alving made Oswald as a boy smoke the large Meerschaum pipe until he grew "quite pale and great beads of sweat stood out on [his] forehead" merely as a joke. Manders is being too generous to see nothing disturbing about the nausea and vomiting which followed,[33] but it is important that Manders believes that nothing but harm can come from destroying a son's respect for his father.

The pipe-smoking incident is the first hint we have of what the Alving marriage was like when Oswald still lived in the house. But precisely what Ibsen is doing with the information is hard to know: is he showing us what can happen when the "joy of life" is perverted? The abuse of children is one of the targets of Ibsen's certain and unswerving disapproval. But the "joy of life"—soon to dominate this act, though not actually named by Oswald until Act II—is the very theme which Ibsen handles most confusingly. Perhaps he is beginning to prepare us for a vision of irremediable sexual conflict in which children are used as both weapons and victims, "things" to be fought over, as Hans Meyer might see it. But because we cannot know this either, a question which appears to half-emerge from the action—namely, "are men and women, wives and husbands, mothers and fathers fundamentally capable of happiness in *any* circumstances?"—is presented abortively. The fact, interesting enough, that both Manders (like Pastor Straamand in *Love's Comedy*) and Oswald think highly of "homes"— though for different reasons—is the kind of thing that rejoiced Georg Brandes when he wrote his preferred and optimistic interpretation of *Ghosts*. It suggests that sensible modification of social arrangements for marriage and divorce could usher in Utopia, preserving all that was best of established institutions while freeing people from interference with their personal liberties by church and state. It is the sort of thing which Torvald Helmer may have some inkling of when the last act of *A Doll's House* ends with his question, "The miracle of miracles . . .?" One wishes that Ibsen had been more diligent in suggesting that internecine strife between the sexes may be inevitable—if indeed he intends to suggest that at all. What looks like the first hint of it is in Oswald's description of his father's behaviour: it suggests a man maliciously using a child to make his wife suffer. Alving's roaring with laughter when Oswald is overcome with nausea suggests something more than a merry prank! But how much more is impossible to infer.

Manders's verbal attack on Helene as wife and mother follows her assertion, after Oswald's exit, that she supports her son's views wholeheartedly. There is evidence in this dreadful quarrel—for Helene replies in kind—to support David Thomas's view of the play as well as the whole array of positive interpretations. The element of troublesome disunity, however, asserts itself right in the middle of Helene's spirited defense of herself, where she explains why she had to take charge and send Oswald away from home as Alving's debauchery grew worse and culminated in his seduction of Regine's mother. In the middle of all the reasonable explanation, the account of sensible decisions made with the kind of courage that is so much admired by those who see Mrs. Alving in a thoroughly positive light, comes:

> Then I swore to myself that this would have to stop! So I took control in the house . . . complete control . . . over him and everything else. Because now I had a weapon against him, you see, and he didn't dare say anything.

Here Mrs. Alving, who appears to many people to accomplish her quest for truth, suggests, like Clytemnestra, a murderous hatred too deep seated in human nature for any recipe of the "joy of life" to eradicate. There is, apparently, gloating triumph in those words, similar, it seems, to the triumphant authority with which Helene orders Regine out of her sight at the beginning of Act II with the curt command, "Go and help with the decorations down in the ironing room." She intends to marry her off, and discusses this with Manders. But first she wants to show Regine who is mistress at Rosenvold.

Usually Helene seems so reasonable, so attractive as a personality that when she looks forward with eagerness to the dedication of the Orphanage and says that it will mark the end of a "long, ghastly farce," we are likely to feel compassion for her—and forget how much of a hand she had in making that farce. Her shock when she hears Regine protesting at Oswald's advances is likely to arouse pity. But can we forget what seems also to have been indicated—that if she is in part a woman with great and stoical courage, she may also be an almost literally murderous matriarch?

It would help us to know whether we are asking the right questions if Ibsen had been more careful in his handling of Oswald's tidings about the "joy of life." These are the very truths, supposedly untainted and associated with a state of innocence, on which Daniel Haakonsen partly founds his claim that Oswald is an "innocent victim," one from whom his mother, the "passionate idealist" and "doomed hero," learns the wisdom upon which her possible recovery of spiritual sight is based. But, in the play, it is hard if not impossible to know whether Ibsen is poking fun at Oswald for being naive or merely being slipshod in his presentation of this crucial motif. We are asked by Oswald to believe that the bohemian artists of late-nineteenth-century Paris invariably spend their Sundays enjoying the company of their chaste, utterly wholesome partners and of their children. No formal marriage ceremonies are called for: trust is sufficient to ensure the triumph of conjugal bliss among this natural aristocracy. No one ever utters a coarse word or indulges in unseemly talk—like that of visiting Norwegian businessmen hurrying, according to Oswald, to Parisian fleshpots. It certainly sounds extravagantly ridiculous when one thinks of the Paris that Toulouse-Lautrec painted and that Gauguin left. Archer pointed out that Ibsen seemed careless to have Oswald assert that Parisian artists could not afford to marry, the cost of licences being very reasonable;[34] perhaps Ibsen nodded on that occasion, or was too rushed to sustain the necessary verisimilitude. The same would appear to be true of the "joy of life" motif: Ibsen may be satirizing it—and all of Brandes's rosy visions—or he may simply have been careless in its development. So the questions which may be implicit in the text are half-formed and unclear.

The harm done in the first act cannot be undone in the remaining two. This is more than just unfortunate because Act II and the first part of Act III—up until Regine's exit to try her chances with her share of the "joy of life"—contain some of Ibsen's finest comedy. Even the comedy, though, does not always function as it can in Ibsen's fully controlled tragicomic work: it *can* be intellectually related to the tragic themes. It is impossible not to laugh at Manders's gullibility when he finishes his planned rejection of Engstrand (for the lies Engstrand has told him about Johanna Engstrand and Regine, and for causing the good Pastor to make a false entry in the parish register) by ridiculously taking Engstrand's hand to congratulate him on his charity to a "fallen woman." This can be seen in relation to Engstrand's successful scheme to betray Manders, whose subsequent decision to travel together with Engstrand after the fire (and Engstrand's manipulation of the Pastor's fears) can be, and has been, seen as either hypocrisy or gullibility. These comic sequences convey much of the action; one can see how they might have been used to penetrate the tragic elements successfully. In fact, the penetration is minimal, which is one reason for the dearth of positive comments on the comedy.

It is only at the end of the play, as has been suggested earlier, that we are presented with one of Ibsen's most stunning realizations of the tragicomic spirit. From the end of Act I until the moment of Regine's departure we have much comedy, some very real horror—as in Oswald's description of the Parisian doctor's diagnosis of his illness—and a good deal of such wisdom as can be extracted from the "joy of life" theme—as when Helene decides that she can tell Oswald and Regine the truth about Alving because she believes he was a splendid man and she must shoulder the blame for having crushed his capacity for joyful living.

Some of Ibsen's recurrent motifs appear. Act II begins with one mockery of a feast: Manders does not know how he managed to eat a mouthful of the dinner intended to celebrate the eve of the Orphanage's dedication. And it ends with another: Regine and Oswald drinking champagne, which seems to be Oswald's idea of the joy of life in bottles, while Mrs. Alving attempts to straighten out their lives. We are told about Helene's two aunts, and we gather that, like Hjalmar Ekdal's (whom Dr. Relling contemptuously calls "crazy" and "hysterical") and Jörgen Tesman's, they did little for their young relation's intellectual or spiritual development. We hear, from Engstrand himself, about his determination to stand on his own feet ("på to reelle ben"—literally "on two real legs") despite his lame leg, and a good deal about Oswald's decaying brains, and this is reminiscent of the head and foot imagery in *Peer Gynt*. But there is little sense of consistent and unified development. In terms of action, Oswald makes a pass at Regine at the end of Act I and so illuminates the title, in whatever sense we understand it. The fire occurs at a dramatically apposite moment at the end of Act II, and seems to offer near surreal suggestions similar to those of such events as the explosion aboard the yacht in *Peer Gynt* and Solness's fall from the tower in *The Master Builder*. But it is not exploited as fully as it might be. Of course we grasp the connections between Oswald's destruction, his father's destruction, and the ominous importance of both in relation to the hypocritical society which produced them, but, by the time that Manders declares that the fire is "a flaming judgement on this house of iniquity," he has made such a fool of himself with Engstrand, and played the tyrant so objectionably with Helene, that it is hard to take his notions of divine judgement seriously, despite the fact that there may be a re-entry of the supernatural in the third act.

There is something to be said, as I have attempted to say it elsewhere (in a context attempting to discover evidence of tragicomic unity in *Ghosts*[35]), for the idea that the tragicomic notes half-sounded in much of the play and fully audible only at the end are to be heard more clearly in some of Ibsen's poetry. One thinks of "The Power of Memory" ("Mindets Magt"), for example, in which a bear in a heated cauldron is taught to "dance," as the heat rises and his pain intensifies, to a tune whose title is "Enjoy Life!" And Mrs. Alving's imprisonment by Oswald in the house she has tried to escape, and his insistence that she take back the life he never asked for, is reminiscent of the central idea in "Bird and Bird-catcher" ("Fugl og Fuglefænger"), in which a sadistic boy takes a captured bird indoors and enjoys its anguish as it tries to escape. The likeness to *Ghosts* is only superficially one of basic situation; above all, it lies in a particular complex of emotions and attitudes, which sees the pain and the ludicrousness of life and is at least half-apprehensive that that is all there is—inexplicable, unchangeable, nauseating. But there is also the possibility of which Ibsen seems rarely, if ever, to despair—that this dreadful vision is itself an illusion, a nightmare from which humanity might wake to something more positive and more certain than Peer Gynt's unknowable crossroads, Hilde and Solness's aircastle, or even Brandes's too elusive "joy of life."

4

The Wild Duck: All Hope Abandoned?

Like *Ghosts, The Wild Duck* elicits statements of passionate conviction. And the depth of feeling is as important as the variety of ethical and aesthetic commitments underlying critical appraisals of the play: it is a measure of Ibsen's success as a poet in the sense that seems to have meant most to him—that of the artist who stimulates spiritual appraisal. On the other hand, the tendency of critics to define univocal interpretations and to defend a supposed monopoly of truth against all comers is just as clearly marked in the assessment of *The Wild Duck* as in that of other plays by Ibsen. And, even though the work is accepted as tragicomic—it is difficult to do otherwise given Ibsen's own statement to that effect[1]—too little attention is given to the fact that one of the principal elements of modern tragicomedy is doubt about virtually all fundamental values which are, in any significant way, inherent in a work. The openness of vision which gives rise to the complex relativism of Ibsen's naturalistic masterpiece appears, therefore, to be still not fully understood, and the most basic division of opinion is between those who believe that the play presents a world from which all hope is banished and those who believe that the play definitely establishes grounds for the renewal of hope even in a world pervaded by hypocrisy, despair, and cynicism.

This division of views is sharpest among those who regard Hedvig as the central character, but it is reflected also among those who regard Hjalmar Ekdal or Gregers Werle as the protagonist.

As one might expect, Karl Guthke is extremely helpful in enabling us to see that the play really does take place in a "borderland between the two major dramatic genres."[2] But in arguing that Hjalmar is the figure "around whom all the characters and the action are rather neatly centered," he unfortunately diminishes the chances of apprehending the play's full range of ambivalences. It is true that Hjalmar has his moments of apparent dignity. Guthke mentions, for instance, Hjalmar's response to Gina's refusal to answer his questions about Hedvig's paternity: Hjalmar turns away quietly and declares, "Then I have nothing more to do in this house." But such moments are usually even more devastatingly interpenetrated by comical implications than Guthke himself explains. It is surely too generous, also, to conclude that, at the end of Act I, "young Ekdal, as he has so far been presented, has enough human worth and dignity to make him a potentially 'tragic' hero." He is, in fact, the not-so-young Ekdal who has just demonstrated his social ineptitude and timorous nature in the conversation following Haakon Werle's dinner party. Moreover, when overwhelmed with confusion and embarrassment at his father's unexpected appearance there, Hjalmar has turned his back on him and then proceeded to talk self-pityingly to Gregers about "the crushing blows of fate" before making a signally unimpressive exit. Here, as elsewhere, the play does not, as Guthke rightly observes, concentrate on making Hjalmar look a buffoon; we are asked to understand him, to sympathize with him, and to appreciate the element of the ludicrous in his situation. But Hjalmar's "worth and dignity" are not sufficiently impressive to rank him even briefly with great tragic heroes.

Seeing Hjalmar as at least substantially a tragic figure—and more so by virtue of being, instead of Gregers or Hedvig, for instance, the protagonist—tends also to distract attention from the very motifs which may be more genuinely tragic than anything that Hjalmar can arrogate to himself as the principal player in what he calls "the tragedy of the house of Ekdal." It is disappointing that a critic whose general theory of tragicomedy is so persuasive does not, apparently, realize that in *The Wild Duck*, the complaints of the most noticeable victim, shot through with dramatic irony as Guthke shows them to be, are not necessarily any more revealing or significant than, for instance, the assertions of the most obvious and apparently detestable victor, Haakon Werle. In confining discussion of *anagnorisis* to Hjalmar, Guthke's approach makes it harder to recognize the epiphanies that seem to offer themselves to other anguished though less histrionic characters.

It is more usual for critics to claim that Gregers Werle is the protagonist, repulsive meddler or flawed hero according to taste and ideological orientation.

Mary McCarthy, who has no inhibitions about biographical surmise and dislikes Ibsen to the extent of detecting a "curious confessional closet-smell" in all his works, sees Gregers quite simply as Ibsen's embodiment of himself "in his tendentious and polemical aspect" and, more luridly, as "a demon that Ibsen is trying to cast out through the exorcism of this play."[3] In effect, these views are an expression, pushed to a splenetic and inevitably disturbing extreme, of the common opinion, fostered by William Archer, for instance, that in the person of Gregers, Ibsen is really castigating himself for injudicious truthtelling.[4]

As Archer states this interpretation of Gregers, it is, more or less, a half-truth, emphasizing the core of what is negative about Gregers and entirely ignoring what is positive.

Like others who dislike Ibsen, or admire him for mistaken reasons, McCarthy gravely underestimates him as an artist and insists, with inadequate evidence, on condemning him as a third-rate thinker. It is not true that Gregers is essentially a walking idea, one as uncomplex artistically and intellectually as Folly or Mischief in a morality play. He is not simply the "grotesque and half pathetic devil" that McCarthy, and Dr. Relling, see. He is—including his aspect of the partially admirable visionary—as much more than that as *The Wild Duck* is more than a *drame-à-clef* to which any *raisonneur* holds the key.

Cyrus Hoy, who, like Guthke, has articulated an impressive theory of tragicomedy, is, partly for that reason, much more persuasive than McCarthy in advancing his view that Gregers is the play's central character.[5] Gregers is perceived by Hoy as a heroic idealist, though, unlike Cordelia, another truth-teller with whom Hoy compares him, he is tortured by a guilty conscience and also "does not himself incur the worst; others are left to reap the tragedy he has sown, which is not the least of the play's ironies." None the less, as Hoy sees it, Gregers's own fate is both grievously tragic and ludicrous:

> He is an idealist, operating in a less than ideal world and, as the world pursues its incorrigible way, becoming ever more disaffected with it. He will also become increasingly out of step with it, failing, as he does, to recognize that his particular ideal of complete and absolute truth-telling is worthless to the average man and woman: that the average man and woman have their own ideals, and that when they fail to live up to these, they are not above pretending to themselves and to others that they have achieved them, or at least reasonably approximated them. . . .

It is evident at once that Hoy perceives Gregers as more of a constituent of a complex dramatic pattern than McCarthy or even Guthke does. Nevertheless, his view does not perceive the whole pattern, and its limitations spring, to some extent, from a lack of full acknowledgement of the thoroughly ugly aspects of Greger's nature that McCarthy overemphasizes.

Despite the distortions which flow from perceiving Hjalmar as the protagonist, the temptation to think of him in that way is understandable: in Gregers's case it is difficult to overcome. And in the case of Hedvig it is almost impossible to avoid, despite the fact that she is carefully presented as being still a child, still in the early stages of puberty when, as Relling warns and Gina naturally understands, she is not necessarily capable of taking mature decisions nor fully responsible for her actions. It is not for nothing that we are told about the dangerous games she plays with fire, nor for nothing that Relling specifically warns Gregers and Hjalmar of her psychological vulnerability. To think of Hedvig, therefore, as though she conforms to a literary archetype—the martyr who dies for love, for instance—has its dangers, one of which is to assume that she is all spirit and no flesh.

Ellie Dunn, in *Heartbreak House*, informs Captain Shotover that the modern view is that the soul and body are one. Hedvig is far from an age (or indeed a century) which could allow her to be so pert, but we are given to understand by Ibsen, as surely as Strindberg informs us that menstruation is one of the factors which loosens Miss Julie's self-control, that the troubled spirit of Hedvig Ekdal is the more easily troubled because, in the ordinary course of nature—which was not infrequently ignored as indecent or misinterpreted before naturalism—she must get used to physiological changes which can produce their own fears and inner turmoils. Hilde Wangel (of *The Master Builder*), though, like Ellie Dunn, well on the far side of puberty, appears as dangerously ignorant of her own physiology and psychology as does Hedvig. Ibsen does not over-emphasize the subject in *The Wild Duck*, but he did not let his nineteenth-century audiences forget it—as they would doubtless have preferred. To regard her as merely, however attractively, an embodiment of spiritual qualities associated with voluntary sacrifice is to risk forgetting Hedvig's specific physical and mental condition. The greatest danger, therefore, about treating her as the play's central character is the minimization of a value judgement which, unusually, is recurrent and completely unambiguous in Ibsen, namely that parents and other adults closely associated with children and adolescents are responsible for them both physically and spiritually and fully accountable for what children do. And Ibsen does, in fact, not appear to regard Hedvig as a fully formed personality: whatever she does may be a hint of the admirable woman she might have become or, with equal likelihood, a reminder of the oppressive childhood out of which she is, when the action begins, quite literally struggling in body as well as in spirit.

The death of a character who is obviously both innocent and loving will inevitably and not inappropriately be associated with sacrifice: to assume that the sacrifice is necessarily unironic, however, is to be too sanguine and insensitive to Ibsen's ambivalences.

Jens Kruuse, in another consideration of *The Wild Duck* as tragicomedy, considers Hedvig as not only the protagonist and a sacrificial figure but one who outshines Iphegenia or Ophelia, who are rightly regarded as essentially passive, and willingly enacts a ritual death which must be considered as a remarkable intimation of atonement.[6] Kruuse is acutely aware of the strangeness of such metaphysical overtones in the dramatic context of *The Wild Duck*, and accordingly argues that Hedvig must be seen as representing "an alien principle in this naturalistic-psychological play," an alien principle which is, according to Kruuse, reconciled to its naturalistic context by Ibsen's sheer imaginative dexterity. The result is a dramatic form in which the "mystic dimension" and

ideas of good and evil stemming from "a given culture's religious conceptions" are held in amazing but none the less convincing union with all that
is mundane, repulsive, or merely trivial. According to this view, Hedvig is
the only guiltless character in the play: she alone acts while others talk,
and as an indication of the full meaning of what Hedvig attempts in her
death, Kruuse refers us to Golgotha.

This view, despite the vociferous opposition that Kruuse himself noted
to the comparison with Christ, has much to be said for it. In effect, no
suggestion of an intact metaphysic is being forced into the play; rather
the idea, sublime in itself, of a child's "crucifixion" reminding adults of
the spiritual ideals by which their own culture once lived is plausibly
offered as an indication of the play's innermost tensions and meaning.
John Northam's most recent reading of the play expresses similar senti-
ments, but from a more certainly humanistic viewpoint: Hedvig, in death
as in life, is seen as the first of Ibsen's *"inarticulate* poets of living."[7]

These positive views of Hedvig are attractive because they stress that
element of the play which implies that life, even in a world of such
fractured values and disparate ideologies as the play represents, is not
necessarily hopeless. Kruuse explains that he can accept Anders Wyller's
view that *The Wild Duck* is a dramatic exploration of a dominant emotion—hopelessness—of which every character is an aspect,[8] only if Hedvig may be seen as a source of enlightenment—tragic enlightenment, that
is, in a world of ludicrous wrongheadedness, lies, and hypocrisy, whose
comic aspects Kruuse himself regards as being as bleak as those of
Molière's *Le Misanthrope, Amphitryon,* and *George Dandin.*

Northam joins those who see Gregers as a misguided schematizer (a
Brand reduced to the proportions of social realism) and Hjalmar as an
egotistical poseur (a Peer similarly stripped of epic proportions) principally, it seems, because he sees Hedvig as the "only truly sensitive,
generous and unspoilt character": She can draw upon powers of intuitive
feeling that outreach the resources of both logic and rhetoric, and she
dies meaningfully for a potentially uplifting love that is dramatically
credible and thematically endorsed.

The association of Hedvig with meaningful sacrifice is not simply
appealing but undeniably present in the play, and the value of such
commentaries upon its non-ironic aspects as Kruuse's and Northam's is
very real. But so is that of commentaries like those of Anders Wyller and,
much more recently, Errol Durbach,[9] which concentrate on the negative
or ironic aspects of Hedvig's death. Wyller argues that the sense of life
projected by *The Wild Duck* is ultimately similar to the wretched state in
which Pascal in his *Pensées* viewed mankind when deprived of God. He
quotes, for instance, Pascal's remark that "human life is nothing but a
perpetual illusion. . . ." And again,

Man is therefore nothing but disguise, deceit and hypocrisy both in himself and in his relations with other people. He does not want people to tell him the truth: he avoids telling it to other people; and all of these dispositions which are so far removed from justice and reason have their natural root in our heart.

The major difference between the *Pensées* and *The Wild Duck* is, according to Wyller, that Ibsen's work envisages no God, no possibility of redemption. Durbach has effectively focussed on those aspects of the play which hint at the possibility that Hedvig's death is a fulfilment of Kierkegaard's fears about the modern world's inability to repeat any such divinely ordained ordeal as that of Abraham and Isaac: what looks like the heroic circumstances of sacrifice and martyrdom is, according to Durbach, in effect, a painful exhibition of nothing more exalted than the stark murder of a child, *kindermord*. In the absence of any metaphysical dimension, Hedvig's demise is accordingly viewed as parodic, and a foreshadowing of absurdism.

The note of anguished ludicrousness is certainly sounded in *The Wild Duck*, as we ought to expect in any Ibsen play, and above all in his tragicomic masterpiece. Whether we refer to absurdism or, like Wyller, to an atmosphere of all-pervasive hopelessness, possibly extending to and including Hedvig, is largely a matter of historical perspective. The implication that life may be utterly senseless and will remain so no matter how many troubled adolescents perish is present in *The Wild Duck* and cannot be dismissed without some diminution of the play's openness, any more than can the possibility that Hedvig perishes to some purpose.

What critics, sympathetic to the play or not, tend to overlook may now be clear: *The Wild Duck* has no protagonist, despite the fact that Hjalmar talks like one and Gregers and Hedvig seem both to speak and behave like one; it also has no endorsed view of life. Instead of characters ranged around a protagonist, it has a pattern of major characters—including Gina, Haakon Werle, and Mrs. Sörby as well as those already mentioned—who are all seen ambivalently in relation to three distinct, though related, philosophies. These philosophies are perceived as the inventions of three highly articulate allegorists—Haakon Werle, Gregers Werle, and Dr. Relling. And the most basic allegory, of which the two others are essentially modifications, is that of Haakon Werle, whose name, ironically or otherwise, suggests kingliness.

Werle's essentially Darwinian view of life (it is as thematically important that one of his guests speaks about "the struggle for survival" as it is that Peer discovers his possible kinship with apes) is what Yeats recognized as the kind of fable without which "all the great masters have understood there cannot be great art." Yeats, in the context of an essay discussing the multiplicity of poetic emotion in drama, is right to point out that Ibsen arouses "the emotion of multitude" by allowing us to see how doubtfully the unfettered impulses of life itself are containable within Werle's mythopoeic allegory, or any other.[10] As we watch and listen to the inhabitants of the Werle and the Ekdal homes, we are invited not simply to judge but also to feel and share the dramatic impulses which attract the mind and heart now to Werle's possibly mellowing determinism, now to Relling's paradoxically negative humanism, and now to Gregers' sometimes perceptive romanticism. All that the spectator can give of himself to the play is, as Yeats puts it, set "wandering from idea to idea, emotion to emotion." And behind those imaginative and indeterminate wanderings is the never-seen and therefore all the more potently suggestive bird, which appears to be behaving exactly in accordance with Darwin's observation, possibly familiar to Ibsen, of its species in captivity,[11] and which has yet become, quite credibly, the inexplicit centre of all those elevated attributes which romantic poets have associated with symbolic birds: the inspiring spontaneity, the purity of soul, the mysterious and benign selfhood of Wordworth's and Shelley's skylarks, for instance, or in Norwegian literature, of Welhaven's wild duck, in his poem "The Seabird" and of the drake in Ibsen's poem "The Eiderduck."

In this play, mankind, no less than the tamed duck, may have lost all pretentions to glory: romantic and anti-romantic attitudes to life are locked into a pattern of fascinating contradictions.

The kind of poetry which Yeats recognized in *The Wild Duck* may also be appreciated as an illustration, as close as Ibsen or perhaps any other modern dramatist has ever come, of what Stark Young evidently had in mind when he wrote: "dramatic poetry is not the dramatic situation poetically expressed: it is the dramatic expression of the poetic that lies in a situation."[12] There is no attempt whatever to compete in this play with the glories of verse like that of *Peer Gynt*, for instance: the poetry is still substantially in the words, as Yeats recognized, but it is the poetry of the difficult art of dramatic prose that Ibsen has now, for the first time, completely mastered. And there is an abundance of "poetry of the theatre" to support dialogue which sounds completely realistic and yet is capable of poetic evocations.

The verbal poetry is fragmented and frequently touched with dramatic irony—like Hedvig's references to "the briny deep," Gregers's to the "sea and the sky," and Old Ekdal's to "the forests' revenge." It is like the bits and pieces of a Keatsian urn that *has* been ravished by the noisy conflicts of the world's strife, particularly the battles fought over the successive dispossessions of its gods: Ibsen passes the shards before the eye and the mind's eye in a manner which may initially seem haphazard and may leave us far more uncertain than Keats is of the meaning of the apparent sacrifice that his urn portrays.

To some sensibilities, *The Wild Duck* is bound, by the very fact of its naturalism, to lack the sense of both ultimate mystery and truth that is

possible in metaphysical plays such as *Peer Gynt* and *The Master Builder.*
Clearly this is the case for Cyrus Hoy, who finds the revelations of *The
Wild Duck* both complex and intriguing but, none the less, finally both
mundane and fortuitous. For others, the play's enduring appeal may
well lie in its ability to evoke mysteries not considered with reference to
any primal and external metaphysical cause. Like Shaw in one phase of
his writing—which would include *The Devil's Disciple* and *Caesar and
Cleopatra*—the Ibsen who wrote *The Wild Duck, Rosmersholm*, and *Hedda
Gabler* might well have consented to Pascal's observation that the "heart
has its reasons, which reason does not know," but only with the modification, which would, of course, have been utterly repugnant to Pascal, that
the seat and origin of mystery is the human heart itself, not any kind of
"Universal Being" to which the human mind, spirit, and imagination are
inevitably drawn.

For those who can respond sympathetically to the idea that modern
man shapes his own gods—and devils and anti-gods—*The Wild Duck* is not
the great work maimed by its own secularity that it is for Hoy. In effect,
this is no more than to say that Ibsen appreciated that the anthropomor-
phic imagination, which had created the Greek pantheon and the Nordic
Asgard, for instance, in the ancient world, had survived, however imperfectly, the upheavals that have deprived Western cultures of their
catholic God, and, for better or worse, remains at work within the minds
of individuals in all Western cultures, however fractured. In *The Wild
Duck*, we come to know several characters who, deprived of God, are yet,
intuitively perhaps, aware that such science as the kind of medicine that
Relling does not practice and the images produced by the camera's
mechanical eye fall short of providing some centre to which the human
need for real or supposed final truth can attach itself.

Molvik, the only theologian in the play—and in fact the only character,
clerical or otherwise, in all of Ibsen's work who is explicitly referred to as
a student of theology—has lost all his faith and is the most pathetic of
Relling's "rescued" souls. He sustains his supposedly "demonic" nature
on drink and, at one dreadfully ludicrous moment, feebly and drunkenly
mouths bits and pieces of what should be the reassuring words of a
Christian burial service over Hedvig's still warm body. He, whose ex-
calling was the contemplation of the ineffable, is incapable of any
mythopoeic vision, and his character, in its context, seems to imply
Ibsen's own impermanent rejection of all gods.

But the natural corollary of what is very probably Ibsen's personal
refusal to endorse any metaphysic at this period is the fascination, more
evident in *The Wild Duck* than anywhere else, with the mythopoeic
capacities of interestingly contrasted human types: the powerful and
educated (Haakon Werle), the educated and unstable (Gregers and
Relling), the intellectually feeble and sentimental (Hjalmar), the

defeated (Old Ekdal), the gifted but vulnerable and deprived (Hedvig), and even, or perhaps especially, the ignorant and abused (Gina).

Elsewhere I have argued that *The Wild Duck* may owe much to the detailed synopsis of Flaubert's story *A Simple Heart* that Georg Brandes provided in his critical introduction to Flaubert[13]: Brandes, himself an atheist, is at his most interesting in commenting sympathetically upon the mythopoeic world with which a deprived and ignorant old servant gives meaning to her life. The ironically named Félicité spends so much time in utter solitude, with no Gregers to alarm her and no Relling to provide her with a supposedly made-to-measure mythology, that she must do as best as she can with the materials to hand. They consist of distorted fragments of Christian teachings—acquired through her interpretation of what she hears when she takes her mistress's daughter to confirmation classes—and the rubbish—literally the unwanted fragments and leavings of other people's lives—which she accumulates in her bedroom. For her, divine authority is vested in an overcoat which once belonged to her widowed employer's late husband and a portrait of the Comte d'Artois. Divine knowledge is represented by an assortment of objects, including a sea shell, a watering can, some copy books, and an illustrated work on geography, all of which are placed on a "chest of drawers . . . draped like an altar," and divine love manifests itself in numerous rosaries, tawdry prints of the Virgin Mary, and a stuffed parrot, which ended its days as Félicité's pet and which, in her most sublime and most ridiculous mythopoeic imaginings, Félicité associates with the paraclete, on the grounds that the Holy Ghost in the guise of a dove would be ineffective because unable to do what Loulou could, talk.

In *The Wild Duck,* we have a whole assortment of psychologically maimed characters, most of whom, in the face of life's afflictions, have formulated or are seen as in the process of formulating their mythologies, simple or complex, comprehensive or fragmentary, intelligent or ludicrous, according to their gifts and circumstances. Only Old Ekdal, the most solitary of all the characters, and in that respect the most like Félicité, has created a personal mythology which is a completely effective sanctuary: in the attic, with his dried-up Christmas trees, the pouter pigeons, the rabbits, and, of course, the duck, he is in his own eyes a mightier hunter than he ever was in the forest at Höidal. And even Hedvig's death—which he interprets as a disaster of a kind that must be risked in his own world of the hunt—does not shake the foundations of his mythology: retreating into the attic after Hedvig's corpse has been removed from it, he murmurs to himself that though the forests have taken their revenge, still he is not afraid. Not afraid because his deity goes with him even into the valley of the shadow of death.

Other mythologizers are less fortunate, if, that is, it is good fortune to escape reality in mythopoeic fictions which are the creations of a brandy-soaked brain, or bad fortune to formulate a mythology in which whatever forces are thought of as shaping life appear, at best, indifferent or, at worst, malign in their relation to humanity. We do not, in fact, know whether Hedvig intuitively fashions some mythus of sacrifice or whether she shoots herself in hideous confusion. And though compassion inclines most of us to be positive, Ibsen the tragicomic artist is more even-handed. Neither do we know that Haakon Werle is the depraved predator that Gregers is so certain about. And though a number of familiar literary attitudes, not least of which is the suspicion, shared by Ibsen, that all businessmen, especially substantial and successful merchants, must be black at heart, militate against Werle, he is not definitively condemned. Much about him is less certain than Consul Bernick's undeniable fraudulence and Borkman's undoubted embezzlement. He may, but only may, share with his future second wife, Berta Sörby, the burden of believing that he has done all that any fallible creature can to make amends for sufferings as deliberately inflicted by him as his son believes.

If the play's structure is regarded as lacking a protagonist and having instead innumerable symbolic suggestions perceived in relation to three fixed allegorical patterns, one of the most paradoxical aspects of its psychology of myth-making is that Gina Ekdal is clearly at least as important as any other character. And this is not so because she is a myth-maker but because she is, like her daughter, an embodiment of central aspects of the play's own mythopoeic capacity.

It is usual to congratulate Gina on her efficiency as a house-keeper—and that indeed was her first calling, which she might have exercised professionally for much longer had Haakon Werle been able to keep his hands off her. Clearly, also, she is good at doing all that is required to provide unpretentious people with slightly flattering (because retouched) photographs of themselves. A certain sense of decency has been observed in her decision that Hedvig's corpse should be removed from the studio and not allowed to lie around "for everybody to see." And inevitably her maternal nature is acknowledged.

It is also generally thought, however, that she has no imagination, and is therefore not included among those characters poetically associated with the duck. Ibsen encourages this attitude by associating her so strongly with photography, which Strindberg, five years after the publication of *The Wild Duck*, was to identify as the very embodiment of anti-art,[14] and by making her ignorant and illiterate. We may wince when Hjalmar talks to Gregers patronizingly about Gina's inevitably acquiring some culture from himself and his family's visitors (Relling and Molvik), and laugh when he shows vexation at her grammatical errors, but, as Ibsen knew, such reactions to Hjalmar will not necessarily prevent educated people from forming negatively condescending views about Gina:

her malaproprisms are, after all, laughable, and Ibsen's treatment of Gina seems far removed indeed from Shaw's of another woman who begins, as Gina remains, unable to speak like a lady: Eliza Doolittle.

But to judge characters by appearances is as dangerous in *The Wild Duck* as in *Peer Gynt*. It is possible to be utterly convinced that Ibsen is himself guilty of overshooting a supposedly straightforward comical mark in his treatment of Gina: having her talk about scrubbing the floor when Gregers sententiously speaks of foul odours, for instance, and making her take the shade off the lamp should mention be made of a dark oppressive atmosphere. At best she seems a good soul sadly out of her depth among a number of other people who, for all their faults, are at least genteel: just another such character as the Cook whose murder Peer does not think worth mentioning to the Devil.

But the Cook who comically, though not perhaps absurdly, died praying for humanity's daily bread, has a good deal in common with Gina. Gina makes several references to God—as when she cries out, "Dear God the child must be somewhere"[15] when Hjalmar, for the fourth or fifth time, wishes Hedvig out of his sight, or as when, in reply to Gregers's question whether she believes he meant everything for the best, she answers, "Yes, I dare say you did. But may God forgive you, all the same." It would be wrong, I believe, to take such mentions of God as evidence that Ibsen is temporarily loosening his commitment to naturalism; there may well be, however, indications that Gina's sense of decency is rooted in residual religious conviction rather than in a prosaic commitment to tidiness and cosiness. And if so, Gina too has her private mythology, which consists of scraps of traditional Christian belief. It is aesthetically unimpressive but significant in relation to her conduct.

In effect, the play's presentation of Gina is intriguingly ambivalent in a way which is very close to the central ambivalence about the duck, and the latter, interestingly, is always spoken of as female (while the bird in Ibsen's poem "The Eiderduck" is male). The correspondences between the duck and Gina, however, are never fully verbalized by anyone, least of all by Gina herself. Relling does comment interestingly—in a remark not usually well translated into English—on Gina's gait: she goes "padding around in her slippers . . . *waggling* her hips and keeping [Hjalmar] neat and cosy," as Rolf Fjelde appropriately puts it.[16] It is for us to see that it is through action such as this and through suffering, not through explicit verbal comparison, that Gina is shown to be like the duck. Werle, who seduced her, brought her down quite as low as the duck fell, and subsequently "raised her up," as Engstrand says of another "fallen woman." Now, it would seem, her experience of the erotic is over. The duck limps but gets around in a lively, contented way, though wounded in one foot as well as one wing. Gina moves in a fashion which is more likely to inspire affection than passion, if Relling's observation is accurate, and she is reminiscent of a mother bird ever attending to her nest and its occupants. Gina's cosy unaesthetic accommodation with reality is, like the duck's Darwinian aspect, ironically prosaic; but her capacity for affection can be deeply moving, especially by contrast with the men's endless talk about feeling. She protects Hedvig with all the instinctive courage that poets (like Shakespeare, for instance, in his reference to the fierce mother wren in *Macbeth*) and ornithologists alike ascribe to mother birds. Her affection for Hjalmar may, finally, be deeper still, and an instance of touching loyalty—or of brainless Darwinian adaptation to circumstance. We must try to decide—since Ibsen refuses to do so.

Gina, then, like the Cook in *Peer Gynt,* may be one of Ibsen's truly "honest workmen," unpretentious, devoted, sticking to her last, to echo the phrase that Ibsen used, as we have seen, when writing about heroism in the letter to Georg Brandes[17]: like the duck, she may be seen as making the best of an unpromising situation. She may also be seen, again like the duck, as just doing what comes naturally and unremarkably— responding to environmental stimuli as a simple mind, possibly devoid of any ennobling intuitions, dictates.

Whatever is the "truth" about Gina and the feathered creature in the attic with whom *she* recognizes no affinity, it is evident that Ibsen is using her, with characteristic slyness, to imply ambiguous attitudes about art as well as life: if Gina, as mother and photographer, does embody some of the most admirable, though unpretentious, aspects of human nature, she does so without the benefit of art, whose allegories and symbols are meaningless to her. If she embodies no more than the chance capacity of dumb animals to survive haphazard changes, then she represents a world where art has no place at all. As is usual in his best work, Ibsen, in *The Wild Duck,* does not fail to raise the most basic question for any artist—whether his calling and art itself are ultimately anything more than vanity.

Gina's actions are more important than what she says. To some extent this it true of the other female characters: Mrs. Sörby, for example, gets things done. And though she is never at a loss for words, can be witty as well as diplomatic—and, apparently, candid—it is her capacity for managing her own life and those of others to some seemingly positive purpose that is ultimately most impressive about her. As his housekeeper, Mrs. Sörby has run Werle's household for him successfully despite their delicate social situation. And she has, she claims, with every indication of truth, worked out the terms of a marriage which will be mutually advantageous. Discreetly Mrs. Sörby acts as Werle's agent both before and after Werle's single, and singularly unsuccessful, intrusion into the Ekdal's residence to sort matters out himself. And the tragic farce of Hjalmar's footling attempts to move house are effectively contrasted with Berta Sörby's: when Hjalmar has reached the stage of telling Gina that she may prepare the sitting room for his supposedly temporary occupation of it and of simultaneously requiring her to pack his suitcase for his imminent departure, Mrs. Sörby has arranged everything necessary for the closing down of Werle's luxurious town residence and the opening up of a more modest house at Höidal, where she and Werle will live for a short time before being married by "a special license" (without the benefit of the Church, that is) and where they will take up permanent residence after marriage. Like Gina's, the behaviour of Berta Sörby may be interpreted in contrary ways, but it is ultimately what she does that is most important.

John Northam's description of Hedvig as Ibsen's "first inarticulate poet of living" is particularly apt: Hedvig's talk, charged with symbolism expressing the half-conscious promptings of her intensely active imagination, speaks volumes to an audience about her state of mind and soul, but it lacks logical connections and reveals her pathetic confusion. She is able to speak quite straightforwardly about her close attachment to the duck (Relling is at his most perceptive when he calls her the "little wild-duck mother"); to give Gregers an account of why she is kept at home, not even attending school or seeing other children; and to tell him a little about her aspiration—to be an engraver—as well as about the eerie sensations she experiences in the attic. But a word which she uses over and over again is "strange" ("underlig"): in her first private conversation with Gregers, she uses it four times, five if the variant "forunderlig" is counted. Gina and Hjalmar refer to the strangeness of things, but it is Hedvig who apprehends that strangeness most intensely and who cannot explain to anyone her feelings about what is for her the endless series of catastrophes laying waste her world. She is, of course, the one who acts most drastically, and the meaning of her apparent suicide is the heart of the play's fully tragicomic ambivalences. Hedvig obviously does not and physically could not say what her intentions are just before she fires the gun: her lack of words, her silence, is the dramatic embodiment of an ultimate "strangeness."

All the men talk—with the exception of the pathetic Molvik, who is in a state of perpetual hangover, and Old Werle, who, for better or worse, does more than he cares to mention. Gregers and Relling argue vociferously, Old Ekdal mutters a good deal and from time to time gives vent to remarks which reveal how completely his pseudo-religion of the hunt absorbs him, and Hjalmar sentimentalizes nearly all the time. With the mentioned exceptions, the men not only talk more than the women, they also cast themselves continuously as protagonists, antagonists, saviours, martyrs, and sacrificial victims in dramas of their own making. In terms of the heroism which the Ibsen of the later plays does seem, though infrequently, to endorse—that of Dr. and Ellida Wangel in *The Lady from the Sea* and Borghejm, the Engineer, and Asta Allmers in *Little Eyolf*—all of the talkative males in *The Wild Duck* are suspiciously histrionic. Their dramatic context never warrants certain condemnation of any of them as human beings, and it is interesting to note that, after four months of intensive daily work on the play, Ibsen spoke of having grown to like all the characters so well that it was hard to part with them.[18] But it is always doubtful whether the talkative males are conceivably the stuff of which heroes are made. Doubtful with two exceptions—Hjalmar, who is at best a mock-hero and perilously close to being what his father, the second exception, undoubtedly is, namely that comparative rarity in Ibsen, an anti-hero.

One fascinating result of being aware of Ibsen's scepticism about the impassioned talkers in *The Wild Duck* is that the comparatively tight-lipped Haakon Werle is shown in a light, which, to say the least, may not confirm that his is a villainous state of mind.

The Wild Duck opens with a feast at which there is much talk, most of it apparently mere social chit-chat, but with here and there some indications of catastrophes that have already struck the Werles and the Ekdals hard, and of others which are beginning to take shape and will strike both families harder still. As Hjalmar is to point out much later, when he declares to Berta Sörby that he will pay back to the last penny his supposed debt of honour to Werle, the "dust of oblivion" had in fact long, long settled over the battle of which that supposed debt was an incidental consequence. Gregers, in the first act, demonstrates that far from being like, or allowing others to be like, the sleeping dogs of the proverb, however, he is more determined than his father's hunting dogs ever were to stir up the dust of battle again. He risks his own soul and those of every member of the two families in a conflict he may or may not recognize as potentially mortal.

The motif of the feast is itself highly significant: it is, for those who will listen to the poetry of Ibsen's prose and see its visual enhancement on his stage, as rich in suggestions as the banquet that the Troll King throws in Dovrë or the feast of life which Hedda Gabler imagines Lövborg as leaving. It has no literal ghost, like Banquo's, to "shake [its] gory locks" at a certain murderer, for this is a nineteenth-century bourgeois household, the home of a prosperous wholesale merchant (or *grosserer*, as Werle's title, which is repeatedly used, is in Norwegian). But just as grievous death precedes and will follow the banquet attended by Banquo's ghost, so it does Haakon Werle's dinner party. And shades of *Hamlet* are almost palpable when Gregers, towards the end of the act, tells a parent what he thinks of a celebration offered, as he understands it, to throw an air of respectability over a second marriage and to bury for good memories of the abused and dead parent:

> Think of the good impression it must create when it is known how the son hurried home—on wings of devotion—to his ageing father's wedding feast. What will be left then of all the stories about the things the poor dead wife had to put up with. Not a whisper! Her own son kills them all stone dead.

The language is not Shakespeare's, but the dramatic poetry of the situation is as intense as that in *Hamlet*. In the Shakespearian tragedy, as is appropriate, wicked motives and evil deeds are revealed by supernatural agency; in Ibsen's tragicomedy, the configurations of motives behind grievous suffering are doubtful, and the only reference to the supernatural in the context of Werle's dinner party, while psychologically revealing, is ironic and dismissive of any metaphysical possibilities: Haakon Werle tells Gregers about his uneasy and superstitious observation that there were thirteen at table.

Two related questions shape themselves in the course of the entertainment following Werle's dinner party. They arise in a manner quite unlike that which shapes the questions in *Macbeth* and *Hamlet*—such as when will Macbeth meet the grisly end he has so patently deserved, and when, if ever, will Hamlet take Claudius's life? In *The Wild Duck* we are asked to ponder, first, what, if anything, this feast really celebrates, and, second, whether its host and hostess and those attending as guests are as deluded or as ludicrously hypocritical as those who, in *Peer Gynt*, are present at the feast in the Hall of the Troll King.

Does the Werle Banquet celebrate the success of a callous predator, Haakon Werle, in imposing his wish (his supposed wish, that is) that his ruthless past should be either forgotten altogether or accepted as a natural consequence of the Darwinian "struggle for existence"? And is there nothing but lack of integrity (represented by the titled guests, Werle himself, and Mrs. Sörby) and neurosis (represented by Gregers Werle, and Hjalmar Ekdal and his father) among those present at Werle's dinner party?

All this is perfectly possible, and indeed, critical responses to Werle seem to indicate that his villainy, at least, is accepted as certain even though its extent may be indeterminate. But in fact the play actually confirms little of the preceding completely negative interpretation: Haakon Werle has survived a strife-ridden marriage in which, as we later learn, he may have been as much sinned against as sinning. The titled guests are all experienced survivors, and the Werle household is only one of many, it seems, where they make themselves agreeable in exchange for a sumptuous meal. (Ibsen risks, and gets away with, the surrealistic touch of having all the *kammerherrerne*—literally, "chamberlains"—not only unaccompanied by women—which might, in itself, be interpreted as a reflection of Werle's wishes as a widower—but seemingly completely unattached to and unmindful of them, other than Mrs Sörby.) Moreover, it seems, from what they have to offer—complaisance, a little wit, and an air of social consequence—that the *kammerherrerne* may be welcome in many homes where the public image of the occupants is of some consequence. The titled guests are not attractive, therefore, but neither are they simply—or certainly—villainous hypocrites.

We have two completely contradictory accounts of the late Mrs.
Werle's sufferings, her husband's and her son's. Neither of them can be
relied upon but one of them, Werle's, achieves a measure of apparent
support from both Gina and Berta Sörby. With regard to Werle's treatment of Old Ekdal, a court has tried Werle and found reason enough to
acquit him, or, as Gregers sees it, insufficient evidence to convict him, of
complicity in Old Ekdal's crimes: it is Gregers alone who is certain that his
father contrived Ekdal's downfall and Gregers who is eager to see what
may be the dross beneath the glitter of his father's banquet. Gregers is
just as eager to reject his own rights as a son and heir, rights that his
father is, not certainly for hypocritical reasons, anxious to have set down
in a will. Werle tells Gregers his allegory of the human hunt, but it is
Gregers who assumes that there is no possibility of his father's being a
fortunate survivor and not a heartless destroyer of life and spirit. And
although Mrs. Sörby gives the impression, like Lady Macbeth (whose
guests are also all men), of having a remarkable capacity of controlling
her "court", Gregers is the only one to regard her as being his father's
companion in the chase, and as red in tooth and claw as Werle may be
himself by being a willing accessory after the fact. It is ultimately as
unwise to accept Gregers's suspicions of his father as certain proof of
Haakon Werle's supposed villainy as it is to accept them as certain proof
of Gregers's supposed neurosis.

As with Gina Ekdal, the play projects a positive image of Haakon Werle
which it is unwise to ignore. When he tells his son, still in the context of
the feast, that the Ekdals are representative of people who like ducks
wounded in flight dive down into a fjord and bite on to the seaweed, he is
not necessarily claiming that the weak deserve to suffer, or worse, are
best dead. Instead, he could be describing a process which he has
observed, and indeed of which he, as one of the strong, has been an
inevitable part, a process that takes place whether or not he, Gregers, or
anyone else likes it. Malthus and Darwin did not need to rejoice in their
theories for those theories to be as possibly true as optimistic readings of
the state of nature; neither does Haakon Werle need to savour or gloat
about his allegory of the hunt for it to carry more weight than Gregers is
prepared to admit.

Of course it would be naive to think of Werle as a detached
philosopher: he certainly seduced Gina, with her mother's assistance,
and he may be Hedvig's father. And as Werle is made to say with an
underlying irony of which he seems unconscious, "Acquittal is acquittal."
The law, that is, is the law, and not necessarily justice; so it is perfectly
possible that he intentionally ruined Ekdal when they were business
partners. But there is much to suggest, in information supplied by Gina,
his wife's ex-housekeeper, and Berta Sörby, his present housekeeper and
confidante, that Werle was, at times, wrongly suspected and accused of

sexual misconduct by his wife and that her harangues on the subject may have precipitated other and undeniable instances of infidelity. But if Werle did marry for money, as Gregers declares, he not only met the nemesis Ibsen himself declared unavoidable in all marriages of convenience,[19] he also, apparently, suffered, like Alving, the stifling of what Georg Brandes and perhaps also Ibsen cherished as "joy of life." As Mrs. Sörby puts it in Act IV:

> Mr. Werle hasn't tried to hide anything either. And that's mainly what's brought us together. Now he can sit and talk to me quite openly, just like a child. The whole of his youth and the best years of his manhood, all he heard was a lot of sermonizing about his sins—a healthy and vigorous man like him. And many's the time, from what I've heard, those sermons were about entirely imaginary offences.

One of Hjalmar's discoveries—made when he finally has the wit to compare his marriage with Old Werle's second one—is that there may be "no just order in the universe."[20] This discovery might have occurred to him at some time before he entered his theoretical manhood, and certainly it should have crossed his mind as a possibility during his father's humiliating trial and disgrace. But, if Hjalmar is right, he is, in fact, confirming Werle's own presumed view that life is a struggle for survival to which justice is alien. Gregers, still in the dramatic context of the celebration at his father's, applies distasteful animal imagery to Werle: he is a creature Gregers has observed "at too close quarters" and whose life, Gregers says, is like a battlefield strewn with his enemies' corpses. It is Gregers who thinks he can impose justice, but he does not explain what natural predators are to do with their teeth and claws while he attends to their wounded prey. And he appears to overlook entirely the evidence that Werle may be doing what he can to make amends.

What never crosses Gregers's mind is a question which should certainly cross an audience's; namely, is there a possibility that his father, whatever the extent of his former cruelties, may now be genuinely repentant and may have realized that "justice", being harder to define than laws and probably lacking any supreme sanction, is as hard to achieve as to understand? The world of *The Wild Duck* is one, even more undoubtedly than that of *Ghosts*, where all values are relative and therefore all ethics situational.

In Kierkegaard's questioning world-view the worst sinners have a better chance of redemption than those who dabble in sin. Werle, in a world where all is questionable, may, but only may, have realized that decency within oneself and among one's fellow men may not, like Mme. de Staël's sun and starlight, flow from naively pure sources[21] but be achieved only by contrivance—deliberate manipulation, that is, of oneself and others to effect what is conceived as good. The view is sophisticated in comparison to Gregers's, and it is not at all romantically heroic.

All the more reason, therefore, why Ibsen may be asking us to ponder its possible truthfulness. Haakon Werle is undeniably a man besmirched by his past. When he invites a number of distinguished gentlemen to his house for a dinner ostensibly given to celebrate his son's homecoming, it is natural for us to be as suspicious as Gregers is that he is being used to lend respectability to the marriage of a man who is possibly still no stranger to lechery and a woman distastefully determined to seize a chance for wealth and security regardless of the cost to others.

Certainly Werle, unlike Stockmann, knows that those who eat at his table and thank him copiously for the privilege are not necessarily companions of the spirit as well as the stomach. Berta Sörby is, unlike Mrs. Bernick, for example, not naive in such matters either. Both seem to know that where others' perceptions of themselves are concerned, what may count most is not necessarily reality nor even the appearances of it, but what influential people—like the *kammerherrerne*—can be persuaded, by one means or another, to say that they perceive as reality. None of these things make Werle undoubtedly evil; they may in fact indicate a man who is learning, in the loneliness he mentions in Gregers's utterly unsympathetic ear, that it is much harder to do good than evil. And if this is so, Werle learns his lesson without the piteous complaints that Gregers utters whilst appearing to learn a similar lesson. Whatever is against Werle, he appears to have the capacity to face the worst without whimpering, a trait which is, for instance, as characteristic of some tragic heroes as of some tragic villains.

Werle is, at least in part, a lecherous and treacherous animal slowed down only by incipient blindness and age, a figure not unlike the Peer who, returning to Norway as an old man, humorously contemplates his inability to do more than admire the lure of maidenly mountains which seem to be beckoning, even in their snowy purity, to the troll in him. Similarly, Mrs. Sörby, the veterinarian's widow, is, in part, as she makes no effort to deny, a woman whose eye for the main chance enables her to make the most of the opportunities provided by widower Werle's wealth, increasing physical incapacity, and loneliness, which to her is real. And it may be that she was unscrupulous to reject Relling in order to take her chances with Werle, though she tells Relling, possibly with justice, that her decision to break with him was a hard one, not made on impulse, and necessary because of his own waste of his talents.

When Mrs. Sörby sat down for what she says was her candid conversation with Haakon Werle (the one she mentions to Relling, Gregers, and the Ekdals in Act IV) it would seem that she was not in any position to listen to his confessions with a pure heart: she was no Solveig— as most positively interpreted—altruistically listening to Werle's sinful Peer. But neither was she, like Hedda—as most negatively interpreted—drawing out the destructive element in a possibly Dionysian male only to exacerbate it. She may or may not have heard an ageing man's confidences to some positive purpose.

Such ambivalences should not be passed over as though they scarcely exist nor, as is often the case, mentioned only in connection with Hjalmar's shocked recognition that the marriage based on mutual trust may be ironically within the grasp of his supposed persecutors, and not within his own.

Shaw drew attention—too much attention—to the discussion between Torvald and Nora Helmer in the closing minutes of *A Doll's House*. He wrongly took it as being the first demonstration of the mode of the "discussion play,"[22] though he was wise enough to see, unlike some modern actresses, that the "solution" for Nora's "oppression" and Torvald's "chauvinism" may not be as simple as delivering a crisp ultimatum to Torvald and then leaving him to sort out his own life and those of the children with the kindly but ignorant nurse who brought up Nora herself, badly.[23] The bridge between minds and hearts that a wiser Nora and a more obviously contrite Torvald might build is foreshadowed in *A Doll's House*, but in critical appraisals it is too often demolished by reductive conclusions.

A similar coming together of souls—those of Haakon Werle and Berta Sörby—is rarely noticed at all, except by Hjalmar, in what may amount to his most unconsciously ironic epiphany. Werle and Mrs. Sörby are no more saints than they are devils. They may be as grimy as Peer when he stumbles in the mud and dreams of starting his life anew, but unlike Peer, they do not, literally or metaphorically, scan the heavens for the sight of majestic visions. It is possible that they do achieve a humbler, unsensational victory, one stemming from candour and offering no grand ethical imperatives or metaphysical vistas, but something resembling the ability which Mrs. Linde and Krogstad may have discovered in themselves at the end of *A Doll's House*, namely the ability to appreciate what is best in each other and to tolerate, whilst trying to get rid of, what is worst.

Werle and Mrs. Sörby achieve no wondrous revelation. But they may have hammered out a bond strong enough to give their lives a positive and undestructive purpose. Gregers is usually thought of as an idiot, when, in quarrelling with his father in Act I, he refers to Hjalmar as though the latter were an innocent child. And there is much to laugh at in Gregers's adulation of his old schoolfriend's obvious childishness. But, ironically enough, Hjalmar is perhaps as truthful as the Biblical babes and sucklings in one thing at least—realizing that the new Mr. and Mrs. Werle really may be the best candidates for heroism among the characters whose acquaintance we share with him. A good second marriage could be better, the play seems to imply, than an abortive Third Empire, for instance.

The double ethical perspective in which Haakon Werle and Berta Sörby are seen, is, interestingly, expressed in imagery: Werle, who in conversation with Gregers sees himself as a hunter, accepts the courage of some human beings and the cowardice of others for what his observations seem to show them to be—natural phenomena. He is, accordingly, viewed by his son as a bestial predator. When Werle comments on Hjalmar's undesirable ignorance about fine wines, however, we have an image which, though still eminently physical, is decidedly concerned with discrimination of a kind: neither beasts—nor trolls—relish a good vintage of tokay, as Werle does, and it is surely not within the range of animal consciousness to be contemptuous of prey, as Werle appears to be when irritated by Hjalmar's apparent stupidity and ignorance on the subject of wines. The feast at Werle's house could, therefore, in terms of its imagery, celebrate simply and revealingly Werle's outstanding success in terms of the struggle for social eminence which, for some, succeeds the struggle for mere survival. It could, and paradoxically also, celebrate Werle's belated discovery of the "joy of life." The imaginative step from the champagne of *Ghosts* to the tokay of *The Wild Duck* is not too large, though the bouquet and savour of both vintages may be soured by dramatic irony.

It is easy enough to see Berta Sörby as a clever woman who succeeds where Gina, also once in service with Werle, had failed. In the first act Gregers refers contemptuously to Gina as the "female" ("fruentimmer") Werle "palmed off on Hjalmar" when Werle had fully satisfied his sexual demands of her. Berta Sörby, whom Gregers eventually tries to intimidate with the threat of revealing her past relationship with Relling to his father, is clearly, in Gregers's eyes, another "female" differing from Gina principally in the extent of her artfulness. In the same place (Act IV), we also learn that Mrs. Sörby had to endure physical beatings from a sadistic husband. Gregers may have a low opinion of all "females," though his attitudes on this subject are not easily decipherable, for while he appears to regret what he regards as the certainty that he will never marry, he seems also to have voluntarily isolated himself from women. But not even Gregers could deny that the conduct of the male animal who was Mrs. Sörby's first husband was other than repugnant. Treated, however, like an animal, as the idiom has it, and, ironically enough, by a man whose profession it was to treat animals, Mrs. Sörby seems to have retained both her self-respect and an appreciation for life.

The image of the veterinarian Sörby thrashing his wife is an important one, therefore. There seems to be genuine generosity of spirit—as well as an unusual degree of objectivity—in the abused Mrs. Sörby's claim that her first husband was not as base as his worst conduct would indicate and that despite his abuse of her, he was preferable to Relling in that he had not "squandered what was best in him" and sought refuge in the bottle.

Like the widower Werle, therefore, the widow Sörby is associated with images concerning animal behaviour and alcohol. Mrs. Sörby, whom tokay reminds of royal courts and regal favour, knows as well how to praise the *savoir vivre* evident in the contents of Werle's wine cellar as to condemn alcoholism in Relling. And there is a distinct possibility that the woman who clung to life with animal persistence—unlike the first and apparently alcoholic Mrs. Werle—has found in her second husband a man who may be beginning to discover that there is something potentially admirable in human nature. Something admirable in Berta Sörby, for instance, and even in Werle himself, despite all that his first wife and Gregers have ever said to the contrary.

That Haakon Werle and Berta Sörby do not conform to any theatrical stereotype should surprise no one familiar with the theory of naturalism as explained—and put into practice—by Strindberg and Chekhov, for example. But Ibsen is sufficiently a practical artist to keep theory in its place and to make use of what E.M. Forster called "flat characters" when necessary. Thus, in the first act, we have five "round" characters and a larger number of "flat" ones,[24] the *kammerherrerne* and the servants. The "round" characters are divided into two contrasted groups: the apparent winners in the struggle of life—Werle and Mrs. Sörby—and the apparent losers—Gregers Werle, Hjalmar Ekdal, and Old Ekdal.

Most of the flat characters are *kammerherrerne*, titled men who comically, but with convincing realism, pay for their supper with their well-bred servility. As type characters, they represent a conventional and substantially unattractive form of success; they are not unlike privileged drones to Berta Sörby's queen bee. And against their lack of humanity and self-indulgence, the spiritual assets, deficiencies, aspirations, and claims of the "round" characters are suggestively measured.

In *The Wild Duck* as a whole every one of the major characters is meaningfully associated with the banquet at Werle's and the departures from it. For Werle and Mrs. Sörby, their lavish dinner party is, it seems, also their farewell to "polite" society: their life together at Höidal will be simpler. It is up to us whether we regard them as leaving life's banquet because they have gorged themselves long enough and now wish to find a bolt-hole where they can escape the sharp tongues of a small-minded community, or because they are people who have reached a point in their relationship at which they are wise and strong enough to afford the luxury of chosen and comfortable isolation. Little has been said by critics about their decision to live at Höidal. What Ibsen is hinting here is indeed a singularly open question. Höidal is the place where there live, according to both Relling and Gregers (who have both spent many years there), materially and spiritually impoverished working people and their families. It is quite conceivable that Haakon Werle and his second wife have chosen Höidal as a place least likely to be frequented by "successful" visitors; it is equally possible that the man and woman who have had a measure of success in helping those apparently maimed by Werle's activities, the Ekdals, now wish to bring to the labourers' doorsteps at Höidal something more palatable than Gregers's "claim of the ideal" and possibly, even, something more uplifting than Relling's "life-lies." Wide open as this question is, there is little room for doubt about Ibsen's posing it. Were Werle and Berta Sörby simply wealthy escapees from a world they no longer choose, in one way or another, to recall, they would hardly go to live "up at the works" at Höidal when they could afford a luxurious villa in some beautiful foreign place and the exclusive hotels where Arnold Rubek, for instance, attempts to overcome his misanthropy.

The exits from Werle's banquet of both Hjalmar and Gregers, however, are more precipitate and more theatrical, and their immediate consequences are easily calculated. Hjalmar is badly confused—even before his cowardly, though understandable, inability to acknowledge his father when the latter appears unexpectedly in Werle's drawing room. His incapacities have been fully displayed and recognized by everyone present (except Gregers) in his painfully funny inability to recite—or even show some of his photographs—for his supper. He hurries home for a generous helping of what some will see as a reassuring love and others as cloying and unwholesome sentimentality. Gregers, in preparation for what he regards as his final departure from his father's household, has a violent argument with Werle. He refuses his offer of a partnership and accuses him of the calculated destruction and spiritual blinding of the Ekdals and, virtually, of full and total responsibility for the death of a woman whose actual experiences are as uncertain as Beate Rosmer's before Rebecca West's arrival; that is to say, Gregers's mother and Werle's first wife.

The more extended consequences of Gregers's and Hjalmar's departures are much more incalculable. Should we judge Gregers as Cyrus Hoy does, or as Mary McCarthy does? Should we decide that Hjalmar is entirely the posturing though not utterly despicable fool that Relling sees before as well as after Hedvig's death? Or is he a man of some humble worth, who, because of a residual capacity to learn a little from bitter experience, is less likely than Relling believes to spout self-aggrandizing sentimentalities about the dead Hedvig before the grass has grown on her grave?

With a beautiful irony, Ibsen, even while allowing the questions about the destinies of the other "round" characters to shape themselves, gives us a slyly cunning portrayal of one ageing and peculiar bird, Old Ekdal. Though not invited to the banquet, Old Ekdal none the less insinuates himself into the after-dinner entertainment—much to the chagrin of all the major characters present, not least that of Haakon Werle—and goes home happy with what he fancies most in all the world (as Mrs. Sörby is informed by Pettersen), a bottle of brandy. He seems largely oblivious to the embarrassment he causes, perhaps intentionally, and he does not stay to hear Hjalmar's pathetic comments to Gregers on his own (Hjalmar's) cowardice, nor the vicious accusations which Gregers subsequently aims at Werle. Old Ekdal misses too, though he has incited, Gregers's tragicomic avowal of having that very moment, found "an objective [he] can live for"—the "redemption" of the Ekdals—an objective which, comically and pathetically, he dare not express to his father in case Werle should laugh at him.

The final irony of the first act, as those conscious of the play's continual use of sight imagery are aware[25], is that Gregers, now so terrifyingly sure that he sees things straight, observes contemptuously to his father that Mrs. Sörby is playing blind man's buff with the *kammerherrerne*! But neither here nor anywhere else in the play can those who, singly, in pairs, or in other groups, may walk in darkness be said for sure to behold a great light. Some unpretentious lights, not necessarily false fires, may, however, illuminate the paths followed by all the characters in the play capable of seeking enlightenment and willing to suffer the privations of the journey. The number is not large, and the nature of such epiphanies as there may be is not certain.

In allegorical terms, the rest of the play is concerned with an elaboration of three distinct views of the animal fable with which Haakon Werle attempts to enlighten (or deceive) his son: none is endorsed or rejected by the play, the unfailing source of dramatic and poetic vitality of which is the tension between their rigidity and the play's evocation of life's more unpredictable motions.

Werle is, undeniably, the hunter who, at some unspecified time before the present action of the play commences, shot down the now ironically fat, contented, and thoroughly domesticated duck to whose natural and, in the minds of several characters, romantic past the title explicitly refers. The creature was badly maimed, in a wing, by gunshot wounds and mauled in one foot by Werle's retriever. Characteristically, Werle decided that as the duck was unfit to cope with its natural life, it should be granted the release it had actually sought when, wounded, it had dived deep into a fjord and clung on to the weeds to drown. It was Pettersen, Werle's manservant, who gave the wild duck to the Ekdals rather than wringing its neck, as instructed. It is also Pettersen, who, in the opening minutes of the play, is called by Old Ekdal, possibly with much more truth than Ekdal realizes, a fool—or literally "a cod" ("torsk"), a creature that is uglier than any duck and unquestionably at home underwater.

Haakon Werle knows nothing of others likening Pettersen to a cod and his son to a "queer fish" (as Gina does at the end of Act II) but he has constructed his own allegory about life on land and death in water. According to him, some people are like the duck: once they "get a couple of slugs in them" they dive into the depths of some lake or fjord and "they never come up again." They drown that is, though Werle, quite consciously it seems, does not speak so explicitly of death any more than he is ruthless enough to hasten the actual demise of any of the Ekdals. Those who were, inevitably it appears, his prey, and life's psychological casualties in general, do not, according to Werle's allegory, actually perish: instead they inhabit a subaqueous wonderland where, out of the compassion or the expediency of their former predators, they may be sustained for an indefinite period, provided they are left undisturbed.

For Werle, then, as for Darwin and, in his pessimistic periods, Tennyson, nature is inevitably "red in tooth and claw." No Biblical lions lie down with the lambs, and specifically Christian contemplation of sheep, young, like the lamb of God, or older, like the flocks requiring good shepherds, is remote from Werle's world: those creatures who are not red in tooth and claw will inevitably find themselves either red in breast and throat, or the inhabitants of some kind of psychological limbo. Haakon Werle does not explain his allegory any more than the lion provides a gloss on its roar or the wolf on its howl. The predatory process, he intimates, is not a simple one, for he acknowledges that defeated human beings are the masters of fantasy: it is a process that the more intelligent naturalistic writers, some of whose attitudes Werle appears to share, regard with as much awe as detachment. It is possible that Haakon Werle, contemplating the fate of the Ekdals, recognizes both himself and them as part of the same pattern of complexity which George Moore described after seeing the fate of the Alvings: "we learn that though there be no gods to govern us, that nature, vast and unknown, for ever dumb to our appeal, holds us in thrall."[26] And it is equally possible that he realizes no such thing but would like to keep Gregers's nose out of what he regards as his own affair.

Gregers's view of matters is, as one would expect of a youngish man still in full rebellion against everything his father does, says, and stands for, precisely the opposite. The irony which must not be lost, however, is that Gregers conceives the direct inspiration for his parable from the fable sketched by his father. Gregers, on hearing more from the Ekdals—about the fate of the actual duck, and about the roles of his father's retriever and Pettersen—casts himself as a clever dog in an "improved" allegory of his own fashioning. He will act not, as Werle's retriever does, in strict obedience to training, nor, as the servant Pettersen does, on mere impulse: Gregers, the saviour, will swim into the water, plunge his head under, and grasp the drowning ducks, however unwilling they may be, and when they are dragged ashore, he will breathe wholesome drafts of idealized "truth" into their lungs, ignoring altogether any hunters who may still be standing by with their guns.

The third allegory is Relling's, though he is not so obviously excited by (and therefore clearly drawn into) mythopoeic imaginings as Gregers. Relling curses Gregers's duck parable soundly, but he also calls Hedvig, tenderly, a "little wild-duck mother" ("lille vildand-mor") and, as we have seen, notices, whether conscious of allegorical implication or not, that Gina's gait has something of a duck's about it. But Relling's mind is, in general, distinctly anti-romantic, and it is unwise to fill out too far the terms of his allegory on the basis of his fragmentary hints. It is obvious enough, from his wish that Gregers had fallen down one of the Höidal mineshafts straight to hell, that Relling has little use for fantasy in itself; only when made according to his own prescriptions and recognized by himself as necessary poisons, do myths, or "life-lies", serve any purpose. But there is a necessary distinction to be drawn here: only for those not able to contemplate the truth—most people that is, in Relling's view—is such "medicine" essential. For those like himself—able, that is, to look loathsome reality in the eye (in the intervals between bouts of heavy drinking) he has a clearly understood variant on Werle's allegory: the heads of all the wounded ducks shall be kept well down in the weeds, by such humane cynics as himself, who, situated between the worlds of reality and escapism, ponder the necessity of the submersion of the majority of mankind, and cordially despise the victors still strutting about on the land they dominate.

In the action of the play, Werle's allegory gains some credence by its emanation from his position of lingering strength, and loses some because Werle may still profit greatly from lies and expediency. Gregers's allegory has the appeal of a doctrine formulated by one who has suffered to attain wisdom and is, consciously at least, devoted to whatever may be positive in human nature; it has the disadvantage of being inextricably interwoven with an irrational feud with his father and, apparently, with his Oedipal ties to the memory of his dead mother. Relling's view of life has the strength of the recognition that it can be dangerous to overestimate human capacity, and the weakness of the assumption that the few people naturally able to recognize truth, however intermittently, should content themselves with the supposedly benign deception of the rest.

In the imagery of the play, all that is revealed through the juxtaposition of mythopoeic allegory and Yeatsian images issues in some way from Werle's banquet and from his son's uncertain apprehension of himself as, in Act I, the man who invited the thirteenth person (Hjalmar) to table, and, in Act V, the singular creature who sees his mission as being himself the thirteenth man at the table of others. Who are the Judases and who the Christs of Gregers's imaginings cannot be known. Neither do we know whether, at the end, he is speaking ingenuously or ironically. All we can know is that Gregers may have received, at the end of Act V, powerful intimations of all that the play communicates to us about the complex psychology of groups of people in unstable and perilous situations. Life, he seems to grasp, may, but only may, have those sufficiently in control of themselves to be effective saviours; it may, on the other hand, be a blind and purposeless process in which altruism and self-absorption are ultimately of equal insignificance. Also, those whose will is to destroy their competitors on all those levels at which people engage in battles, cannot always gauge the final outcome of their endeavours.

Ultimately, what we have in *The Wild Duck* is a dramatic translation into human terms of the glory of ducks in flight, the ungainliness of their waddling on land, and the intriguing uncertainty of their underwater meanderings. Tragicomic intimations such as these raise anguished questions as readily as affirmations of faith or opinion. Within the aesthetic pattern of *The Wild Duck* itself, large truths are as elusive for the audience or readers as they are for the play's allegorizers.

Act I shows Werle's house as a centre of apparent control where numerous decisions affecting the Ekdals have been made and will continue to be made, for better or worse, as the action develops. These decisions culminate in Berta Sörby's arrival on the eve of Hedvig's birthday, with a deed of gift. Such a present is, without doubt, far beyond what any adolescent might be predicted to expect; however, it is entirely appropriate to the needs of the Ekdals, and, if used with discretion, might even have been sufficient to make a blind Hedvig's life comfortably endurable, if not happy. It is money made available, in the first instance, to Old Ekdal, and after his death, to Hedvig. There is enough of it to sustain the entire family, it seems, even if Hjalmar continues to be incorrigibly negligent in his work and even if there will be no more copying work for which Ekdal can be overpaid once Werle and Mrs. Sörby leave town.

It is mistaken, therefore, to believe that Hedvig alone is capable of action. Werle and Mrs. Sörby are arranging matters for the Ekdals until only hours before their departure for Höidal. Whether their efforts are best viewed as hypocritical scheming or honest attempts to ensure some kind of security for the Ekdals (after Gregers's efforts have had their effect) is impossible to know.

Act II introduces us to a place where only the female characters do anything practical while the men divert themselves (or "pervert themselves", as Archer nicely renders one of Gina's malapropisms) with talking, dressing up, playing in the attic, and drinking beer or brandy. If the image of social reality presented by Werle's dinner-party is substantially disagreeable, the never ending party-time over which Hjalmar and his father preside in the attic also has its repugnant aspects, not the least of which are its effects upon an isolated and vulnerable adolescent's grasp of reality. There could scarcely be a more apt illustration than Ekdal and Hjalmar's games of Åse's reference in *Peer Gynt* to escapism achieved through romanticizing or drinking. In the case of Ekdal and his son, however, the two activities are not alternatives but are complementary. Only Gina works more or less constantly; she runs the business, such as it is. (Ironically, her work is to take and touch up photographs of people anxious to look their best, such as engaged or newly-wed couples, and Gina is not one to puzzle herself about whether appearances lie.) She also keeps the household and its accounts efficiently and is helped by Hedvig, especially in the demanding and some would say humiliating task of humouring Hjalmar.

The Ekdals are, in terms of their social status, reminiscent of what Shaw called his family after their descent from gentility was well under way—"downstarts." They have already sunk very far, however, and seem to have been saved from the confines of what is now referred to as the "submerged tenth" mainly, perhaps only, by Werle's ambivalent charity. Hjalmar is fond of calling himself a "breadwinner": the Norwegian term is *'familieforsørger'* and means, literally, "family provider." Hjalmar provides for his family by "allowing" his wife to run the business, complaining piteously about exhaustion if he is required to do any retouching, and supposedly pondering an invention whilst actually sleeping in his study. It is possible to see the Ekdals' family life as attractive—founded on kinds of affection and loyalty, for instance. And it is equally possible to see it as loathsome—the disingenuously shared lives of a group of people in retreat from the outside world and subsisting on the "generosity" of the man who appears to have done most to harm them. They turn a blind eye to an old man's alcoholism, a younger man's gross appetite for unmerited adulation and butter, and a girl's obvious need for better guidance than her hard-working and well-intentioned but ignorant mother can provide. Gregers Werle is not a fool to detect spiritual poison in this house, however disastrous his attempts to eliminate it may be.

With a master-stroke of irony, Ibsen places this superficially happy haven for stagnating lives high up in an attic apartment: whatever the spiritual condition of the Ekdals, they literally inhabit a higher plane than most of their fellow mortals. Its physical aspects are special: the photographic studio has "a pitched roof and big skylights," and there are skylights in the roof-space where the duck and its companions live. The sun, moon, and stars are closer to the Ekdals than to most of us, and the life of the streets correspondingly more remote. Such supposed duplications of reality as issue from the photographic studio are much less important, to Hedvig in particular, than this strange place where they originate; we discover that it was during a period of frightening darkness in this peculiar home that Hedvig taught herself to pray when Hjalmar, with a fever and leeches on his neck, told her, with customary tactlessness and hyperbole, that he was at death's door. In Act III she discusses, with Gregers, the effects of light and darkness on her emotions. In Act II we are given glimpses of the bizarre menagerie. A sense of the limited dimensions of human comprehension is induced by our seeing the lamplit studio so near to vast external darkness. Every inch of the Ekdals extraordinary home is fertile soil for myth, and there is a kind of beauty in the fantasies of the Ekdals as there is in those of Flaubert's Félicité. As the second act opens, Gina and Hedvig are awaiting Hjalmar's return. While the mother sews, the daughter "shading her eyes with her hands, her thumbs in her ears" is reading. Before the arrival of Gregers, with his own highly particular notions of reality, reading appears to be Hedvig's only remaining contact with life outside her home, especially since Hjalmar has decided that she must no longer attend school. In Gina's gentle but firm insistence that Hedvig should stop reading, her genuinely maternal concern and her apparently natural evasiveness are evident; she gives Hedvig no hint of the truth but offers a reason the ridiculousness of which is apparent later: "Your father doesn't like it; he never reads himself in the evenings." There is a real need that someone should tell Hedvig the truth about her eyesight. It is a human need to which none of the adults seem to know how to respond. Gina appears to have given no thought to how a blind daughter will live, and this is one of the play's strongest intimations that Gina functions by adaptation to what has occurred rather than by any attempt to control, heroically or otherwise, the future. Hjalmar, who, in Act III, tells Hedvig that she must take responsibility if her eyesight suffers as a result of doing the retouching Gina has requested of him, has got as far as puzzling Hedvig with the recommendation that she should take up basket-weaving. Relling has said nothing, perhaps out of commendable tact, perhaps because he can think of no "life-lie" to conceal the horrifying reality of blindness. And Gregers seems never to get as far as thinking about what Hedvig should be told. Here is the most pressing human need in the play: it is as desperate as little Eyolf's craving for affection, or, even less demanding, for mere acceptance. The avoidance by every adult of Hedvig's need to be prepared for what is inevitably coming is the principal factor militating against the heroic pretensions, stated or not, of every other character. And Hedvig's own ability to act as a free agent cannot be regarded as undiminished when she is already manifesting signs of weak sight and has been made to feel unusual when told that continued attendance at school will "spoil [her] eyes."

As Gina and Hedvig discuss the household accounts, at least two realities emerge: one is that we are watching a mother and daughter who may be evading realities neither can cope with by going through mundane rituals which are reassuring, however seemingly trivial; the other, more surprising and perhaps fully realized only in retrospect, is that, as Gina and Hedvig talk about the groceries and what efforts must be made to pay for them, we are being given the play's first indications of real, however unexalted, sacrifices. "The amount of butter we [euphemism for Hjalmar] go through in this house," says Gina. Quantities of ham, cheese, and salami are also bought, though not easily, nor, it seems, mainly for Gina and Hedvig. They, it transpires, have had little or nothing to eat on this particular evening. As Hedvig put it, "Daddy was going to be out, so there was no need to cook a dinner just for the two of us." It is not certain, that Hedvig has not had a piece of ham or cheese with bread and butter, but the evidence is against it, because her willingness to eat little for Hjalmar's sake has been reinforced by his promise to bring her some delicacies from Werle's table. The abstinence she and her mother accept, perhaps ill-advisedly, as a virtue has, on this occasion, helped her to save her appetite.

Hedvig will soon gladly endure having her ears crammed with Hjalmar's foolish talk about his supposed success at the dinner-party before asking, tentatively, for the food he promised. When she is offered instead a verbal substitute—a description of what each course on the menu tasted like—it is clear that Hedvig understands a basic form of sacrifice: hungry and mortified by Hjalmar's irritation, she "swallows her tears" and instantly sets about doing all she can to jolt Hjalmar out of the maudlin self-pity into which his selfishness has thrown him. And, in doing so, she may be seen either as sacrificing her integrity to his disingenuousness or as demonstrating kinds of love and tact that must be supplied in order to sustain Hjalmar's damaged ego.

If Gregers were capable of seeing that his "claim of the ideal" could usefully put down some tentacular roots in the Ekdal family's grocery bills, there would be more certain hope for him and them. As it is, Gina and Hedvig continue to practice self-denial whilst "buttering up" Hjalmar's sickly morale and, when possible, keeping his father away from "Ma Eriksen's," his drinking haunt when he has not managed to secrete a bottle of something potent in his room.

Hjalmar's homecoming is, dramatically speaking, worth waiting for. It reveals, with unsparing comic irony, aspects of the "tragedy of the house of Ekdal" that Hjalmar, who coins that typically sententious phrase, has never dreamt of. It is predictable that Hjalmar will come home for reassurance after his humiliation at Werle's, predictable that he will be unreasonably vexed when he becomes aware of Hedvig's disappointment at his broken promise, and just as predictable that he will behave as though he, and not, as is more reasonable to believe, his father, is the protagonist of the domestic tragedy—or, more appropriately, domestic melodrama—which Hjalmar has in mind. It is just as predictable, too, that Erhard Borkman, in very similar circumstances, will not allow his life to be blighted by his father's crime because Erhart's self-esteem and will are stronger.

Ibsen's attitude is perfectly consistent in both plays. Rightly it would seem, to judge from a lay knowledge of contemporary psychological theory, Ibsen, in both *The Wild Duck* and *John Gabriel Borkman*, attaches more significance to the influence of parents or guardians than to hereditary factors. Hjalmar, we learn gradually, was brought up, after the death of a mother he cannot remember, by two maiden aunts highly regarded by Gregers for their championship of altruism and despised by Relling for what he considers their hysterical idealism. Relling and Gregers agree that his father always had the highest expectations of Hjalmar, without understanding him, so that when he eventually entered university, no one had higher hopes of Hjalmar than Hjalmar himself. In the first act he speaks of his family's financial ruin as having deprived him of academic distinction; we are given good reason to suspect that he is fortunate to have been spared the humiliation of failure. Like another protégé of two doting spinsters, Jörgen Tesman, Hjalmar has been long conditioned to consider himself destined for high accomplishment, but he lacks even the pedantry which helps Tesman to achieve his questionable victory over Ejlert Lövborg.

Nearly always, Hjalmar plays at being a great man: his notions of distinction are both ludicrous and pitiable, and the price his illusions exacts of others, particular Hedvig, is immense. To restore Hjalmar's withered ego, the Ekdals must accept all the supposed glory of the satirical witticisms and cutting remarks of Berta Sörby, Old Werle, and the *kammerherrerne* as his, for that is how he deceitfully recounts them while imputing to himself also a high-souled spirit of rebellion against social injustice as his reason for not entertaining the guests in some way more agreeable to them.

Hjalmar is certainly a pathetic figure: his self-respect is soon restored by his family's reception of his supposed conduct at Werle's. As for the trolls in the Dovrë, so for Hjalmar, what the credulous can be made to accept as true is true enough for him. A few compliments on his appearance in evening dress, which is borrowed, and on his own jacket, into which Gina helps him, and a few more on his curls or, as he prefers to have them called, "waves", and he is ready to be good-natured—until, that is, he is faced with Hedvig's disappointment.

The tantrum into which Hjalmar then flies is extremely comical. His talk of selfless endeavours, of his "working till [he's] fit to drop", and his absurd criticism of Gina for not being diligent enough to find a tenant for the spare room, is amusing—except, that is, for the fear this piteously inadequate man can be seen to arouse in Hedvig. And the significance of the tantrum deepens when it can be recognized, in retrospect, as the first open manifestation of Hjalmar's undeniable paranoia.

Just before Gregers's knock at the door—which has the same surrealistic quality as Hilde Wangel's arrival in *The Master Builder*—Ibsen shows the kind of reconciliation of a "truth" and an "ideal" that is certainly within Hjalmar's range of understanding and capacity of execution. When Hedvig, repeatedly, has protested her love, offered him beer, and embraced him, Hjalmar is ready to forgive and to receive forgiveness. When, that is, the three people whom he has just deceived, raged at, and played Affronted Virtue for are prepared to accept most of the blame for the ugly scene that has just occurred, he is ready to deliver a maudlin speech:

> And even if I am a bit unreasonable now and again, well . . . heavens above! You mustn't forget I'm a man beset by a whole host of troubles. Well, now! [Dries his eyes.] This is not the moment for beer. Bring me my flute.

He just has time to play a funereal rendering of what should be a cheerful folk-dance when Gregers arrives to require of this poor creature an altogether more exalted kind of reconciliation.

It would be wrong, however, to see Hjalmar as merely an unconscious buffoon, not simply because Ibsen said that he is not a farcical character,[27] but because there are moments, later in the play, when he does show some lingering ability to recognize unpleasant truth about himself. Moreover, the play does indicate that if Gregers were more aware of Hjalmar's limitations than he is, there could be a possibility of the Ekdals making a fresh start. The not unconvincing but highly specific combination of Hjalmar's limitations and Gregers's apparent inability to translate what may be sound principles into effective practice may be the greatest negative force in the play.

Long ago, Hermann Weigand suggested that if Gina were able to play the role of remorseful sinner, writhing in anguish and craving for Hjalmar's forgiveness, Hjalmar could play the part of the noble husband, ready to pardon her for deceiving him—and even to "forgive" Hedvig for not being indubitably his daughter. It is appropriate that Weigand, who emphasizes the comic aspects of the play, should see such a melodramatic subterfuge as wholly ridiculous.[28] But in the context of the play, it would be no more ridiculous than Relling's sustaining life-lies. And there might have been enough truth in it, if injected into the Ekdal's domestic situation at an appropriate moment, to have enabled Hjalmar and Gina to make a fresh beginning, as is vital for Hedvig. The melodrama would have its ludicrous aspects, but Hjalmar, in the first two acts of Ibsen's play, shows sufficient talent for a good melodramatic male lead, and even Gina, like Hedvig, demonstrates some skill in modifying her emotions for Hjalmar's sake. If Gregers had any talent as a theatrical director, he might even have been able to devise a few scenes—"A Breadwinner's Discovery," "The Wife's Confession," "The Husband's Pardon"—which, however absurd in themselves, might have had salutary effects. Tragically and ridiculously, however, Gregers makes as big a mess of his task of reforming the Ekdals' attitudes to life as he does of lighting the stove in his room, though both tasks seem essential. As Act II closes, Gregers, emotionally overwrought by his final confrontation with his father (as both Relling and Gina observe), invites Hjalmar to accompany him on a long walk. We never know precisely what is said, but Hjalmar clearly promises Gregers that he will reorganize his family's life in accordance with "the claims of the ideal," and clearly also, he is told about Werle's sexual relationship with Gina and is taken to task for allowing his honour to be called into question by accepting Werle's charity and Gina's perhaps knowingly disingenuous devotion.

One of the most sardonic jokes in the play is that having expressed these opinions, which are substantially true, Gregers leaves Hjalmar to get on with it, and comes back, full of naive confidence that he will witness the Ekdals' transformation. He is like a psychiatrist foolish enough to tell a patient all that ails him and then to expect the patient to devise his own cure or like a priest who believes that the mere naming of sins will effect their extirpation. Another such cruel joke is that the Hjalmar who is eventually able to realize, after Hedvig's death, that he "drove her away from [him] like some animal" is not a total stranger to real remorse and painfully accurate self-appraisal. And in reproaching a God, whose existence he doubts, for his woes, Hjalmar in fact reveals that if someone more capable than Gregers of succeeding Werle in the role of Providence had stage-managed the Ekdals' hypothetical new beginning, Hjalmar might have maintained, and even managed to begin to deserve, Hedvig's love and Gina's devotion. Crucial issues might then have been presented to the Ekdals in terms comprehensible to them, rather than in an idiom as foreign to them as grand opera or as a Kierkegaardian meditation on heroic theory. Chance, therefore, plays a considerable part in the events that lead up to Hedvig's death, the chance that the man in the play most obviously concerned with trying to help the Ekdals lacks the far from superhuman skills necessary to combine idealism with practical contrivance. Gregers, like Stockmann, has lived long enough in the wilds to have attained noble visions, but, again like Stockmann, he has spent too long in isolation to recall that, on returning to the lowlands, he must deal with humanity and not the angels, or the devils, of his imagination.

Constantly, after Act II, we are invited to contemplate a situation, the Ekdals', which is very much like Old Ekdal's description of the underwater world of drowning ducks that he describes to Gregers: the birds are said to "hold on with their beaks to the weeds and stuff—and all the other mess you find down there" and "never come up." In Norwegian the "mess" is said to be "devilish" ("fanderskap"), and we have good reason to see perversity in the Ekdals' home before as well as after Gregers's arrival. We are also asked to separate the truth from the sentimentality in Hjalmar's description of Hedvig's approaching blindness: "Happy and carefree, just like a little singing bird, there she goes fluttering into a life of eternal night." Gregers has the wit to see much of what is wrong but not the skill to put things right.

By the end of Act II, when Werle has almost certainly seen the Ekdals and his son, quite literally, for the last time, and Gregers has taken up residence in the Ekdals' spare room, the world-views of father and son are shown in their full contrast. To aggravate the situation and increase its potentially mortal danger, all that is required is the arrival of another character as deprived of love and of hope for himself and as unyielding as Gregers himself is: Dr. Relling, a cynic at once more consciously well intentioned and more potentially dangerous than Dr. Rank, is shown at work and at loggerheads with Gregers in Act III.

It will not escape a good director that just as, in Act I, Ekdal ruins Werle's feast by his unexpected appearance, Werle destroys whatever feeble chance of success the Ekdals' luncheon for Gregers, Relling, and Molvik has by his sudden and equally unexpected interruption of it, in Act III. As the feasts in the play become ever more fragmented—until Hjalmar alone is shown, in Act IV, chewing on bread, butter, and coldcuts (when not playing Injured Innocence)— we may well be reminded of Shaw's most successful tragicomedy, *Heartbreak House*, in which characters are never shown as eating a formal meal but give the impression of being sustained by whatever Nurse Guinness chooses to provide at random intervals. And the latter's habit of referring indiscriminately to those around her as "ducky" is the least of the resemblances between *The Wild Duck* and *Heartbreak House*: the best and most significant is that both plays give us horrifying and yet amusing images of lives which may already have foundered even while characters express, in their behaviour as well as their words, their apprehensions of approaching catastrophes.

The House of Hushabye and the House of Ekdal have more in common than their differences disguise, which is not surprising since it was Shaw who, in the English-speaking world, pre-eminently recognized Ibsen's ability to match Shakespeare in knowledge of the human mind and heart, and Shaw also who proclaimed Ibsen's ability to capture, perfectly, representative nineteenth-century situations.[29]

Shaw also described what it was like to find oneself impelled, simultaneously, to laugh at the comedy and weep at the tragedy in *The Wild Duck*.[30] It could be expected, therefore, that he noticed how, in Act II, the motifs of sacrifice and redemptive reconciliation are slyly introduced in strikingly unromantic guises. He would not have missed, either, that Act II ends with Hjalmar and Gina carrying off-stage the besotted body of Old Ekdal, just as Act V ends shortly after the same people carry off the corpse of Hedvig.

In terms of visual theatre, these similar events are an encapsulation of the tragicomic spirit. We know, for sure, no more, it seems, than Ibsen did whether the life of the drunken ex-lieutenant or the death of the pathetic adolescent are worth more than the simple acts of kindness or of mere conventional decency their bodies receive at the hands of Hjalmar and Gina.

When Act III commences, we see the first daylight that illuminates the play and are reminded that in the preceding acts we have been watching, by artificial light, extraordinary events in the lives of both the Werles and the Ekdals: in Act I, where the dining-room itself was brilliantly lit, a dinner-party has been attended by a son who had been absent for sixteen years, by his only friend, whom no one other than Gregers wished to see, and by the friend's father, who took everyone by surprise; in Act II, where the attic's eerie light was striking, the extraordinary homecoming of Hjalmar and the equally unusual arrival of Gregers have occurred. In Act III we have the appearance of normality—or at least of what is normal in the Ekdal home—and it is in this act that, with dreadful because entirely unconscious irony, Hedvig is to tell Gregers that, by day, she has nothing to fear and therefore nothing to pray about.

But despite the daylight, things are not quite normal, for Hjalmar has thoughtlessly asked Gregers, Relling, and Molvik to lunch at short notice, and Gina is therefore even busier than usual, in the kitchen rather than in the studio. And Gregers has already succeeded in making a disgusting mess (the Norwegian term is *svineri*—"swinish mess") in his room in his hopelessly impractical attempts to heat it. Other suggestive images now begin to emerge: Gregers, to whom Gina refers specifically as "the pig" ("grisen"), is about to show what a mess he can make of human relationships, producing results which may well be considered worse than the "devilish mess" to which Old Ekdal referred the night before; Hedvig, however, becomes the instrument of a fine touch of dramatic irony when, at Gregers's appearance in the studio, she apologizes for "the mess," the untidy room that is, which he has just entered. The association of Gregers with disgusting confusion of various kinds is suggestively connected with fire images: Gregers disastrously fails to light his stove; we already know that Gina has to keep an eye on Hedvig, who likes to play with fire in secret, and on Old Ekdal, whom, she fears, might absent-mindedly set the house ablaze while drunkenly trying to light his pipe. The suggestive references to messes and fires culminate, of course, in Hedvig's firing the pistol which kills her. And the death occurs in the attic, which, for all its mythopoeic associations, is very much a product of confusion. Whether the fiery associations of the gunshot are in any way suggestive of spiritual purification or, like the burning of the Alving Orphanage, reminiscent of hell, is another question that the play never answers.

When Gina provides the herring salad Hjalmar had asked for, and beer and a decanter of brandy, we are free to imagine how many a frugal meal Gina and Hedvig will take to balance the Ekdal budget—and to wonder whether any of the men present deserve such sacrifice or have anything worth celebrating.

Before the meal is served, Hjalmar appears at his worst—complaining bitterly about a little retouching Gina asks him to do and getting out of it—whilst pretending, for Gina's benefit, to be doing nothing of the sort—and, worse still, foisting the eye-straining work on to Hedvig. Despite the extenuating circumstances—the attic must be prepared for Hedvig's birthday party, which is to be held on the following day—it is perfectly clear that it is Hjalmar and his father who really have fun rigging up their ridiculous contrivances in the attic. They are only ostensibly for Hedvig's delight, though doubtless Hedvig would, given the opportunity, have supplied the elaborate manifestations of gratitude expected from her.

In fact, what we see of the Ekdals at home reveals the troll in every one of them quite as much as the loving and likeable human being: even Hedvig is not left quite unscathed. As in *Peer Gynt*, human trolls, unlike their folk-tale relations, do not necessarily burst in the sunlight; in Act III of *The Wild Duck* a number of apparent trolls appear before us as clearly as the Woman in Green and her bastard son in *Peer Gynt*. Spiritual deformity identifies them: it is easy to understand Gina's happiness at having escaped from the sexual liaison with Werle into which her avaricious mother coerced her, but there is a suggestion that her loyalty to Hjalmar may be servility, and therefore grotesque. And such lack of self-respect, if that is what it is, is not only repugnant but also, it seems, infectious: Hedvig's adulation of her supposed father is completely uncritical. Hjalmar's egocentricity and thoughtlessness would be obviously reprehensible if he had the intelligence to be fully conscious of them. And while Old Ekdal is beyond moral reproach, like all others whose sanity is questionable, this mighty hunter of rabbits, like the inhabitants of Begriffenfeldt's asylum, is so steeped "in the barrel of self" as to be beyond recall. Looking at these people, it is tempting to remember Hermann Weigand's view that there is a sense in which Hedvig's death is a necessary escape from a life not worth living and enduring blindness for. One of the factors set in the balance against Weigand's view, however, is that the Ekdals are far from untypical. So to condemn them from some lofty peak may be to condemn Relling's "average man" and therefore, quite probably, ourselves.

When Gregers enters the studio, he has his first opportunity of speaking in private to the girl he believes is his half-sister. Clearly he sees in her one who is in real danger of being injured, as he was himself, at about the same age, by a parental relationship built on deceit. He is also strongly drawn into Hedvig's mythopoeic world, in which the contents of the duck's attic, both animate and inanimate—the rabbits, the poultry, the stopped clock, the exciting and frightening pictures in the old copy of Harryson's *History of London*—are the embodiments of mystery and wonder. So strongly indeed is Gregers attracted by Hedvig's talk of how much she likes pictures which show great sailing ships at sea and of how much she fears the picture of Death with an hourglass and a girl that we can almost forgive him for apparently not lessening his adulation of Hjalmar when Hedvig informs him, innocently, that when her father decided she must not go to school, he promised her lessons, but has not yet found time to give her any. If one is willing to see what may be positive, Gregers's silence at this point may be part of his routine of work as the abnormally clever dog of his allegory. Soon, indeed, he does tell Hjalmar that there is a good deal of "the wild duck" in him, and that he must get away from "a poison swamp."

In terms of dramatic poetry there could scarcely be a better illustration of Stark Young's remark about the poetry in situations themselves[31] than Gregers's conversation with Hedvig and Gina's eventual interruption of it—to set the table for lunch. For we are shown the quite different perspectives of three characters in a complex situation and invited to take an objective view of the whole, but discouraged from making any facile judgements.

It is clear that Gregers's perspective is an ethical one, despite his lack of objectivity. For him "the briny deep," a phrase he first uses to describe the attic as a refuge for all wounded ducks, feathered and human, has a strictly allegorical application, and yet the emotional excitement he shares with Hedvig releases in him the terrors of a baleful world not accessible—at least for him—to analysis in accordance with the ethical theories on which he pins his hopes for salvation. At Hedvig's age, he saw his mother living in what seemed to him just such a hellish atmosphere. And, ironically enough, it is Gregers's very insistence on a total cleansing of human relationships which seems more likely to fix him fast in just such a grotesque underworld than to set him or others free.

Conversely, Hedvig, whose apprehension is primarily aesthetic, appears to see "the briny deep" as an intriguing paradigm of both the duck's past, present, and future, and her own: the beauties and the terrors of the ocean depths represent, for her, ineffable mysteries and, simultaneously, the most basic of human needs. As for Flaubert's Félicité, so for Ibsen's Hedvig, at the centre of a collection of what is rubbish to others but wondrous to her, is a pet bird which embodies simultaneously an ignorant, sensitive, and deprived girl's need for love and her capacity to return it. Yet when Gregers obliges her to ponder "the briny deep" it is she who is clearly and sadly puzzled by Gregers's ethic of spiritual liberation, who is most likely to be thought of as gaining some sort of emancipation.

So complex, however, are the psychological interrelationships glimpsed in this and in the second conversation of Gregers and Hedvig (in which the topic is sacrifice) that, in its context, "the briny deep" is entirely appropriate as an illustration of what Yeats called "the emotion of multitude." And in that multitude, the specific contrast between Gregers's ethical orientation and Hedvig's aestheticism is only one limited perception. It may be significant enough, however, to remind us of similar spiritual enrichment—or pollution—experienced by Brand and Agnes in relation to the "sacrifice" of their child. *Brand*, like *Paradise Lost*, deals with the mysteries of love and justice, both human and divine and on an epic scale. In *The Wild Duck*, though metaphysics are absent and the scale diminished, the intricacy remains—which is one reason for not reducing the play by simply taking sides with either Hedvig or Gregers in their struggles to see things clearly.

The sight of Gina setting the table and answering the questions of the would-be clever dog, Gregers, underscores both amusingly and affectionately Gina's relationship with the duck. Gina's answers are brief, not now, it seems, out of evasiveness, but because she has a job to do and Gregers is in her way. Gregers, of course, has a whole approach to life in mind when he asks Gina whether she has learned retouching. Gina gives him a side-long glance when she answers affirmatively, for she is instinctively suspicious of him, but there is not, at this point, any indication that she comprehends what Gregers is driving at; she seems, at least at any level of consciousness at which she might turn vague anxiety into coherent ideas, as oblivious to Gregers's implications as the duck itself is to the variety of attitudes to life which others project upon it. And yet, Ibsen is not content to let her seem merely insensitive: she is no thinker, no artist, and certainly no poet, but, as she pads around getting things done for her husband and his guests, she seems to have the pathos and the dignity of the unassuming few to whom life gives little and who are yet, like Flaubert's Félicité, capable of giving others much more than they receive. Paradoxically, Gina, who shares with Werle the invidious distinction of being known to have been "immoral" in the narrow sense, is perhaps the best approximation to the Christian beatitudes that the play has to offer. As with Werle's humanity, however, Gina's humble service is not presented as undoubtedly admirable: in its context it is permeated with irony stemming from the element of concealment in her relations with both Werle and Hjalmar.

Shortly after this, Hjalmar, having emerged from the attic, where a shot has just been fired, becomes engrossed in a conversation with Gregers about the duck: their talk is heavy with the weight of Gregers's allegorizing. Gina, in her impatience to get the preparation for the meal done, is made to utter a remark, charged with dramatic irony of the utmost potency. It is an observation, however, which does not usually find its way adequately into English: in Norwegian it is "Den velsignede vildanden, ja. Den gjøres der da krusifikser nok for." If the translator aims for the literal meaning, he will produce something like Rolf Fjelde's "Oh, that sacred duck—there's been crucifixes enough made for her." Even this translation, admirable in its attempt to make English do, without obvious strain, what the Norwegian does with great ease, falls short, for the "velsignede" means "confounded" as well as "sacred" or "blessed" (as Einar Haugen points out in his *Norsk Engelsk Ordbok* with reference to the phrase "velsignede villanden"). If the translator decides that idiomatic liveliness is worth more than literal meaning, he will produce something like McFarlane's, "That blessed wild duck! All the carrying-on there is about that bird." And one of the characteristically sly indications that, as Kruuse is aware, Golgotha is not absent from *The Wild Duck* disappears.

In the original, Gina herself appears to mean no more than *The Oxford Ibsen* gives her words to say. But behind what she means is the poetic meaning of what she says—that the duck, which may be a source of blessedness or damnation, has already become associated with numerous sacrifices: the Ekdals may need no more crosses to carry, for neither they nor others will necessarily be enlightened by further sacrificial suffering, real or supposed. No one in *The Wild Duck* shows any sign of serious belief in the Crucifixion, and when Gregers, at the end of the play, seems to realize that the comparatively minor offering he asked of Hedvig (the killing of the duck) may have become a contemporary "crucifixion" enacted by a child seeking to sow love where there has been deceit and misunderstanding, he is judged a fanatic and a madman. But the play does not conclusively take Relling's side when he curses the departing Gregers any more than it permits any character to dilate on the poetic power, in its specifically naturalistic context, of Gina's remark about crucifixes.

Significantly, Gina and Hedvig go into the kitchen almost immediately after Gina's comment: a hard-working housewife and her daughter go into another room to prepare food, and, for the rest of the act, Ibsen parades before us a succession of men who fancy that they have a genuine claim to heroism or, at least, heroic self-denial. Gregers appears to conceive of himself as deriving some kind of particular zeal from his celibacy, a sense of mission to his fellow men, which he may regard as a destiny for which he is specially suited by his ugliness and afflicted conscience. Hjalmar can—and does—define several "heroic" roles, all, as he expresses them, seemingly the promptings of some exalted destiny. And in Act III, he gives Gregers the fullest account of the "tragedy of the house of Ekdals." He makes his lineage appear utterly ridiculous by explaining that his father descends from two lieutenant colonels "not both at the same time of course." He also attempts to impress Gregers with an account of his father's mental debility as indicated by the fact that when Old Ekdal had the chance to put a bullet into his brains, he did not. But he expects Gregers to admire his (Hjalmar's) own singular mental fortitude for daring to "choose life" in circumstances so similar to Old Ekdal's that both men toyed with the same gun whilst meditating suicide.

Relling seems to regard himself as having a quietly heroic stoicism, and his room-mate, Molvik, absolutely believes himself singled out and raised above ordinary mortals by virtue of Relling's pronouncement that he, Molvik, is "demonic!" Gregers keeps interrupting the meal-time pleasantries with talk of marsh poison. Old Ekdal emerges during the course of the luncheon to demonstrate his hunting prowess—by showing off a rabbit skin—and even Haakon Werle appears, not to talk about heroism but to make a final attempt, for characteristically shadowy motives, to influence Gregers's thought and conduct.

The men's heroic pretensions range from the barely credible to the ludicrous. But in this male-dominated part of the act, in fact right in the middle of the full-blown comedy of Hjalmar's account of the "tragedy" of his family, a note of unpredictable authenticity is sounded. Hjalmar's language is less hyperbolic than usual when he describes his sense of incredulity after his father's conviction. And the emotion he refers to is both believable and revealing:

> When they had taken him away, and he sat there under lock and key—oh, that was a terrible time for me, I can tell you. I kept the blinds lowered at both windows. When I looked out and saw the sun shining the same as usual, I couldn't understand it. I saw people walking about the streets, laughing and talking about things of no importance. I couldn't understand it. I felt that all creation ought to have come to a standstill, like an eclipse.

Gregers is never closer to Hjalmar, and perhaps also to the audience, than when he adds, "I felt just like that when Mother died." This interchange, surely, expresses the real sufferings which, for good and all, seem to have left Hjalmar incapable of life without patently ridiculous illusions, and life for Gregers unbearable without messianic ambitions. In the manner of Ibsen's tragicomedy at its best, the observations which convey to us the most intense past sufferings of the principal male characters appear within a context the tone of which is predominantly satirical. The memory of these psychologically crippling experiences should stay with us whenever we see Hjalmar and Gregers struggling to impress each other and themselves with some sense of their own significance. The reason that these men wish to be convinced that suffering must bring some kind of wisdom may be that they have experienced, in sobering reality, anguish which did no more than induce feelings of incomprehensible futility.

Appropriately, what we witness among the adults—and particularly the male adults—in Acts IV and V is the tragicomedy of inadequacy. It is foreshadowed by the darkly ridiculous suggestion of the fish image with which Act III closes: Gina tells her daughter that Gregers has "always been a queer fish" (literally, the phrase in the original, "en fæl fisk," means "a disgusting fish"). Hedvig, who "stands by the table and looks inquiringly at [Gina]" remarks, as she often does, that "this is all very strange." For better or worse, the "queer fish," who is also the "pig" who made the revolting mess in his room but who prefers to think of himself as "an absurdly clever dog," has joined the other inhabitants of the "briny deep." It is entirely consistent to think of Gina herself as having no ocean depths in mind when she refers to Gregers in this way but to envisage Hedvig as visualizing those depths and their latest protean inhabitant. Whether Gregers, in any shape or form, should be there at all is a question that continues to pose itself, but from this point on the central question concerns the nature and value of Gregers's presence once his jaws, whether piscine, porcine, or canine, have closed upon those he regards as his father's prey, and Relling regards as Gregers's.

There are no finer passages of sustained tragicomic writing in Ibsen than the last two acts of *The Wild Duck*. All there is to admire and to despair about in all the characters is juxtaposed in situations kaleidoscopic in their revelations of dramatic nuance. And most of the horror, which emphasizes the unintentionally comical aspects of grown-up behaviour, arises from a growing consciousness among the audience or readers of Hedvig's peril.

It is in these acts that we see Hedvig fluttering into the eternal darkness of which Hjalmar has spoken. But, with dreadful irony, it is Hjalmar himself who, more than anyone else, creates that darkness by causing the girl's anxieties to turn into a terrified conviction that she has lost and can never again deserve his love, and that she, in some way wholly incomprehensible to her, has caused his apparent anguish. And, while this hideous nightmare descends upon Hedvig, Gregers and Relling intermittently score points off each other in their battle of abstract theories, and Gina behaves like a mother bird hard put to know how she can fight off those who have come, it might seem to her, simply to ravage her nest and endanger her offspring.

In this situation, which develops a momentum that seems surreal, even Werle's attempt to play his last card—the deed of gift which Berta Sörby brings for Hedvig's birthday—does not prevent the working out of a process of the costly revelation of uncertain truths. By the end of Act IV, Hedvig is already speaking of death, and at the end of Act V she has used the gun which twice previously figured ineffectively in the Ekdal family's "tragedy." Handled now for a third time by a truly desperate Ekdal, the gun is fired to devastating effect.

The opening of Act IV, like that of Act I, finds Gina and Hedvig worrying about the absent Hjalmar, and, as usual, concerned about his stomach. When Hjalmar appears, the first sign that real trouble may ensue from his long conversation with Gregers is that Hjalmar goes without his dinner. He resolves to make an entirely new start: from the very next day he is going to "get down to things in real earnest." But, comically, he immediately encounters a setback—the next day is Hedvig's birthday and a party is planned. Even Hjalmar must be vaguely aware of his ridiculousness when he defers the spiritual regeneration of his family till "the day after, then!" But the possibility that he feels a little foolish does not stop him from vowing never to set foot in the attic again—and again, immediately, having to eat his words because Hedvig's birthday party is supposed to take place there.

Perhaps it is this second false step that causes Hjalmar to lapse from his heroic stance into petulance: "That damned duck. I'd like to wring its neck." Hjalmar is, it seems, so overwrought by what Gregers has told him about his circumstances that playing the hero, though his conscious wish, is simply beyond his capacity. He wants to demonstrate that he has understood Gregers's allegory. With terrifyingly funny effects he tries a little allegorizing himself. He speaks of the duck as not simply symbolic of humanity but as actually human! Alarmed at Hedvig's terror when he threatens to wring the duck's neck, he cries out, "Not a hair of. . . ." And only then does he remember that it is people who have hair, whether wavy, like his own, or soft and pretty, like Hedvig's, presumably. "Not a feather of its head shall be touched," he rephrases it, hugging the child, hinting his continuing love, but asking her to "run along" so that he can concentrate his attention on Gina. Between this point, at which he gives Hedvig the last embrace she is ever to receive from him or from anyone else, and the end of the play, Hjalmar's feelings for the girl, which seem to run much deeper than most of his pronouncements on the subject, have no chance against his struggles to play the hero, which cause him, several times, and with more and more brutality, to reject her.

To see Gregers as wholly wrong in advising Hjalmar to reorganize the Ekdal household is mistaken. It is true that Gregers has been told by his father to expect little of Hjalmar, but Hjalmar himself insists on being regarded as a man of real promise. He claims an ability to take responsibility. Because he encourages Gregers to overestimate him, Hjalmar must share the blame for the disasters which follow.

In his conversation with Gina, after Hedvig's departure, Hjalmar's pettiness—which he is usually canny enough to conceal in Gregers's presence—emerges. He says no more about the photographic work, because he is not really interested in ascertaining whether his profession could in fact provide sufficient money for the Ekdals' needs. He wants—and does all he can to start—a melodramatic scene about Gina's "past" and about the payments (which, according to Gina, amount to no more than subsistence pay and a little pocket money) which his father receives for doing copying work for Werle. Hjalmar's rage about his wife's sexual relationship with Werle is understandable, though anything but heroic. He pays no attention at all to Gina's explanation, which has the ring of truth, that her mother virtually forced her into bed with widower Werle despite his reputation for lechery, in the hope, presumably, that a lucrative marriage would follow. He does not choose to acknowledge Gina's evident affection for him nor wonder for an instant what he has done to deserve it. All he sees is that he is married to a woman who deceived him, and, in addition to the stain on his honour, there is the blow to his vanity—which even Gina detects as such. The Ekdal household is not, as Hjalmar has stupidly imagined, self-sufficient: "You liked to think [your father] got everything from you," says Gina, truthfully, it seems.

Hjalmar, calling out for the lighting of lamps—the better to see the naughty deeds of others—kicking a chair to demonstrate his "fiery temperament," and becoming angrier than ever when Gina reminds him, gently, that her practical nature has been an asset to him, is, at one level, a splendid illustration of the comic type which sees all that is worst in others and none of its own grievous faults. If the play were as purely comic as Weigand maintains, Hjalmar would be a Norwegian relation of Sheridan's Mrs. Candour. But *The Wild Duck* is tragicomic, and there is dreadful danger in Hjalmar's utter lack of self-knowledge at this comical point.

Not to want to laugh as Hjalmar indulges in the stalest of stagey language—the reference, for instance, to Gina as a spider who trapped him in her web of deceit!—would be inhuman. But not to feel like weeping at the harm he is doing would be no less inhuman. As Hjalmar mounts from one absurdity to another—from accusing Gina of stifling his gift for invention and him with it to, in the next breath, reproaching her for not allowing herself to become the wealthy widow he had wished to leave her—Gina, who takes his accusations absolutely literally, weeps and declares, with every appearance of sincerity, that she hopes he will not die and leave her alone. Nowhere is the tragic inability of human beings to live up to the heroic expectations of others more evident than when Gregers, his face suffused with joyful anticipation, now bursts in upon Hjalmar's attempts to be the hero with his hands extended as though to embrace two shriven penitents.

But to conclude from this, and all that follows, that Ibsen is giving us an authenticated picture of swamp-life is unduly pessimistic—even if, like Weigand, we regard the swamp as made aesthetically acceptable by the sublimity of a comic perspective. Neither is *The Wild Duck*, like Molière's *George Dandin* and *Tartuffe*, a brilliant demonstration of evils which are perceived and presented as indubitable facts. It is, rather, a study of the psychology of disingenuousness among people, most of whom (Werle,

Berta Sörby, and Relling being the possible exceptions) are not aware of the consequences of their own behaviour. They are, for the most part, fools rather than knowing liars and hypocrites. And fools who, if made conscious of the misery they cause, can become perceptive in their wretchedness even though their epiphanies are brief and inconclusive.

As the last two acts of the play unfold, we watch a series of events so emotionally overwhelming that they may shock the intellect into inertia. If they do not, and if we remain aware, for instance, that the situation of the Ekdals, though broadly representative of universal human failings, is yet one in which highly particularized characters are worked upon by the chemistry of particular events to extremes less typical of ordinary experience, the play may be seen as shaping questions. Questions about the validity of Social Darwinism as an interpretation of the human condition, about the nature and capacity of the human will, about evil in a non-metaphysical world and whether it can be eradicated.

Social Darwinism, as we have seen, appears to be the truth as Haakon Werle perceives it: Social Darwinism, that is, with the rough edges camouflaged by the victor's supposed commitment to sustaining, at some minimal level, the lives of the vanquished. Werle apparently thinks of such succour as being effective only if made available through subterfuge: one does not invite the inmates of the casualty ward round to dinner—though one's son may be fool enough to do so. One works instead through tactful intermediaries. This view is persuasively presented not only because Werle gives it clear allegorical expression but because it seems to explain so much of what we see: the strong survive, though with no particular or inevitable nobility, and the weak are sunk in their murky though possibly enthralling depths. But it is as well, when thinking of Werle, to remember that the story told by the victors is not necessarily good history.

Werle's experience is broadly representative in that it embodies responses to the competition for social and economic advantage, the reality of which Ibsen denies no more than Shakespeare or the Old Testament do. But life is not presented in *The Wild Duck* as having results which are inevitable in the competition that is: perhaps that is the truth that is dawning upon Werle and causing him to detect the hollowness of his lavish dinner parties. Helene Alving, in the end, seems to learn that she must accept a considerable measure of responsibility for lost "joy of life." Haakon Werle also may learn that he must accept responsibility for wrongs done and happiness lost.

If he does, then he is seen as acknowledging that even in a godless world, life does not necessarily deprive us of will and the intelligence to use it. If Werle married, as his son alleges, for money, it may not have been beyond his capacity to realize that a woman unloved before marriage and, it seems, neglected in it could become bitterly resentful and destructive. Similarly Werle appears to have the wit to see that a son brought up in a home where his parents were in a state of perpetual strife might grow up full of self-hatred and yearning for impossible perfection in others. If Werle has realized these things, then he is possibly moving towards an acknowledgement that his opinions about determinism have been his excuse for unscrupulousness but not a justification of it. The loneliness he mentions to Gregers could therefore be real. And if Werle's unsuccessful attempts to win Gregers's regard and his successful attempt to gain Berta Sörby's illustrate anything more than expediency, the play hints that the human will may have its positive as well as its sordid triumphs.

Part of the tragedy of *The Wild Duck* may be that Haakon Werle can find no way of speaking as frankly to his son as he has, it seems, to Berta Sörby. If this is the case, Werle's situation is interestingly similar to that of Aline Solness: she speaks with complete candour to Hilde Wangel about things she is never able to tell her husband. Gregers's entrapment in the utterly negative view of his father which his tormented mother impressed upon his adolescent mind is another aspect of this tragic alienation of father and son.

Ibsen, however, differs from Zola, for example, in that although he makes extensive use of the theme of the infection or paralysis of the will, he rarely discounts the possibility of its recovery. The effects of neurosis, solitude, and social humiliation, for instance, are all taken into account, and in *The Wild Duck*, as, generally, elsewhere, characters are rarely represented as villainous. Studies in perfidy, like Bishop Nicholas in *The Pretenders*, are rare in Ibsen. Rarer still are studies in unalloyed virtue: Haakon Haakonsson, also in *The Pretenders*, appears to be the nearest approach. And even when, as in the case of Gregers, insanity seems about to claim a character, he does not cease to be of interest in terms of the theme of will.

Ibsen, as we have seen, wrote to Frederik Hegel that he was reluctant to part with the characters he had created for *The Wild Duck* because they had become dear to him despite their multifarious failings.[32] He made no exception. But what endeared the characters to him was not, surely, their vices, but the fact that, however unsuccessfully and however uncertainly, all of them attempt to make some sort of sense of their lives. Their attempts may be demonstrably foolish or wrong-headed. None of them, it seems, arrives at what Peer Gynt refers to as the "arcana of truth." But in one way or another and in accordance with their more, or less, feeble lights, they exercise a degree of will and are not mere automata responding only to complex environmental stimuli.

What we witness in the two last acts of *The Wild Duck*, therefore, is no more inevitably a demonstration of hopelessness and absurdity than it is a reliable vision of meaningful sacrifice. As is appropriate to tragicomedy, these two responses are simultaneously evoked, and audiences and readers alike must endure the uncertainty of Ibsen's refusal to endorse either of them. The degree of dramatic tension aroused in this way is the very life of tragicomedy.

A similar ambiguousness is achieved in Ibsen's poem "The Eiderduck," which is, appropriately, regarded as a source. Here, a drake who has three times lined his nest with his down, and three times had his nest pillaged by a heartless fisherman, spreads his wings and flies south to heal his wounded breast in the sun. The poem conveys perfectly the suggestion that he left his home in Norway and fled to southern Europe (like Ibsen himself) as an act of protest against spiritual violation. But how far Ibsen's drake has the capacity to control or substantially modify his destiny is a subject as dense as the mist or fog ("skodden") into which he flies. The extent to which the will may be exercised by any individual creature, and responsibility apportioned to him or her by those who must try to make value judgements, is as much an enigma in "The Eiderduck" as in *The Wild Duck*. And the enigma is present in the majority of Ibsen's plays whether their ethos is metaphysical or naturalistic.

In the last act of *The Wild Duck*, there is a fascinating array of characters with some kind of claim upon the imagination to be identified with the principal occupant of the attic menagerie. Haakon Werle and Berta Sörby, who seem at first so much like victorious hunters, have withdrawn to Höidal when the act begins, and we have been given reason to think of them as more vulnerable, more in retreat from the harsher aspects of life—and therefore more like the duck—than they at first appeared. Old Ekdal has become so clearly associated with the duck in its newfound safety as to have lost all sense of responsibility and of reality. And Hjalmar, for most of the time, is far closer to his father in spiritual terms than he cares to admit. But not so close as to have lost all capacity to catch a glimpse of worlds less comfortable than his father's. Gregers, who is closest to the vision of the duck's past, has, fixed perpetually before him, a romantic view of a sunlit heaven of a kind which Mme. de Staël would admire; but, intermittently, it is obscured by visions of depravity and death. Relling, voluntarily inhabiting a borderland between the world of realities where he has failed and of total retreat from them to which he consigns others, sees the duck as part of a world that is full of menace—menace that the strong, like himself, supposedly, can acknowledge and that the rest must be taught not to see. But what we become more and more able to see in Relling is the vulnerability which underlies his cynical humanism. Gina is, in Gregers's terms, the most draggle-tailed of creatures; in Relling's, a cosy, maternal soul devoted to her nest and indifferent to everything else. Hedvig is, in Gregers's terms, the chosen instrument of sacrifice, inviolate and capable of bringing redemption; in Relling's, an endangered adolescent and pathetic in her confusion. All these are duck images. None of them is necessarily more true or valuable in absolute terms than the others.

It is Berta Sörby who, ironically enough, sets in motion the final "hunt" of which Hedvig's death may be considered the "kill." She intends to contrive precisely the opposite—the security of the Ekdal family in so far as it can be guaranteed by Werle's deed of gift to Old Ekdal and Hedvig. The candour of Mrs. Sörby seems, if viewed objectively, admirable. She does not hesitate to tell the Ekdals, Relling, and Gregers that the plans for her marriage to Werle are complete. Candidly, she admits its advantages to herself and, without false modesty, claims that Werle's share of the bargain is equally good. Her statement of how she will help Werle will appear to some as genuinely moving, to others, sardonically amusing: "Well I shall try to use my eyes for him as best as I can." Whatever else may be said of her, Berta Sörby claims that she will be performing willingly and for no undeclared reason what we may be asked to see, without any sentimentality or glorification, as one of the most admirable of human functions, caring for others. Several women in Ibsen (and a few men) are called to such service: some refuse it, harshly as Regine Engstrand refuses to nurse Oswald and Gunhild Borkman refuses even companionship to her husband; others, like Ellida Wangel in *The Lady from the Sea* and Rita Allmers in *Little Eyolf*, grow in stature as they learn to care; still others become at least half comical and pathetic, trapped in the confines of seemingly negative self-sacrifice, like Juliane Tesman or Lona Hessel after her return to the Bernick household. But Mrs. Sörby's attachment to Werle is strong enough to cause Gregers to threaten, irrationally, to destroy the marriage if he can, and to cause Relling to plunge into his deepest bout of cynical despair.

After Mrs. Sörby's exit, the ideologues, in their different ways, struggle to take possession of Hjalmar's mind. He is the seeming focus of that element of the action which is, predominantly, sardonic comedy: Hedvig moves in ever-increasing tragic isolation. Their dramatic worlds coalesce, transform, and illumine each other perfectly.

Hjalmar, holding forth about paying off every penny of his debts to Werle and about the irony of Werle's second marriage being an agreement for the mutual forgiveness of sin, is very obviously echoing phrases he has learned from Gregers whilst understanding little of their significance. He is genuinely puzzled and remarks to Gregers, "But from what you said, you had to go through all this difficult business before you could found a true marriage." Gregers is never more pathetic and ridiculous than when he asks Hjalmar, "wasn't it a good thing I came?"

The dark forces that have already been set loose now become vaguely evident even to Hjalmar when he talks about an "implacable power" that he sees as working in Werle's life. There *are* forces at work now which do seem to be beyond the characters' control—but, agonizingly, only just beyond the control of the more intelligent and partly as a result of chance. These forces are not supernatural, however, as Hjalmar imagines—much to Gina's anxiety—but are the devastating and blind psychological impulses which drive men to live out their fantasies. Hjalmar becomes convinced, with no conclusive evidence, that Hedvig is not his daughter. Ironically, it is the sight of her reading, as he has told her to do, the deed of gift from Haakon Werle which convinces Hjalmar that he is not her father; her eye-strain is obvious, and Mrs. Sörby has talked, indiscreetly for once, about Werle's approaching blindness.

Gregers is now genuinely apprehensive: there is desperation in his attempt to persuade Hjalmar to stay with his family, and horror in Hjalmar's retort, "I don't want to. Never, never!" We never know whether he is right to conclude that, in the biological sense, he has no child. But we do see the horror of his cruel rejection of Hedvig and of his ignoring of Gina's impassioned plea, "Look at the child, Hjalmar! look at her!"

There is poignant irony in the fact that Act IV ends with the two most sensitive, most vulnerable, and most unstable characters, Hedvig and Gregers, who may be half-brother and -sister, drawing together conspiratorially to discuss prayer, death, and sacrifice. Ridiculously, as they do so, Hjalmar has not gone to fight a great and solitary spiritual battle, as Gregers imagines. Instead he has set out with Relling and Molvik for a long night of drinking.

Act V of *The Wild Duck* is perhaps the finest piece of sustained tragicomic writing produced for the nineteenth-century stage. We have been given every opportunity to become thoroughly familiar with characters, all of whom are complex both individually and in interacting groups. A situation has now developed which is so ambivalent that its culmination, a child's death, has tragic aspects which draw together everything in the play associated with idealism, sacrifice, and meaningful suffering, and comic aspects associated with all the play has shown us of human inadequacy, confusion, and disingenuousness.

The death itself is a master-stroke of tragicomic multiplicity: the only thing about it which is certain is that a girl is killed by a gun which she fires. Even Dr. Relling's "expert opinion" that Hedvig must have intended to shoot herself because of a powder-burn on her dress is, according to information available to the audience but not to Relling, inconclusive. In effect, it seems that Hedvig could have committed suicide—for a number of reasons—or she could have accidentally shot herself while attempting—again for a number of reasons—to shoot her pet. We never know what actually happened. This lack of all certainty is deliberate and Ibsen's principal means of ensuring an open ending.

The final act opens with Hedvig and Gina worrying, yet again, about Hjalmar's whereabouts. There is a comical contrast between Relling's slurred talk of being a "be . . . east" in charge of other beasts, including the drunken Hjalmar, and Gregers's concern about the state of Hjalmar's soul. It is important to remember that before Hjalmar struggles up the stairs to stage his last attempt to be a hero, he is snoring out the last hour of a drunken stupor on Relling's sofa.

Before Hjalmar arrives, there is time for another pitched battle between Gregers and Relling, for a last chance for Gregers to give Hedvig further instruction about sacrifice, and for Hedvig to ask Old Ekdal for some practical advice about shooting ducks. The dramatic importance of this advice is often overlooked.

From the argument between Gregers and Relling, which concerns Hjalmar's upbringing, we learn that Gregers is convinced that the faith in Hjalmar shown by his father, his aunts, and his fellow university students is justified. But Relling's view is that nothing that can be called heroic can be expected from a man nurtured on a diet of unceasing flattery. Relling's opinion that Hjalmar must have illusions to live by is persuasive, but it does not, in fact, prove Relling's notion that the "average man" must be sustained by life-lies, for Relling's "professional" services seem confined to, or at least concentrated upon, people who are obvious or disastrous failures. Similarly, Gregers's idolatry and mistaken opinions of Hjalmar do not disprove Gregers's view, not an uncommon one in the nineteenth or twentieth centuries, that heroes may exist and should be emulated.

How much Hedvig really understands of Gregers's talk about "the genuine, joyous, courageous spirit of self-sacrifice" is hard to know: it appears that she probably believes that giving up the duck for Hjalmar's sake might well have the same effect—a favourable modification of Hjalmar's mood, that is—as going without food and enabling him to have beer and butter. There is no indication at this stage that she regards killing the duck as some kind of altruistic rite. And certainly, as yet, she has not thought of literally sacrificing herself.

When Hedvig asks the man who may be her grandfather how to shoot the duck, Old Ekdal tells her that ducks must be shot *against* the lie of the feathers . . . never with the feathers." And because Ekdal is speaking on the one subject, other than how little water he takes with his brandy, on which he may be regarded as an authority, this information needs to be carefully weighed. If it is, it is clear that Relling's opinion that the powder-burn on Hedvig's dress proves that she shot herself deliberately is not conclusive: a young girl who had never fired a gun before, and who is afflicted with such poor sight that she has to hold a letter very close to a lamp to read it, is not likely to be able to take a distant and safe shot at the bird and fire the bullet in against the lie of the feathers. It seems likely, therefore, that Hedvig, possibly trying to make sure that she killed the duck instead of just maiming it (again), may have been holding the struggling bird while trying to kill it. This is hardly a practical proposition. But Hedvig, from all the evidence, is not in a practical frame of mind when the pistol is fired. The duck is also heard quacking just before the shot sounds out. This is the only time that we ever hear the duck, a fact which in itself suggests that something very unusual—like Hedvig struggling with the bird—may be going on in the attic.

It is certainly clear, from the question that Hedvig asks Old Ekdal, that, when she enters the attic, it is probably with the intention of killing the duck. Before Hedvig dies, however, some of the most horrifying and horribly amusing episodes of the play occur.

Hjalmar, obsessed with the heady delight of acting out his last crude notions of a hero, comes in to announce that he is going away—for ever. Between ridiculous considerations—of whether he needs to take with him his completely unused technical magazines, for instance, and the whereabouts of the notes he claims to have made in preparation for the writing of his autobiography—Hjalmar cruelly rejects Hedvig several times. And Hedvig is fully aware of Hjalmar's meaning, though she does not always understand his phraseology: when Hjalmar speaks of "those who have no business to be here," Hedvig asks, "In a low trembling voice," "Does he mean me?" Moments later, she is in the attic with the gun.

There seems little doubt that Hedvig can hear all or some of what is said in the studio while she is in the attic. Certainly Gregers and Hjalmar hear sounds which they take to be the duck quacking in the attic while they are in the studio. If she can, then all certainty about the manner of her death disappears. We do not have the evidence that Hedvig deliberately kills herself in an act of loving self-sacrifice, and neither do we know, for sure, that the death is the result of Hedvig's mental confusion or a mere accident.

What we do know is that Hedvig probably entered the attic believing that if she killed the duck, Hjalmar would love her again, as Gregers had instructed her. But she may overhear clearly Hjalmar's monstrous claim that Hedvig never truly loved him, has been in league against him with Gina and Mrs. Sörby all along, and is only waiting for the signal from others to leave him. If she is not now too desperate to hear or understand anything, she may hear Gregers's claim, in reply to Hjalmar's ridiculous outbursts, that Hedvig will soon offer him the proof of her love. And she may hear Hjalmar's doubtlessly unintentionally ambiguous remark in which he claims that Hedvig would never give up "this life" for him. He means the life of ease he claims to believe that the second Mrs. Werle will offer her; in its context the phrase can well mean—and could certainly be taken by a desperate weeping child to mean—life itself.

When Hedvig pulls the trigger, she could be trying to give Hjalmar the proof Gregers says he needs, and so shoot herself accidentally while holding the duck close and peering at the lie of its feathers. She could be so horrified by Hjalmar's ludicruous accusations that she shoots herself in sheer despair. Equally she could be responding directly to what sounds like a challenge to give up her life for Hjalmar. And there is no reason to discount the possibility that she is no more responsible for her own safety with a gun than for the safety of the house when Gina catches her, as she has done on several occasions, playing with matches. Hedvig may carry through a deed comparable with the central sacrifice of the Christian religion or with those of martyrs for other noble causes; she may, equally, die in some pathetic travesty of martyrdom, and the death could just as well be neither exalted nor absurd, but a pathetic accident.

Gregers, of course, is convinced when he hears the shot that Old Ekdal has killed the duck at Hedvig's request, and that all has gone according to his plan. He is not totally foolish to exclaim that he knew redemption would come through Hedvig, for he cannot predict life's ironical chances—like Hedvig's apparent decision to kill the duck because of Ekdal's inability to take the hint that she wishes him to do so; or Hedvig's overhearing, clearly or not, the conversation in the studio; or, most significant of all, Hjalmar's talking, within Hedvig's hearing, enough dangerous nonsense to unhinge the mind of the child whom he has just rejected repeatedly and with all the signs of lofty contempt.

We do not know enough about the circumstances of Hedvig's death to make them the basis of any certain value judgement. Ironically, in fact, Hedvig's last moments of life are as much of a mystery to us as the fate of the duck itself. Is it waddling around distractedly and missing a few tailfeathers as the play ends? Or is it settling down in its basket after a good feed and a splash in the trough? We do not know, and as with the precise facts of Hedvig's death, Ibsen artfully determined that we never should.

Hedvig's death does not confirm the view that sacrifice is both possible and meaningful in modern life, and it does not confirm the opinion that all action is equally useless and meaningless. The final argument of Gregers and Relling is accordingly utterly inconclusive.

Equally inconclusive is Gina's remark to Hjalmar, as they carry out the corpse, that they must help one another, for now Hedvig belongs to them both. For what does such a conclusion show? Does it demonstrate that Gina, having made sure that the body should not lie in the studio "for everybody to see," can adapt to her changed circumstances as readily and as brainlessly as, according to Darwin, wild ducks do to domestication?[33] Or does it show that Gina, even though shocked, intuitively grasps that she must now protect Hjalmar from realizing the full horror of what has happened—assuming, that is, that she realizes it herself? The play merely shapes the questions. It answers them no more certainly than it confirms that Hjalmar—whose most significant *anagnorisis* is the realization that he drove Hedvig away from him as an animal might—will be a wiser man or more of a sentimentalist than ever for the experience.

The Wild Duck offers no assurances; it opens many perspectives—optimistic, pessimistic, deterministic, nihilistic—but it ends, as it begins, with human beings not too far removed from ourselves in their talents and their vices, struggling to make some sort of sense of their lives. We should feel reluctant, it seems, to be prepared to take the place of either Gregers or Relling and commence the philosophizing again. And Werle, the man who may, but only may, have acquired inner vision to compensate for his blindness has, perhaps wisely, retired to a place where, presumably, he does not intend to philosophize, or alternatively, where philosophy may be the truest and most dearly bought gain he can share with his second wife.

5

How Firm a Foundation?— The Doubtful Triumph of *The Master Builder*

The Master Builder opens by showing us three people, blood relations, quietly working in an architect's office. Within minutes we are given good reason to detest the architect for his calculated oppression of the two men and for his sexual abuse of the woman. At the end of the play we have been given grounds to consider the same architect a hero. He has, as Maurice Valency sees it, reaffirmed his manhood and the validity of his vocation.[1] He may be, as Orley Holtan, for instance, persuasively argues, a new Prometheus,[2] while others view him as a martyr for Dionysus. In terms deriving from George Steiner's view that Ibsen created a modern mythology to replace those which were discredited in nineteenth-century Europe,[3] he may also be seen, as James Hurt sees him, as the architect of his own existential "recovery of wholeness and peace."[4] And there is even a real possibility, as has been suggested, too, that we are meant to see him as a Nietzschean superman.[5] The last words of Christ, according to St. John's gospel, are used to describe his supposed triumph, and the victims of the first act have apparently sunk into insignificance—small people of no ultimate consequence, it seems, in the presence of such a god-like being and that of the woman who has urged him to "climb as high as [he] can build."

The questions upon which the play is structured—the firmest foundation in the work—are all concerned with whether, in the play's own terms, any single positive or negative response to Solness can be taken as wholly valid, whether some synthesis is feasible, or whether, as will be argued here, a substantial number of diverse and contradictory reactions are all justified but inconclusive. Successive readings or particular productions may draw attention to what seem indisputable answers, but, as we should expect from Ibsen, ultimately, even though the scope of *The Master Builder* is wide enough to include, as Maeterlinck emphasized,[6] strong

155

intimations of metaphysical forces, we are not allowed the solace of any clear verdict.

Since the play is rich in evocations of myth, folk-tales, the Bible, and Nietzsche, and of Ibsen's own work (especially *Peer Gynt*), similarities to Freudian theory and foreshadowings of *Little Eyolf, John Gabriel Borkman*, and *When We Dead Awaken*, some discussion of sources, literary parallels, and historical milieu might seem essential here. Considered in isolation from the play, however, apart from the exact contexts which establish their particular and not easily predictable tone and relevance, discussion of such matters is likely to be unhelpfully abstract. This in itself is a reminder of the quality of the work, for *The Master Builder* is to Ibsen's late metaphysical prose plays what *The Wild Duck* is to the naturalistic works and *Peer Gynt* comes close to being for the verse plays, namely a perfectly unified whole composed of the most disparate parts yoked together not by the violence that Dr. Johnson thought that he detected in English metaphysical poetry but by the skill of a first-rate imagination.

The first sound we hear after the action has commenced is one of distress—Knut Brovik gasping for breath and exclaiming pathetically, "I can't stand this much longer." After Kaja Fosli's sympathetic reply—from which we learn that she is Brovik's niece—he explains that "it gets worse every day." The vagueness of the pronoun (the "this" and "it" of Brovik's remarks are both "det" in Norwegian) arouses curiosity. What is wrong with him? There is nothing in the room itself to cause discomfort, and, within seconds, Brovik is talking about suffocating even if he goes home to rest.

His appearance, like that of his son and his niece, tells much, however. He wears "a rather threadbare but well preserved black coat," and his cravat has yellowed. A man of his years, working late (it is evening), with a son who has "a slight stoop" and a niece who is "slightly built" and "delicate looking," probably endures more than merely physical affliction; in fact, as frequently in Ibsen, physical and spiritual health are closely related. Old Brovik cannot sleep—trying to do so brings on the feeling of suffocation he refers to. Within hours he is unconscious and dying after a stroke suffered as a result of his confrontation with Solness: the only sleep which can bring Brovik peace is death.

All this is perfectly straightforward, it seems, exactly what might be expected in a realistic work with a symbolic dimension. But Ragnar's advice to his restless father that he should "try and get some sleep" is the introduction of a motif that the play develops extensively and far beyond the limits of realism. We are to learn that Brovik is only one of the restless souls in *The Master Builder*. Halvard Solness and Hilde Wangel have recurrent dreams of falling in the foetal position, and their conscious hours often seem like extensions of dream worlds. We have every reason also to see Kaja's and Aline's minds as equally troubled. Indeed, the only people who are specifically referred to as sleeping peacefully—dreamlessly, like children after a long day of satisfying play—are the Vikings, who are one of Solness's and Hilde Wangel's favourite topics of conversation. The worlds of wakefulness and dream thoroughly interpenetrate each other, as in *Peer Gynt*, and it is useful to note that there are no easy equations of consciousness with reality or dream with illusion. When Brovik, trying to sleep, suffers the stroke which literally stifles him, the sleep which becomes death is the plainest indication of the reality of his waking hours. Though, when we first see him, Brovik struggles fitfully to regain his lost vitality, he is, even then, one of Ibsen's living dead. Asleep or awake, he endures a living, continuous nightmare of his fall from his former status as a successful architect. He has, we quickly realize, suffered a blow very similar to that which Haakon Werle in all probability dealt Old Ekdal—but for Brovik, there is no brandy, no dressing up, no self-deluding fantasies. He works for the man who admits destroying him, and every hour he spends in Solness's drawing office is a further humiliation.

It is obviously important that Brovik has decided upon a settling of accounts with Solness—"Tonight there's going to be some plain speaking," he declares. Perhaps, after all, he is capable of heroic resistance, of wresting back his self-respect? But, though Brovik's announced intention of airing his grievances with Solness suggests heroic battle, the mood of the play changes in a way that deprives Brovik's last stand of any certain grandeur just before it occurs. As Solness is heard mounting the steps, Brovik, Ragnar, and Kaja all hurry back to their work, the two men re-entering the office behind the one where Kaja is employed as a bookkeeper, and all of the hastening to their duties like the mice of the proverb anxious not to be caught exercising any freedom when the cat returns.

When Solness enters, he looks the picture of success. He is "strong and vigorous," his clothes, including "a grey-green jacket buttoned-up with a high collar and broad revers" and "a soft grey felt hat," suggest that he has achieved the difficult synthesis of successful artist and respected citizen. The two folders he carries under his arm give him the air of one suitably occupied with important professional matters. As we soon discover, however, it is quite appropriate that the sight of Solness with his folders brings to mind that of Alfred Allmers returning from the mountains with a case of blank paper, having written not a word of his book about "Human Responsibility." Even Solness's *coiffure* looks just right: although he is "of mature years," he has a fine head of curly hair, complemented by a dark moustache and bushy eyebrows. If there is a hint of the Dionysian here, the Victorian gentleman in Solness, conscious of appearances, keeps his hair "close cut."

Naturally the audience is waiting with some curiosity the battle which

Brovik has spoken of, and it comes, but not before Solness has demonstrated to Kaja that he is in a seemingly amorous mood. Told by Kaja that her relatives are in the drawing office, Solness raises his voice to give Ragnar and Knut Brovik the idea that his attentions to Kaja are entirely professional before indulging in a brief interval of dalliance with her, which brings the mood of the play close to farce. Kaja puts an end to it with her warning, "Sh . . . They can hear you," which in itself suggests a ridiculous situation: however powerful the spell which Solness has cast upon her, it has not overcome Kaja's concern with appearances! Whatever may be deeper and darker about Solness's relationship with Kaja, it is important not to overlook the ironic treatment of his lechery, her gullibility, and the deception practised by both of them.

Before Brovik tackles Solness, there are other intimations that complicate the dramatic mood. We learn that a young couple have commissioned a design for a house from Solness at a place called Løvstrand. The name, which refers to foliage and a beach, is interesting, and taken together with the name "Solness" (*sol* means "sun," and *nes* is a headland or a promontory), is obviously as evocative as that of Lövborg (referring to foliage and a castle) in *Hedda Gabler*. Master Builder Solness, however, is in a state of some anxiety about a commission which, on the surface of things, sounds inspiring—to design one imagines, a house which will complement a landscape as beautiful, presumably, as its name. And it is this anxiety which prompts the first implicit questions about Solness: how genuine and how great is the talent of this man who is clearly zealous about his reputation as an artist, and what is the nature of the crisis he appears to be approaching? There are hints of unflattering and sardonically humorous answers to these questions in the sight of Solness taking refuge from his frustration by flirting with Kaja and bullying the Broviks. These are Gyntian tactics: they do not prove that Solness is a mere poseur, but neither do they give any confirmation of underlying spiritual distinction.

When challenged by Ragnar, who has, it transpires, been doing some work on his own initiative for the Løvstrand couple, Solness admits, "I haven't got the plans straight in my mind yet." He never does get them straight, and we are, even as we learn more about the tensions between employer and employees, beginning to learn why he perhaps never could. We may be expected to sympathize with Solness when he responds with annoyance to Knut Brovik's assurance that there are no financial difficulties in this instance. But his admission "I don't know anything about these people" is damaging, especially in the light of what Solness later has to say about the importance of "knowing people," and taken together with the word "home," which appears frequently in this context, it may be seen as the introduction of the play's central theme: what can Solness truly know about his fellow creatures and where, if anywhere, can they be really at home? Are churches with or without high towers (the parallel with the old church and the new in *Brand* springs to mind here) suitable? Are substantial suburban villas where children may be conceived in joy and raised in love really more appropriate? What place in the scheme of things does a house like the one to be built at Løvstrand have? Perhaps a sound bank balance and a desire for beauty (all we know about the Løvstrand couple) are all that an architect should look for in clients? Perhaps, on the other hand, he should be building castles fit for royalty or for supermen for some people, and altogether humbler dwellings for others—Aslaksen's "compact majority," for instance? Solness does not know the answers, though he may be tormented by such questions as his vexation about the Løvstrand commission, and the rest of the play, demonstrates.

Solness's doubts and doubts about Solness are central themes, and many of the doubts are implicit in the contrast between the Dionysian evocations of the names "Solness" and "Løvstrand" and other aspects, psychological and philosophical as well as metaphysical, of building homes for all the kinds of people who live in a fractured culture such as Solness's and ours. We ought not to overlook, either, especially in the context of Norwegian preferences for first names which make less use of saints' names than other Western cultures, the irony that Solness's first name, Halvard, associates him specifically with Christianity in Norway, St. Hallvard being the patron saint of Oslo.

Because there is so much in the names in *The Master Builder*, it is worth noting the evidence which suggests that Ibsen seems to use the character named Borghejm (in *Little Eyolf*) to imply an ironic contrast and implicit negative commentary on Solness. Borghejm, an engineer, has all the confidence and certainty of purpose that Solness lacks. The first syllable of his name means "castle," "fortress," or "stronghold," and suggests the famous hymn which, in Norwegian, declares that "Vår gud han er så fast en borg" "A mighty fortress is our God"); the second syllable means "home," and there is every indication in *Little Eyolf* that Borghejm is both at home in a world no less permeated by metaphysical uncertainties than that of *The Master Builder* and that he can establish a real home for a family with or without the benefit of an architect's design. This probability is supported by Borghejm's positive and unaffected relations with other people, which are also singularly free of fantasy. Without any heroic posturing, he succeeds in extricating the woman he loves, Asta Allmers, from a situation of real psychological and spiritual peril. And he is also the only character in the play whose approach to little Eyolf is based on completely straightforward and unforced affection: he plays with him seeking nothing but the child's happiness. But, as we shall see, the "castle in the air" which Solness and Hilde seem to regard as their spiritual home is not "en borg" but "et slott." When Hilde taunts Solness by telling him that castles in the air ("Luftslotte") are good places to take refuge in, she is echoing the Norwegian proverb "Han bygger Slotte i Luften," which, according to Ansten Anstensen's *The Proverb in Ibsen*, refers, unlike the similar English proverb, in a wholly negative way to people who indulge in dreams or visions.[7] Significantly, also, Solness and Hilde's "luftslott" is reminiscent of the famous folk-tale collected by Peter Asbjørnsen called "The Golden Castle that Hung in the Air." But the certainties of the folk-tale become questions in *The Master Builder*. These uncertainties, charged with tragic irony, are an integral part of the play, as will be shown: they function quite independently of the link between *Little Eyolf* and *The Master Builder*. But Borghejm, none the less, has a special relationship with Solness, as he has also with those other questionable heroes—Alfred Allmers, John Gabriel Borkman, and Arnold Rubek.

Borghejm is undoubtedly Ibsen's closest approach to that genuine but completely unhistrionic heroism which he seems to envisage in the letter to Brandes in which he implies the need for an unpretentious shoemaker who will stick to his last.[8] No one could be more down-to-earth than Borghejm—who builds roads on rock foundations, roads that will, it appears, link the communities of Norway physically as effectively as Haakon Haakonsson seeks to bind them spiritually in *The Pretenders*.

Wrestling with similar doubts to those which torment Allmers, Borkman, and Rubek gives Solness his primary claim to heroic stature. When, however, Solness shows confusion and anger about the designs for the Løvstrand house, we have the first indications not only that he may be, unlike Borghejm, actually as well as nominally unqualified for the tasks he sets himself,[9] but also that, even if he once had great ability, he is now suffering its irretrievable loss. Having declared his frustration, he insists that the young couple who want the house "can go to somebody else—anybody they like—I don't care." He does, of course, care both because his apparent inability to design the Løvstrand house may signal a falling off of his imagination and creative power and because he realizes—at those times when he can surface from brooding self-immersion—that Ragnar Brovik is longing to take his place.

Having dismissed Ragnar and Kaja, Brovik starts the struggle with Solness rather unheroically by trying to play on Solness's assumed sympathies—"I don't want these poor children to know how bad I am," he confides. But aware of Solness's obvious hostility, he goes on to the offensive with signs of lingering vitality. He refuses to be bought off—more completely than he is already—so he impatiently rejects Solness's offer of a pay rise for Ragnar, insisting that it is time that his son had the chance to do some independent work. In the verbal battle which follows, much of the sense of tragic loss experienced in Ibsen's work by those who doubt themselves and their calling is apparent. The Solness–Brovik relationship is much like a photographic negative of the John Gabriel Borkman–Vilhelm Foldal friendship. Solness and Brovik do all they can to destroy each other by exchanging painful assertions of apparent truth, while Borkman and Foldal oblige each other's self-esteem, for most of their time together, by telling comforting lies. One feels that Ibsen might, when writing *The Master Builder*, have been amused if Archer, for instance, had told him about the English idiom "home truths!"

There are suggestions that the battle between Solness and Brovik has a certain epic quality, but equally there are suggestions of low malice and meanness of spirit. This is evident in the cunning with which Solness seeks to undermine Brovik's faith in his son's ability. The tactic is reminiscent of Bishop Nicholas's shrewd assaults on Earl Skule's self-confidence, also strongly associated with his son, in *The Pretenders*. And though Brovik's defence of his son attracts admiration, there is malice in the sadistic pleasure which Brovik seems to derive from informing Solness that Ragnar's designs are distinguished from Solness's work by their originality: "Aha! *New*! Not the sort of old-fashioned rubbish *I* generally build!" exclaims Solness, obviously enraged and wounded. To all that can be said about the heroic quality of this quarrel between two long-standing enemies, must be added a comment on its element of Social Darwinism. Here, at one level, we have two old dogs struggling for the last time over an ancient bone.

There is much that is appalling about this battle, whether we view it from a mythic perspective (Brovik as an overthrown Cronos to Solness's Zeus, for example) or from a deterministic viewpoint. Each old foe utters a curse upon his rival. Solness tells Brovik that he must "die as best as [he] can," and Brovik leaves the field of battle with the wish, which is fulfilled, that Solness shall from now on know nothing but troubled dreams. "Sleep well," he says, adding, surely with all the menace he can muster, "if you can."

But it is the aura of inscrutability which gives the battle of Brovik and Solness its strongest dramatic appeal, and this element of the unknowable seems to derive, ambiguously but undeniably, from the supernatural. Solness, doubtful, preoccupied with self, yet seemingly aware of dreadful and ultimately cosmic discord, has as good a claim as Peer Gynt to the title of poet (*digter*). Seen in this light, the struggles of Solness affirm both life and spiritual health, and Brovik, for all the pathos of his situation, is ultimately closer to all that is negative—including the malevolent aspects of supernatural forces that seem to operate at subterranean levels in the play.

A man who is simply a callous sadist would not cry out "half in desperation," as Solness does to Brovik, "Don't you understand? There's nothing else I can do! I am what I am! And I can't change myself."

Solness realizes, though the thought terrifies him, that there may be a kind of fate which has made him what he is: it has shaped his sense of vocation. He is not a villain who cannot get rid of his cloak and dagger, but a tragicomic figure who does not understand why "things just ran [his] way" or feel certain that he has in fact accomplished what may be expected of him. There is perhaps something admirable about his stoical endurance—which to the Broviks looks like mere self-centered obstinacy. It is as though he cannot relinquish a task which he still hopes to envision clearly and to carry through, even if all the Ragnars in the world come to ask for their chance to advance.

Brovik is not evil in any obvious sense. Essentially he is presented as a kind of moral cripple, a man maimed by Solness's destruction of his career and able to retaliate only fitfully and with as much rancour as justified anger. But there is something repulsive about his success in using Ragnar for his purposes. It is true that Ragnar never shows any sign of resistance. But that in itself is suspicious in a world where vocation, if it has any meaning at all, seems unlikely to coincide exactly with parental aspirations. The negative intimations of Brovik's association with lasting and perhaps more than merely human evil reside in his determination not just to restore the name of Brovik to its former honour but to ensure that his son and his niece shall complete the task for him after his death. His ill fortune complements the "good luck" of Solness and allows for the operation of unknowable agencies, which, ultimately perhaps, override personal human responsibilities.

It is perfectly clear, as the action proceeds, that the strong mutual attraction which once existed between Kaja and Ragnar is utterly spent. It is entirely possible to blame Solness for destroying it; it is equally possible to blame Brovik for exploiting it to an extent that caused Kaja to yearn for freedom from both her male relatives. Thus she could have become as easily susceptible to the will, spoken or not, of Solness as little Eyolf, his mind unseated by the pressures of his parents' conflicting demands on him, is lured away by the Rat Wife. Indeed, when questioned later by Solness about the marriage which is going to follow a five-year engagement, Kaja remarks, with obvious apathy, that she will marry because that is what her uncle and cousin expect of her. In fact, the last and dreadful image we have of Kaja is that of a niece sitting by the bedside of an unconscious and dying Brovik mentally resigning herself to entering a loveless marriage to his son. And Ragnar's reigning passion at that point is, naturally enough, not love at all but hatred for the man who, permanently it seems, alienated her feelings from him.

In Ibsen, dominant characters like Earl Skule and Gregers Werle obviously foist their ambitions on to the young with disastrous results, or endanger them in the attempt, as Karsten Bernick and John Gabriel Borkman do. Sometimes, also, apparently weak characters, whose lives are full of self-denial, like Martha Bernick and Juliane Tesman, for example, steer the young along uncertain paths. Like Martha and Auntie Julle, Brovik has much to complain of, but, ironically, he succeeds where a character as cunning as Bishop Nicholas fails in determining the future of others even from beyond the grave. The extent to which his influence upon Ragnar and Kaja is a baleful one may be measured by the lack of any indication that the new order—in life as in architecture—to be presided over by the new Mr. and Mrs. Brovik will be joyful. Indeed it seems certain that whatever evils marred the rule of Solness, its horizons were wider and its hopes more inspiring than those of Ragnar Brovik.

The episode immediately following Brovik's departure is so saturated in what Arne Røed has aptly termed "sterile sex"[10] as to preclude anything but negative interpretation. The sardonic humour characterizing the feigned sexual interest which Solness shows in Kaja reveals an undeniably fraudulent element of his character. We learn, very soon, that his only aim in pretending love for Kaja is to make use of her influence with Ragnar: she alone can oblige him to stay on as a subordinate in Solness's employ. Accordingly, there is dark humour in Aline's interruption of the "lovers." Kaja, or "Miss Fosli" as Aline, with some acerbity, prefers to call her, has hardly had time to stagger or totter (the Norwegian word is *vakler*) back to her desk from the kneeling position in the middle of the room where she has been literally idolizing Solness, when Aline appears! There is dark humour also in the speculation which the idolatry prompts whether Kaja succumbs to Solness's evidently hypnotic appeal of her own volition or as a refugee from Uncle Knut and Cousin Ragnar. And there is dreadful irony in the similarity of some of Kaja's remarks to Solness (such as, "Oh, you know very well there's only one person I care about now! There's nobody else in the whole wide world!") to the vows that Solveig makes to Peer when she comes to him in the mountains. Solveig utters a promise of enduring love which is as close as Ibsen ever comes to spiritual certainty[11]: Kaja's words, though similar, seem wrung from her in a travesty of love and they sound cheaply exaggerated.

Solness's remarks to Kaja, about his loneliness and brooding, have a maudlin and self-pitying ring. They are loathsome in the context of his dishonest motives and deceitful intentions. Ibsen comes as close here as he ever does to an endorsed condemnation of a character by showing us in Solness's treatment of Kaja utter disingenuousness and complete disregard for a helpless victim. There is horror in the fact that Solness, who talks so much about the importance of "knowing" others, so shamefully abuses the one woman whom he appears to understand completely. *The Master Builder*, however, is not, at least in any narrowly puritanical sense, a didactic work about sexual misconduct. Thematically as well as dramatically speaking, the illustration of the influence that Solness exercises over Kaja is most important because it demonstrates that he does

have exceptional powers. Whether they are merely hypnotic or extensions of the forces which, later, he claims, literally possess him is left,
fascinatingly, open to question.

Aline's interruption gives Solness an opportunity to display his acting
talent more fully still: one moment he is assisting Kaja to her desk, having
himself given the alarm about Aline's arrival, the next he is back in his
normal place, turning to his wife and asking, "Oh, is that you, dear?" To
Aline's acidly self-deprecating, "I'm afraid I am intruding," his lying
answer is, "Not at all. Miss Fosli only has a short letter to write." There is
well managed comedy here—as Peter Wood's 1964 production for the
British National Theatre made clear.[12]

The comedy continues even after Aline's departure to keep Dr. Herdal company. Solness has been rather too convincing in his protestations
of regard for Kaja, and she, anxious to deserve his supposed affection,
offers to terminate her engagement to Ragnar. It is hard when seeing a
production which runs true to the play not to laugh at the discomfiture
which causes Solness to exclaim, "Break it off! Have you gone mad!
You'd break it off?"

There is comedy also in the moment when Kaja emerges sufficiently
from her idolatry to suspect Solness's motives. Timid and badly frightened as she is, she manages to get out the partial question, "Is it mainly
because of Ragnar that you . . .?" Evidently even such a master of
charisma as Solness can be made to lose his head when his performance
as Casanova is not only interrupted by his wife but disturbed by an
unexpected demonstration that Kaja still has one or two of her wits about
her. The humour here, incongruous as it is with the sympathies one feels
for Kaja, foreshadows the comic aspects of Hilde Wangel's onslaught
upon the sensibilities of Solness. He still finds it easy enough to send Kaja
off with a few words spoken in a kindly tone—and specific instructions to
arrange her affairs with Ragnar to suit Solness's professional convenience. But the time is already approaching when Hilde will show him that,
like Peer Gynt, he risks all he has in erotic entanglements with exotic
young women.

But before Hilde Wangel arrives with a head full of ideals and fantasies, and powers of enchantment to match anything that Solness can
offer, the play spends some time with its feet firmly on materialistic
ground in the uninspired company of Dr. Herdal. It is not accidental that
in this play we have Ibsen's least enlightening physician. Dr. Rank can
teach us much about the psychology of frustrated love, and Nora learns
more from him than she bargains for. Dr. Relling, philanthropic even in
his deepest cynicism, is widely regarded as the voice of good sense in *The
Wild Duck*. And wise physicians do not cease to be useful even when
Ibsen's naturalistic phase is over: Dr. Wangel, combining compassion
and trust with his medical skill, is able to summon up the courage to allow

his second wife the freedom in which to purge herself of a psychological or possibly literally devilish nightmare. Dr. Herdal, however, is a bumbling creature, so inept that he twice admits, when Solness is trying to explain (honestly it seems) his mental anguish, that he cannot understand a "single, blessed word of all this."

Ibsen's use of Herdal is one of his most skilful feats of thematic orientation. In most of Ibsen's metaphysical plays, doctors of medicine are not really at home: the Doctor in *Brand* undoubtedly knows what is wrong with little Alf, but the malaise of the soul which afflicts Brand, like the spiritual affliction which Brand diagnoses in his countrymen, lies beyond the terms of the Doctor's competence. In *The Master Builder*, Dr. Herdal is shown as understanding nothing beyond Aline's well-grounded antipathy towards Kaja Fosli and, later, beyond the indubitable fact that sufferers from vertigo must not, when in high places, be subjected to loud noises. With a subtlety that makes Shaw's ironic treatment of the medical profession seem like noisy axe-grinding, Ibsen introduces several of the most intriguing aspects of Solness's mysterious world of aspiration and torment in the long duologue between Herdal and Solness, while making the doctor's incomprehension quietly but insistently apparent. And, with exquisite irony, the nature of Solness's "good luck"—the word is "lykken," as in *The Pretenders*—is spoken of blithely by Herdal, who is utterly oblivious of the horrible doubts the very term sets loose in Solness. Also without Shavian trumpet blasts but with results just as effective, Ibsen hints through Herdal's choice of words the limitations of his pragmatic mind and probably also of any kind of merely materialistic approach in the presence of possibly mystical phenomena.

Herdal has no coherent philosophy: the unpleasantly Darwinian implications of the word he uses to refer to Aline's intuition about Solness's relationship with Kaja Fosli would therefore seem either not to occur to him at all or merely to express his commonplace grasp of reality. The word is "sporsans" and its denotations are, in the words of Einar Haugen's *Norsk Engelsk Ordbok*, a "dog's ability to track" and "sense of smell." Animal images should not be overlooked in *The Master Builder* any more than in Strindberg's *Miss Julie*, in which the heroine's physiological condition on the night of her downfall is implicitly compared with that of her pet bitch, ironically named Diana. There is a level to *The Master Builder* at which Aline Solness, though pale, dressed in mourning, and wearing her hair in faded ringlets like those of a worn doll, sniffs out evil in her husband's life. It is the same level at which Herdal speaks of Solness's rise to the top of his profession in terms which belong to the jungle. The image he uses is a perfectly ordinary colloquial idiom in Norwegian, but it has no precise equivalent in English—as is evident, for example, in *The Oxford Ibsen*'s translation. Herdal, speaking to Solness, uses the phrase "swang your way up" ("svang Dem da op"). The means of ascent to which he is referring is the financial opportunities which were available after the burning of Aline's family home. Herdal congratulates Solness on his ape-like achievement with no apparent consciousness of irony. Ibsen, it seems, wishes to remind us that, as Arnold Rubek knows very well, human beings have not purged themselves of unpleasant animal characteristics. Rubek also has reason, however, to suspect that mankind may be capable of transcendence; Herdal, on the other hand, is at home among the swinging apes and the sniffing hunting dogs. It is a dimension of human experience that Ibsen knew well and, unlike Herdal and other more conscious Darwinian determinists, could not endure for long.

It is revealing, as Herdal's myopia is made ever more obvious, to note how frequently the word "grunn," meaning "basis," "grounds," or "cause" and also "foundation" or "groundwork," is used in his duologue with Solness. It is used three times in the discussion of Solness's relationship with Kaja and appears again in the verbal compound "grunnmuret" (literally "on a foundation wall") at the climax of the conversation, when Herdal asserts that Solness's career is more firmly established than ever before, while Solness, not in the least reassured by him, insists that a terrible reversal awaits him and that it will come through the young. Ibsen juxtaposes Herdal's talk of firm foundations and Solness's reiterated comment "Omslaget kommer"—literally "the change (or reversal) is coming."

Significantly, in the last act, it is Solness who insists to Hilde that their "castle in the air" shall have a firm foundation beneath it—"med grundmur under." Hilde, the instrument of the ambivalent reversal in Solness's fortunes, knows, or seems to know, much more about the reality of their foundations than Herdal.

Two other key words, also repeated frequently in the rest of the play, are emphasized in the Solness–Herdal conversation. There is every sign that to Solness himself they are indications of his spiritual torment, while to Herdal they have no intensified meaning whatever. The words are "lykke," to which reference has already been made, and "forferdelig," which means "dreadful," "horrible," or "terrible."[13] Herdal's inability to grasp the nature of the master builder's terrors and apprehensions prepares us well for the arrival of the young woman who seems better qualified for the task. Significantly, her first name closely resembles that of one of the Valkyries[14] and is also reminiscent of the noun "hulder," which refers to a kind of a siren frequently encountered in Norwegian folk-tales, and which, according to Haugen's *Ordbok*, also has the specific literary connotation of *femme fatale*. And her entire name is the same as that of the disturbed adolescent who is excited at the prospect of the death of a young would-be artist in *The Lady from the Sea*.

Hilde's arrival itself is a skilful tragicomic contrivance. It has and is meant to have, no less than Nora Helmer's slamming the door when she leaves home, distinctly melodramatic overtones. Ibsen is using a familiar theatrical device (one borrowed from the purveyors of popular plays to whom Ibsen referred as "Scribe and Co."[15]) in a characteristically inverted fashion, much as both Shaw and Brecht frequently adapt melodramatic techniques for their own purposes. When Hilde Wangel knocks and then walks boldly into the room with "her skirt hitched up, a sailor's collar open at the neck and a small sailor hat on her head," an audience may be as stunned as Solness, who has, the very moment before, been holding forth about the retribution to be brought by youth knocking at his door.

For Solness, the knock and Hilde's arrival seem to confirm his premon-itions of fateful intervention in his life; for an audience watching him and the young woman with the eccentric dress, a rucksack, and alpenstock, there is more than a hint of absurdity. Solness, so solemn, so thoroughly absorbed in portentous self-analysis, is jolted out of it in a fashion which amusingly emphasizes one of Solness's most distinctive characteris-tics—his lack of humour, especially on the subject of himself—the very attribute which may be Peer Gynt's literally saving grace. The appear-ance of the young woman on his doorstep is itself wrily amusing and creates an impression of oddity which is deepened when she announces that she has a quantity of dirty underwear to wash! Hilde, in effect, combines the determination and eccentricity of Lona Hessel with the predatory nature and seeming affinity with supernatural mystery which distinguishes Brand's half-sister, Gerd. We are very quickly made to see how Solness and Hilde complement each other, but it is important to remember that there is a considerable measure of the ludicrous in their first encounter (within the present action of the play) because Hilde's aspirations and ambitions are, like Solness's, ostensibly impressive but ultimately of no certain worth. Together, in their fascinating duologues, they, like Peer with his onion, lay bare all that we can know of their souls. And, as in Peer's case, the tragicomic possibility that nothing of ultimate value may reside at the very centre of their beings is as strong as the possibility that in those innermost recesses is the wellspring of some high and shared destiny.

The laying bare of Solness's innermost being has begun before Hilde's arrival and is fascinating for those with sharper ears than Herdal's. There is, for instance, that aspect of Solness which resembles an "ashlad," the folk-tale archetype who is as remarkable for his astuteness as for his good fortune.[16] The rags-to-riches motif, which is part of the stock-in-trade of the modern novel, is equally at home in *The Master Builder*. Whereas, however, in such novels as *The Mayor of Casterbridge* or *The Great Gatsby*, the motif is adapted to a predominantly secular vision, in *The Master Builder* the supernatural element is still present. There is nothing to suggest the supernatural about Herdal's unwitting introduction of the motif:

> But you yourself . . . you saw your chance and took it. Started out as a poor country lad, and now look at you—at the top of your profession. Yes indeed, Mr. Solness, you certainly have had all the luck.

The certainty that Solness and Hilde gradually come to see themselves as an "ashlad" and a princess does not emerge clearly until they begin to elaborate their vision of a castle in the air. But before that, in fact from the moment of Herdal's reference to the "poor country lad" who made good, implications about Solness's career in comparison to an "ashlad's" begin to emerge. We learn that, like an "ashlad," Solness starts with nothing but his native—or God-given—wit, and, also like an "ashlad," he receives what he takes to be divine reassurance of the value of his calling—the building of churches, that is. "Ashlads," like the one in "The Golden Castle that Hung in the Air," set out to rescue princesses, kill trolls, and inherit kingdoms. Solness marries Aline, presumably for love, and the differences of social rank and wealth between them resemble those of "ashlads" and the princesses they marry; he inherits the large home of Aline's parents and with it a "kingdom"—a large estate which, divided into building lots, provides the economic basis of his career. But there resemblances between "ashlads" and Solness end, and ironic differences begin.

Solness, unlike "ashlads," seems cursed in his marriage, and the ambition which he first had dedicated to God leads him, after the fire, to turn his back on conventional Christianity. And it is in this mood of rebellion that he turns his attention from building churches to building "homes for people"; that he turns to women other than his wife (he admits to Herdal that he has been interested in several women before Kaja); and that he finds himself a new princess. And as we see him trying to satisfy the wishes of the Princess Hilde, we are in the gravest doubt whether Solness is in some way re-establishing all that once had been positive about him or is hastening himself to death in the mere guise of a hero to satisfy what may be the perverse desires of a woman who, like Rebecca West, could well be more troll or witch than princess.

The discussion of Solness's luck or fortune (*lykken*) is another hint of how widely the play is to range over the relationship of the supernatural to the human. There is, even when he first appears, much that indicates that Solness may be a Faustian figure doomed to pay with his own soul and that of Aline for sacrilegious denial of his vocation. This is one feasible explanation of the guilt that he tells Herdal he feels towards his wife. And yet, if Solness could be sure that there were a deity as definite, for example, as Aline's conception of Him, much of his anguish could be dissipated at least in so far as it might be interpreted in the light of a received body of doctrine by the church on which Solness has wilfully turned his back. Solness might not then be in a state of uncertainty about his "luck." As it is, he feels impelled first to build "homes for people" and then, regarding that task as worthless—for unclear reasons—obliged to build for himself a large house with a tower. Perhaps this structure indicates a commitment to both humanism and unspecific supernatural forces or, as Egil Törnqvist plausibly suggests, to the Nietzschean ideas of aristocratic individualism and the superman.[17] On the other hand, it may represent nothing more profound than the aspirations of the many prosperous Victorians who built large "family houses" solidly, in brick or stone, but with enough eclecticism in their design to achieve a degree of the exotic not exceeding the proprieties.

The horrifying and tragicomic nature of Solness's situation in life and metaphysical orientation is the uncertainty of both. The dread he feels may be a result of, paradoxically, not accepting a Christian conception of divine justice whilst simultaneously fearing that a tyrannical Jehovah has demanded more of him than, for instance, of Abraham, whose son He spared. In other words, like Peer, he experiences what may be the Kierkegaardian *angst* which can precede salvation; but instead of turning to Christ, he, possibly abortively, drives his terrors inwards, to the peril of his soul. And it is while Solness is in a state of doubt such as this—the full extent of which we learn only gradually—that Hilde convinces him that only by again defying a deity, to them possibly even more unknowable than to others, can he regain his manhood and assert the right of mankind to honour not only the *lares* and *penates* but also the Dionysus both within and beyond themselves.

It is just as possible, however, that the deity whom Solness defies is, if not entirely non-existent, a satanic force or some malign entity utterly dissociated from any established theology. From what he says after his conversation with Herdal, it is clear that Solness has been long preoccupied with the half-formulated notion that evil forces emanating from or using his own will, forces that may be in no way identifiable with a deity who cherishes the building of churches, had caused the fire in Aline's home and indirectly her misery and the deaths of the twins. His mind has become, as he subsequently tells Hilde, a place where trolls and, more strangely still, good and evil devils hard to distinguish from each other hold sway. The master builder appears, therefore, to be in a state of utter confusion about the supernatural. If it exists as more than some kind of uncanny telepathic extension of his own innermost wishes, Solness is unsure how and tormented about why it seems to use him for purposes which are indeterminate and unrelated to any ethic which he can discern. And when he makes his second ascent of a tower, it is perhaps as much to discover the identity of the "Almighty One" he believes is there as to dispute with him.

There is then, a part of Solness's soul which is an unwilling metaphysician—and he seems at times to be living out a version of the Cairo madhouse scene, where Peer suffers some of his worst tortures. This is especially true at the end of the play, where the sight of Solness apparently arguing at the top of his tower with an invisible force as Hilde and Aline watch him should surely remind us of Peer battling with the Boyg; like Peer, Solness has "women behind him," though to what avail, if any, we do not ultimately know.

It is the ill-defined nature of the territory where Solness must fight for his soul that the Solness–Herdal duologue suggests. Later we are to learn of the Promethean identity which Solness seems consciously to envisage for himself and of the specifically Dionysian and later Nietzschean perspectives in which Hilde appears, as though by instinct rather than learning, to view him. But before moving on to those heroic possibilities, it is necessary to observe that Solness makes some admissions to Herdal which could strip him of every shred of dignity and all substantial claim to heroism. As with Peer, Allmers, Borkman, and Rubek, there is more than a chance of a verdict of partial or total spiritual inauthenticity in the eschatological judgement of Master Builder Solness.

There is a point in the last act when Solness seems so fearful that Hilde comments sarcastically, "You seem pretty afraid altogether." If there is a suggestion there of Rosmer's kind of hesitancy in situations of crisis, it is not accidental. Nor are the hints, which are also reminiscent of Rosmer, that Solness may be more generally ill-equipped for the heroic tasks he sets himself. And in Solness's case, the evidence is just as potentially damning as in Rosmer's. It is not until the second act that Hilde asks the pointed question why Solness does not call himself an architect, but in the Herdal–Solness duologue there are substantial hints that Solness may be fundamentally incompetent in his profession.

There are certainly at least two reasonable responses to Solness's observation to Herdal about how useful he finds Ragnar and Knut Brovik, the latter being "so extraordinarily clever at working out stresses and strains and cubic contents . . . and all that damned rigmarole." The last phrase, which is literally "devilish stuff" (*dœvelskap*) in Norwegian, could, of course, be the kind of airy talk predictable, though undesirable, in a person of superior talents. It is possible therefore to ascribe to arrogance Solness's assigning to underlings all the precise calculations which assure the structural safety of buildings. And it is equally possible to see in it evidence that Solness cannot cope with the laborious and unglamorous work which is part of all undertakings of any consequence. It is useful to recall, also in this connection, that Brovik has already reminded Solness (how truthfully it is impossible to judge) that he (Solness) was far from thoroughly acquainted with his craft when he seized power from Brovik and began his rapid rise to the top of his profession.

Solness is less specific about Ragnar's talents in the conversation with Herdal, but there could be a touch of both envy and fear in Solness's apparent understatement that Ragnar is, like his father, "pretty clever." Later, of course, he admits to Hilde that there is no doubt whatever about Ragnar's abilities and that he foresees immediate success for him if Ragnar begins to work independently.

The suspicion exists, therefore—and it stems from Solness himself—that he may be little more than a figurehead in his own company: Knut Brovik seems to be dealing with all essential practical matters; Ragnar, to be providing ideas to satisfy both conservative and more radical tastes in the styles of homes commissioned from Solness. The accounting is done by Kaja—when she is not otherwise engaged by the master builder. It is surely of some consequence that we never see Solness handle any of the specific tools of his trade. And the only thing he actually *does* which is undeniably related to architecture (excluding his ambiguous performance in the topping-out ceremony) is to raise a pencil—with the greatest reluctance—to sign Ragnar's drawings. He looks like an architect, of course. It is easy to imagine that his grey-green jacket and soft grey felt hat must cut quite a dash on building sites. The folders under his arm would probably give confidence to anxious clients, too. Indubitably, therefore, Solness plays the role of architect superbly, but whether he is truly talented is another matter. And even if he is not guilty of sheer incompetence there is much to suggest that, like Peer during the threadball scene, he may be guilty of having never properly developed his talent. Just where has Solness been before he returns to his office to behave as absurdly as he does when the action opens? What could he have said that had anything to do with philosophical attitudes appropriate to architecture that would not sound ridiculous in the light of what we see him do?

Solness's confusion is such that there is at least one point in his conversation with Herdal at which the latter cannot be blamed for being baffled at the master builder's state of mind. Solness claims that he derives a feeling of relief from allowing Aline to believe that his relationship with Kaja is more than expedient pretence: it is "rather like paying off a tiny instalment on a huge immeasurable debt. . . ." But how? If Solness really believes that he is spiritually indebted to Aline, he is unlikely to pay off the debt in any sense comprehensible to her by convincing her that he is unfaithful; all he does is to increase the debt because the infidelity that Aline suspects hurts her deeply. He seems also to think that he can in some way "pay" by being judged evil by a mystical judge of some kind in a situation where no real evil exists. But it does exist: Solness does not need to abuse Kaja physically in order to besmirch his soul and hers by his treatment of her. Indeed there is much to suggest that, judged in terms of the effects he produces—Kaja claims that he has taken complete and permanent possession of her mind—what he does is worse than physical abuse. And yet, to think of Solness as a mere masochist, and a slow-witted one at that—relishing the pain of resentment he wilfully nurtures in Aline—seems shallow and unconvincing. Undoubtedly this is one of the moments which foreshadows Solness's vision of himself as a Promethean figure—tormented by some god enraged by Solness's supposed commitment to humanity in general. But it is a suspicious and inauspicious foreshadowing.

When Hilde breezes into the room, she behaves in what seems like a deliberately unconventional manner. She walks up to Solness, who shows every sign of not recognizing her, and, "her eyes shining and happy," exclaims, "Good evening!" as though she were confidently expecting Solness to experience an instant epiphany. He does not. In fact what happens instead is the commencement of an intriguing process of revelation through which positive and negative aspects of both Solness and Hilde are revealed and dramatically juxtaposed. And from the very beginning of this process—which is made theatrically manifest and not simply conveyed by words—it is virtually impossible to find anything within the text which endorses any particular features as more valid than the others. When the odd young woman marches across the room to the confused middle-aged man and addresses him as though their relationship is an intimate one, what are we to think? Are the mysteries to be unfolded sacred or profane, spiritually uplifting, perverse, or banally predictable? Has this man, about whom the play has so far suggested more to censure than to admire, in some way assisted by the young woman with the shining eyes, triumphed over the darker elements of his own nature in a way of which we are yet to learn; or are we watching another Peer Gynt haunted by a survivor of one of his excursions into lustful fantasy? Although the bulk of criticism of the play supports the first reading, the outstanding modern English production of the play —Peter Wood's—appeared to pay some attention to the alternative, and it is the conviction of the present writer that the alternatives are presented in the text itself with equal dramatic emphasis. Just before they make their very last remarks to each other about their castle in the air on a firm foundation, Solness, "with bowed head," asks Hilde, "How did you become as you are, Hilde?" And she replies, "How did you make me as I am?" Those are questions to which no simple answers are appropriate. If we do have variations on Pygmalion and Galatea in Solness and Hilde, the complexity of their souls and the alchemy of their relationship is, in all likelihood, infinitely more subtle than anything Ovid gives us cause to ponder. From the time of Hilde's arrival with her alpenstock and dirty underwear to that of Solness's departure for the tower with the man—perhaps even the god or the superman—in him inflamed and his vertigo possibly all ready to strike, the play vacillates constantly between suggestions that Solness and Hilde are in some sense supreme and that they are comical victims of their own delusions—an ageing man who should know better than to fall prey to eroticism and a giddy young woman too headstrong to consider that her fate may be as ultimately inglorious as Solness's if he loses his grip on everything else in blind desire for her.

The climax of Act I is Hilde's account of Solness's ascent of the tower in her home town of Lysanger (*lys* means "light," and *anger* means both "fjord" and "sorrow" or "remorse"). Only in Act III is the Promethean relevance of this climb made absolutely explicit by Solness, though the Prometheus motif is foreshadowed by imagery in Act II. In the last act he tells Hilde that at Lysanger he was consciously defying God by renouncing the building of churches and starting instead to design "homes for people." In Act I we must surmise whether it was the godlike aspiration of the handsome man ascending the tower that caused Hilde's exultation or whether the "harps in the air" she heard had more to do with her puberty—she was "twelve or thirteen" at the time, and some critics, most notably Hermann Weigand,[18] have not hestitated to see Hilde's sex hormones as giving rise to her ecstasy. And we must also decide as best we can how meaningful Solness's possibly Promethean climb at Lysanger was in the light of his subsequent behaviour to Hilde—in so far as we ever learn what it really was.

The actual climb at Lysanger contains some of the most unambiguous indications of heroism. We know that Solness was grief-stricken after the death of his sons, shocked by Aline's subsequent withdrawal from an active interest in life, and preoccupied with the idea that he had in some way been responsible for the fire that burned Aline's family home: to climb the Lysanger church tower at such a time, when mental stresses were added to his habitual vertigo, shows unusual courage—even if it may be associated with negative motives such as a secret desire for death. What happens after the topping-out ceremony is much more ambiguous.

In a meaningful way the thematic nub of *The Master Builder* is contained in the scene either remembered or fabricated (there is no way of establishing which) by Hilde, in which Solness is said to have arisen from a banquet in his honour, gone into a room in the Wangel household where he found Hilde alone, still wearing the white dress she had worn, like all the other schoolgirls, for the topping-out ceremony, called her a princess, promised her a kingdom, and embraced her passionately, kissing her "many times."

Solness, when he hears Hilde's bold account, is astounded. He denies it, claims that she dreamt it, or that *he* must have "willed it . . . wished it . . . desired it" and conveyed the whole sense of the imaginary experience to Hilde by telepathy. But finally, with a show of impatience suggesting that he will say anything she pleases to satisfy her, he declares, "All right, damn it . . .! So I *did* do it then!" And later Solness avows, when he has had plenty of time for thought, that if he did not in fact do what Hilde claims, he ought to have.

The question of the significance of the passionate encounter, real in whatever sense, is far from answered when both parties agree to its desirability, however. Here, as elsewhere, we have, implicit in the action, two opposed evaluations of events. The heroic one is that a man who had dedicated his life to the service of humanity, and defied a vengeful deity to establish his right to do so, rose from a joyful feast and encountering an exciting girl, who was clearly drawn to him in admiration of his courage, did not hesitate to embrace her with an uninhibited passion for her youth, vitality, and beauty. Perhaps also, her white dress drew Solness to her—as Solveig's white apron attracted Peer—because he thought that he recognized in the girl the purity he had lost and a manifestation of *the Eternal Feminine* for which he may have yearned. In ardent embrace, he defied Victorian propriety and even much more recent standards of decency, but he asserted a Dionysian capacity for joy and perhaps also, and contradictorily, a desire for atonement. Respecting Hilde's virgin white, he promised the consummation of their union—physical, spiritual, or both—in ten years' time. The unheroic reading emerges as follows: an unscrupulous builder (or building contractor[19]) who destroyed his business rival by some means unwholesome and unmentioned, having decided that church-building was not the way to the prosperity and renown he wished for, saw his chance to profit by some speculative building of private houses on land inherited as part of his wife's estate. His conscience was uneasy, however, because a fire he had willed but not actually started had not only facilitated his commercial ventures (themselves as shrewd as Lopakhin's in *The Cherry Orchard*, which they closely resemble) but indirectly killed his children and crippled his wife's mental health. Coming in a state of grief, shock, and remorse to dedicate a new church tower, he imputes to God all the evil—including that in himself—of his situation and vaingloriously casts himself as a martyr and a philanthropist. Mentally drunk on such heady pretensions, he becomes physically drunk at a banquet (a mockery of a feast, like those in *Peer Gynt*, *An Enemy of the People*, and *The Wild Duck*) and encountering a girl alone in a room in her home, virtually assaults her in a way which causes her to become obsessed with violent erotic fantasies and which is reminiscent of Peer Gynt's troll threats to Solveig. The whole incident, being too shameful to be remembered, is suppressed, though for ten years afterwards, the man, whose wealth and renown as a domestic architect are now considerable, goes around "trying to identify . . . some experience [he] felt [he] must have forgotten." By this time, when in fact the girl, now a woman, comes to claim her "kingdom" he is as anxious as she to see his behaviour in a heroic light, and it is certainly to his advantage that her reading of life is sufficiently liberal to see the sexual conduct of "the worst of trolls" or of the most abandoned Viking plunderer as "exciting."

If the heroic reading is accepted alone, then all one sees is high romance, Promethean and Dionysian glory, and the courage of lovers whose adultery is nothing compared with their challenge of a joyless, duty-bound society, possibly itself possessed by Nietzsche's "slave mentality." If the unheroic reading is accepted alone, then there is only an arrogant lecher who comes as close to seducing a curious but strangely vulnerable adolescent as circumstances will allow, and struggles with his conscience for years until at last the girl, now as predatory as he was, comes to take her revenge, and like a parodic May to his overblown September, compels him to emulate March with the result that he makes public fools of them both.

To state opposed visions of Solness and Hilde as baldly as this might suggest that *The Master Builder* is closer to *Rosmersholm* than it is, however. In *Rosmersholm* the heroic and mock-heroic antitheses are clear—to such an extent, indeed, that the play, in performance as well as in reading, can rightly be seen as, at one level, a play about the difficulties of writing heroic plays at a time when the consciousness of theatre audiences was influenced to a depressing extent by utilitarian and non-theistic values. This is less true of *The Master Builder*, for although it has much in common with *Rosmersholm*, its vision is much more kaleidoscopic and its presentations of heroic and unheroic possibilities more numerous and less rationally structured.

The intriguingly multidimensional nature of the principal characters in *The Master Builder* is evident in the entire play, not simply at its climaxes. Thus Hilde's conversation with Herdal, just before his departure in Act I, associates her with mountains, but not as might be expected with heights inaccessible to most people but with a hostel where she evidently enjoyed flirting with Dr. Herdal (a choice singularly unflattering to her) and other unspecified men, relished the scandalized reactions of a number of staid old ladies busy with their knitting, but none the less managed to ingratiate herself sufficiently with Aline, also a guest at the hostel, to receive from her an invitation to stay with the Solnesses should she visit their town. Hilde, therefore, seems as intriguingly unsure of herself as we are likely to become in trying to allot her any particular and exclusive dramatic identity. She is part troubled adolescent—as troubled, perhaps, as her namesake in *The Lady from the Sea* or Hedvig in *The Wild Duck*—part, like Gerd, the bold adventurer in dangerous places that her rucksack and alpenstock suggest; part the young woman with dreams of unconventional love; and part the girl who would like to find in Aline a confidante and friend with whom she might nurture the gentler aspects of her nature which do, however surprisingly, exist. It is not until much later in the play that we learn that Hilde has run away from home, never to return, she believes. But even without that knowledge, it is possible to see in the Hilde of the first act a singular but not incredible character whose troubles are as complex as her dramatic identities.

It is no wonder that, confronted by this strange young woman and her tale of their supposed encounter, Solness should review reasonable explanations of why Hilde could be deceived, just as earlier he has attempted to discover whether Hilde has come to town to seek work, spend money on clothes, or register as a student. What is more interesting, however, is that eventually Solness is as convinced as Hilde that there is some kind of reality in her account of events at Lysanger. And in this moment of agreement, both of them, before starting their journey to a possibly higher reality or the heights of illusion, share one of the play's few moments of relatively unironic humour. To help him remember Lysanger and his promises, Solness should, says Hilde, mischievously, "have tied a knot in [his] handkerchief." But responding to Solness's reply that he would have forgotten what the knot was for, Hilde, with darker humour, informs him that she knows there are absent-minded trolls as well as amorous ones.

By the end of Act I many, though not all, of the points of reference that are available to gauge the nature and doubtful worth of the master builder's soul have been established. It is certainly noticeable that trolls are much in evidence as the act draws to a close. Not only does Hilde poke fun at the idea of Solness as a stupidly forgetful troll, she is excited as well as amused by the idea that Solness should have returned to her respectable home in Lysanger to abduct her, the daughter of the town doctor, "just like a troll." Perhaps the talk of trolls carrying off and ravishing women (which is strongly reminiscent of Peer's abduction of Ingrid) is an indication that, at heart, both Solness and Hilde have much in common with Ulfheim and Maja in *When We Dead Awaken*: they, like Solness and Hilde, speak of palaces and folk-tale royalty but, in the end, are content to settle for an essentially physical relationship quite low down on the slopes of aspiration. Perhaps if Solness were free of a woman he comes to think of as a corpse bound to him (Aline)—as Ulfheim is free of a woman who tormented him—he and Hilde could enjoy the troll in each other and forget about more exalted ambitions, as Ulfheim and Maja do when he shows her the hovel he pretended was a castle fit for a princess. Certainly, in the last act, Hilde seems particularly enthusiastic to hear the accounts of rape and brutal treatment of women which, as Solness informs her, are characteristic of the sagas. But at the end of Act I, as elsewhere, there is nothing that definitely associates Solness and Hilde more strongly with Ulfheim and Maja than with Rubek and Irene. Indeed, there are several clear foreshadowings of Rubek and

Irene—those apparent aspirants to spiritual redemption—in *The Master Builder*. And one of the most striking of these occurs when Hilde, stunned, it seems, by Solness's disbelief of her account of his behaviour at Lysanger, "remains silent and motionless," and is told by Solness, "Don't stand there like a statue." Ibsen's ambiguous treatment of the Pygmalion myth—ambiguous partly because there is no certainty that the Galatea figure's transformation is permanent or for the better—begins in *The Master Builder*, which very clearly looks forward to *When We Dead Awaken* in this respect also.

Having established the uncertain nature and worth of the relationship of Solness and Hilde, Act I concludes on a note of approaching catastrophe—of the very "reversal" which Solness forecast even though now he seems, ironically enough, not to recognize its certain approach. Caught up in the prospect of another expedient to save himself—by setting "youth against youth" (Hilde against Ragnar)—and rejoicing when Hilde declares in reply to his fervent assertion of his need of her, "Then I *have* my kingdom," Solness appears to overlook Hilde's reservation, "Almost—I was going to say." Hilde, it seems, wants something more than the knowledge that Solness needs her to sustain his battle with life. She may wish to possess him utterly—an impression which subsequent predatory imagery reinforces. And if she does, there is something to be said for the conviction that Solness, in welcoming Hilde, is unconsciously embracing a death that he both fears and secretly desires at the hands of Youth. Whether that makes him a genuinely tragic figure—the victim and accomplice of a *femme fatale* of his own making, for instance—is unclear, however, for nowhere in the first act or elsewhere in the play does Hilde indisputably demonstrate that she is possessed of the aura of sublime malignity of soul which distinguishes such representatives of that literary archetype as *la belle dame sans merci* or Dolores, Our Lady of Pain. Indeed, it is feasible that, as Hermann Weigand suggests, Hilde's behaviour and visions flow from "abnormal infantilism" and Solness's from an advanced case of paranoia.[20] Of course, this interpretation is no more conclusive than others, and to some it may be objectionable, even offensive. But there is evidence for it in the text, evidence that should establish that in *The Master Builder*, as in *Peer Gynt*, Ibsen is intent upon the contemplation of the dross as well as the gold of human experience. And as a miner in the gold-fields he mentioned to Brandes,[21] Ibsen had, by the time of writing *The Master Builder*, long since discovered that as well as obvious dross, there is also the fool's gold to distinguish from the genuine article.

The most striking thing about the opening of Act II, set in "one of the smaller sitting rooms of the Solnesses' house," is the sight of "flowers and plants in rich profusion" and Aline Solness watering them. The implications of this particular piece of "poetry of the theatre" are as clear here as in *Rosmersholm* and *Hedda Gabler*. Women with a passion for life, like Rebecca West, tend growing plants and are symbolically associated with them; women who are in retreat from life or who have reason to dread some aspect of it—women such as Beate Rosmer and Hedda Gabler—dislike flowers and have them taken away. Aline's appearance, the same now as it was in the previous act, suggests a faded doll, oddly clad in mourning. What are we to infer from the sight of this figure as she "walks noiselessly about with a little watering can"? Perhaps there is some significance in the silence—reminding us, as it does, of the opening of the first act, for here too there is ultimately nothing peaceful, and the silence merely precedes clashes of will which continue the play's revelation of souls.

Kaja Fosli appears briefly, to report her own arrival, her uncle's illness, and Ragnar's decision to come to work late. Aline, still "over by the plants," links for us the presence of death in both the Brovik and Solness households by declaring, with reference to Brovik, "I shouldn't wonder if he, too, died": the "too" relates to nothing that has been said but to an unspecified death, perhaps her own, about which she has been brooding even whilst fostering life.

No better reminder of Ibsen's refusal to allow easy judgement of characters could be found than Aline's tending flowering plants while dressed in mourning and contemplating mortality. As we are to discover, the nature of her grief is neither what Solness believes nor easily predictable (though her doll-like appearance is a clue to the mysteries that lie deeper than Nora Helmer's association with dolls). And she is not as dead as Solness at least has come to believe by the end of the play, though his hopes of reviving her spirit by presenting her with an imposing new house are to be dashed within minutes of the opening of this act. In fact, what the sight of Aline in the second act does is to establish that we have scarcely begun to understand her. Perhaps we may never do so, any more than she comprehends fully the husband she is to claim knowing so well, or he understands her, despite his similar assurances. The enigma is more complex than in the naturalistic plays where choices, though contradictory, are more within the range of the knowable. The surrealistic quality which pervades *The Master Builder* no less than *When We Dead Awaken* is particularly evident here. There is a good case for suggesting that Aline Solness does not just share with Knut Brovik the horrible distinction of being the first of the living dead in the four last plays (which, Ibsen told Moritz Prozor, formed a series with its own epilogue[22]). She is also, by contrast with Brovik, one of the characters who, dead as they are in one way, may yet have attained some glimpse of the reality that the Button-Moulder promises for those who slay themselves and thus mystically become themselves. In this respect she anticipates, in a manner different from Hilde's, Irene in *When We Dead*

Awaken. If Aline were ultimately a mere dead soul, she would have no
need of flowers, nor would she struggle, physically, to rush to Solness's
aid when he climbs the tower in the third act, and faint in terror when he
falls.

It is as mistaken to judge Aline a spiritual non-entity as it is to judge
Solness and Hilde as undoubted champions of spiritual vitality. And
essentially all that happens in Acts II and III is a dramatic manifestation
of the kinds of dread and enlightenment that stem from not knowing
anything for sure about the spiritual worth of all three characters.

What Aline and Solness do together after Kaja's departure and before
Hilde comes down from her bedroom is to talk to each other as they have
never done before about the anguish each has endured since the fire. It is
as though Hilde's presence in the house—and her having slept in one of
the three never previously occupied nurseries—has stirred the mutual
life, even the mutual love, still seemingly left to them as a married couple.
Aline invited and Solness seems in some way to have summoned Hilde to
the house. Towards the end of the first act, both husband and wife seem
quietly happy that they have found a foster-child, as it were, for their
nurseries. And, in the second act, Hilde is to speak of herself as dreaming
like a princess in her child's bedroom. Nothing in the play is more
moving than the moments of apparent calm shortly after the commencement of Act II, in which Solness and Aline agree that their anguish
is lessened, however briefly:

Solness [after a short pause]. So we did find a use for one of the nurseries
after all, Aline.
Mrs. Solness. Yes, we did.
Solness. And I think it's better that way than having everything
standing empty.
Mrs. Solness. The emptiness is dreadful, you are right.

But foster-children are not easy to take to one's heart, as Ellida Wangel
knows of Hilde's namesake in *The Lady from the Sea*, and Hilde is soon to
arrive with accounts of her strange dreams just as Solness and Aline
seem, in the confidences they continue to share until the moment of
Hilde's return to them, to have destroyed all hope of peace for themselves.

What we discover, horrifically, is, first, that both Aline and Solness
have, each in their self-imposed solitudes, blamed themselves wholly for
all the sufferings of the other. Solness, though he does not tell Aline this,
believes that he willed the fire, possibly in league with agents of mystic or
diabolic forces. Aline believes, and she comes very close to telling Solness
this, still in the diologue early in Act II, that she lacked the will to keep the
children alive (though she gives not even the slightest hint of the relation
of her lack of will to the "deaths" of the dolls). Moreover, we may infer

with equal horror, that each has come to believe, grotesquely, that, having no right to happiness, he or she is condemned to live in a nightmare of fantasies. They never, in this conversation or elsewhere, describe the substance of their nightmarish imaginings to each other. As the subsequent action shows, their fantasies seem to each so peculiar that they may not be spoken of, though, in fact, they may contain quintessential truths. Solness, we already know, has half convinced himself that he is mad because of his dark broodings—and he suspects Aline of believing him so. Aline contemplates death and diverts all her vital impulses into nostalgic reverie rooted in her infancy.

One of the most intriguing and agonizing questions which the action of *The Master Builder* shapes for us is whether Hilde realizes that both Solness and Aline confide to her, and her alone, what they perceive as the causes of their private convictions of guilt. There is, at the deepest level of the play, the suggestion that if Solness and Aline could be as candid in speaking to each other about their guilt as they are to Hilde, they might effect a mutual catharsis and even a reconciliation in a renewal of their love. It is only to Hilde that, in Acts II and III, Solness confesses what he believes about the pollution of his will, for which he cannot disown responsibility. And it is also to Hilde only, in Act III, that Aline confides that her will to keep the children alive was sapped by the destruction of those symbols of her girlhood happiness—the nine little dolls with which she secretly played even after marriage, and without which her womanhood became misery. Perhaps because Hilde too is spiritually blinded, because she has ambitions for Solness which preclude any possibility of the reconciliation of husband and wife, or even because she is too inexperienced to see the consequences of her actions, Hilde does nothing to heal the wounds of the Solnesses, though she alone could. And ponderings such as these call into question everything about Hilde herself—including whether we should admire her or detest her for seeming to see glory in asking Solness to achieve "the impossible" whilst appearing to neglect one great opportunity to perform, as an intermediary between Solness and Aline, a difficult, though apparently possible, act of wondrous healing.

Before Hilde joins them, however, the Solnesses move from their moment of harmony to the anguish of mutual misunderstanding and recrimination. It is as though the "fosterchild" they had imagined sleeping peacefully were a troll, infecting their house, which is no home, with the sinister peculiarity of her dreams. As we discover subsequently, Hilde has been experiencing, in her nursery room, the excitement of a recurrent dream. It is of a kind that would interest Freudian analysts, for it is centered on falling from great heights in the foetal position. In strictly dramatic terms, Hilde's dream is strikingly evocative: it suggests the children possibly endangered by Solness—Hilde herself as an adolescent as well as the two sons for whose deaths Solness has long felt responsible; it suggests a fascination with death and, because Solness will tell Hilde that he has similar dreams, implies that the most fundamental bond between them may be a longing for death; it suggests trollish perversion of the will because Hilde, like Solness, finds "exciting" what to others would be ghastly nightmare. And yet this shared recurrent dream also suggests the triumph of a victorious death—a *liebestod*.

Solness, who is soon to assent, with every show of gladness, to Hilde's demands of him, gives, in his quarrel with Aline, every appearance of being cut to the heart by her insistence that, build as he will, he can never build her a home. Aline, believing apparently that Solness has not truly built the new house for her happiness, as he claims, but for some other reason known to him alone, seems equally devastated.

What we witness in this duologue in Act II—the only conversation of any consequence between Solness and Aline—is the dramatic enactment of the raking among ashes of the poem "They Sat There, Those Two," which Ibsen left among his preparatory notes for the play. In McFarlane's literal translation, it reads as follows:

> They sat there, those two, in so snug a house in autumn and in winter days. Then the house burnt. All lies in ruins. Those two must rake in the ashes.
>
> For among them a jewel is hidden, a jewel that can never burn. And if they search diligently, it might perhaps be found by him or her.
>
> But even if this fire-scarred pair ever do find that precious fireproof jewel—she will never find her burnt faith, he never his burnt happiness.

In the play, the Solnesses do seem to have been truly happy in the early days of their marriage. There is no hint whatever that Solness married Aline as Allmers marries Rita, for money. During the action they seem actually to expose the lost jewel of their mutual trust and love to our eyes, as to Hilde's, but—with dreadful irony—not to their own. Also we, like Solness, continue to doubt whether he will ever rediscover happiness; and we are as unsure, ultimately, as Aline herself, about her lost faith—which, in its context, seems to mean faith in a vocation.

The duologue ends in horror. Aline's insistence that Solness alone can explain why he has built the new home drives him back into what he perceives as guilt and causes him to shout that he is, "A madman . . .! A lunatic!" Aline seeks to understand—"What is behind all this?" she soon asks, genuinely wishing to know and probably not, as Solness seems to imagine, implying a reproach—but she can neither comprehend nor help him in his suffering. Solness's protestations, in which he dare not be specific, only give Aline, not unreasonably, cause to believe that he really is insane:

Solness.	There's nothing behind it. I've never done you any wrong. Never knowingly, never deliberately, that is. And yet—I feel weighed down by a great crushing sense of guilt.
Mrs. Solness.	Guilt . . . on my account?
Solness.	Mainly on your account.
Mrs. Solness.	Then you are . . . sick after all, Halvard.

The ultimate horror consists of more than the apprehension of possible insanity, of more even than that Solness and Aline have suffered a diabolical infection of the will. It is rooted, as we are to learn, in the doubtfulness of any worthwhile purpose for living at all, for either Solness or Aline. It is manifest in Solness's conviction that the demands of his supposed vocation have lain waste Aline's, and in Aline's apparent fear that she has never truly entered the adult world.

Aline's calling, as Solness, not she, describes it, is also the one that Ibsen insisted, when addressing the Norwegian Women's Rights League, was the most appropriate for the female feminists of his day and for women in general—motherhood.[23] Solness never speaks with more ardour or more lyricism than when he declares to Hilde, in Act II, that Aline had a

> . . . talent for building children's souls. . . . So building their souls that they might grow straight and fine, nobly and beautifully formed, to their full human stature.

Just as St. Paul, in the parable of the building of the immaterial Church in Corinth (I Corinthians iii, 9–23), perceives as vested in himself, a master builder, a gift of grace from God, the supreme architect, so Solness seems to see in Aline a similar divine gift for building souls. One of the most dreadful ironies in the play is that Solness, whose words seem to echo the Pauline parable, appears to apply its judgements so imperfectly to himself. There is, according to St. Paul, a promise of salvation even for those whose ill-conceived buildings, misusing the foundation of Christ, will be destroyed by fire. But destruction awaits those who "defile the temple," as Solness seems to do in declaring himself a master builder with no allegiance to any deity.

His belief, unshakable it seems, in an essentially Christian vocation for Aline necessarily throws all Solness's convictions about his own vocation, which he himself defines in anti-Christian terms, into appalling doubt. If he has, in the pursuit of his own supposed calling, turned Aline's "talent for building . . . souls" into "a charred heap of ruins", as he also asserts, what certainty can he have that he was truly called to build anything? And if he was so called, must it not have been by some other god (or even devil) opposed in every way to the goals of Aline's at once common and inspired calling, as Solness sees it?

What Solness saw, or believes he saw, in Aline was the capacity to make a home which would have been a spiritual fortress or castle (*en borg*), built on the bedrock of religious faith and human love—a home such as those which Pastor Straamand convincingly extols in *Love's Comedy* and which Peer envies the uncomplicated sailors in the last act of *Peer Gynt*. (None of these homes, by the way, has any kind of architectural distinction.) Yet he is half convinced that he was right to defy the God of Aline's supposed calling because, as Solness perceived it, He was inscrutably associated with the death of the twins—so that Solness would dedicate all the energies of his own soul to the building of churches. So he attempted to build "homes for people" without reference to any deity. And Hilde persuades him that his final interpretation of his vocation—building a paradoxical "castle in the air on a firm foundation"—is both god-like and possibly a tribute to metaphysical forces other than those acknowledged by Aline. Only Hilde can ever feel certain of his victory.

The orientation of Aline's life is, however, much more dubious than Solness generously believes. And when she confides to Hilde, in Act III, that what she found hardest to accept about the fire was not the loss of the twins but of her "nine lovely dolls," the doubtfulness is fully evident. Ironically, it is all the more clear because it seems to indicate that, like Hilde herself, Aline is strongly attached to a girlhood dream. But whereas Hilde's dream is passionate, daring, and full of action, Aline's is peaceful, retiring, and suggestive of emotion recollected in tranquillity. The conversation about the dolls is so moving—and so charged with irony—that it deserves full quotation:

> Mrs. Solness. No, no, Miss Wangel. . . . Don't talk to me any more about my two little boys. We need not be sad about them. They are happy where they are—so happy now. No, it's the small losses in life that cut deep into the heart. Losing things that other people think nothing of.
>
> Hilde [puts her arms on Mrs. Solness's knee and looks affectionately up at her]. Dear Mrs. Solness, tell me! What things?
>
> Mrs. Solness. Just little things. Like I said. All the old portraits on the walls were burnt. And all the old silk dresses were burnt. Things that had been in the family for years and years. And all Mother's and Grandmother's lace—that was burnt too. And even the jewels! [Sadly.] And all the dolls.
>
> Hilde. The dolls?
>
> Mrs. Solness [choking with tears]. I had nine lovely dolls.
>
> Hilde. And they were burnt too?
>
> Mrs. Solness. All of them. Oh, I found that hard—so hard.

Hilde.	Had you put them all away, then? From when you were little?
Mrs. Solness.	Not put away. The dolls and I had gone on living together.
Hilde.	After you had grown up?
Mrs. Solness.	Yes, long after that.
Hilde.	And after you were married, too?
Mrs. Solness.	Oh, yes. As long as he didn't see, it was . . . But then they all got burnt, poor things. Nobody thought of saving *them*. Oh, it's so sad when you think about it. Now, you mustn't laugh at me, Miss Wangel.
Hilde.	I'm not laughing.
Mrs. Solness.	Because in a way they too were living things, you know. I carried them under my heart. Like little unborn children.

Hilde appears to doubt Aline's capacity for any kind of positive adult life. Her question about putting the dolls away suggests St. Paul's remark, which also appears in the First Epistle to the Corinthians, about the need, as an adult, to put away childish things (I Corinthians xiii, II). Aline had gone on playing with the dolls, secretly, after childhood had passed, even after marriage had begun. She is perhaps therefore much closer in spirit to Lord Sebastian Flyte in *Brideshead Revisited*, who is so deeply attached to his teddy bear, than to Solness's ideal of motherhood.

And yet playing with dolls does not make Aline a certain victim of infantilism any more than her wish to be a princess inevitably makes Hilde one. There is the suggestion in the very number of the dolls—nine, (which brings to mind all the nines that Sylvia Plath manages to incorporate into her poem about pregnancy, "Metaphors") and in Aline's last, profoundly touching remark about carrying the dolls, "in a way . . . too . . . living things" beneath her heart "like little unborn children," that had the Solness marriage ever been essentially right, the dolls of Aline's fantasy could have become children who would have grown to physical and spiritual maturity rather than the two little boys who lived only twenty days and were, dreadfully, poisoned by their mother's own milk. Of course, we cannot know this, but the theory of psychological "displacement," according to which a minor matter (like the burning of dolls) looms largest in a grievously troubled mind while traumatic experience (like the death of one's children) is suppressed, could apply to Aline, and would support Solness's belief in her maternal vocation. In its context, in the third act, what Aline's fantasy about the dolls does is to confirm nothing but to leave us wondering whether Aline is a woman never loved sufficiently to become the mother she might have been or is an over-grown child unable, even with a husband's love, to grow up.

Similarly, of course, we may be wondering whether Solness could have succeeded as a husband and father where his various achievements as a master builder are all questionable, and even, perhaps, whether Hilde could have found a more genuinely fulfilling life in the village where all her schoolgirl friends, for all we know, stayed. She alone, it seems, conceives a need to leave home, to wound her father by defying his authority, and to seek her fortune in a strange kind of adultery.

When, in Act II, Solness and Aline conclude their verbal raking among the ashes, they do so because Hilde has arrived, and Aline's almost immediate departure is marked by a barbed comment that recognizes only the danger in the guest who slept in the nurseries. Hilde will have much to tell Solness about her dreams when the two of them are alone, Aline suggests, because he has "known [Hilde] so long. Ever since she was a child. . . ."

After Aline has gone, Hilde and Solness commence their first great duologue, and in it, as Aline foresaw, he reviews his life with very different results from those which emerged from his heart-searching with her. Rarely, even in Ibsen, is it more difficult than it is here to distinguish between what is truth—exalted or mundane—and what is illusion, pretence, egomania, or *folie à deux*.

There is, within the pathos of a husband's lingering loyalty to his wife, an intense dramatic irony: Solness assures Hilde that she would never detect hostility in Aline "if only she [Hilde] could get to know her [Aline] properly . . ." But it is Aline's reference, shortly before her departure, to "duty" that stings Hilde into a display of what can be either admired as her daring independence of spirit or viewed as a demonstration of the fearfully tenuous nature of her grasp on reality. The word "duty" (*pligt* in Norwegian) sounds "cold and sharp and prickly" to Hilde because it is associated with conventional ethics and conventional religion, which she despises. As we see in the conversation about the dolls, Hilde is appalled to see that Aline believes literally that God brought about the deaths of the twins so that He could receive them into heaven. But long before that, it is clear that Hilde, though she is apparently too ill-read to name such deities herself, wishes Solness to affirm with her that Dionysus, not Jehovah, should triumph, or at least that the Dionysian element in human nature is worthier than any deity who demands denial of self and duty to others.

Hilde, it seems, has, or believes she has, nothing to learn from a priest any more than from her father, a doctor, whose house she is eventually to describe as a cage. Moreover, she and Solness both affirm that there is nothing they can learn from books: discussing reading specifically, they agree that they "can't really see any point in it." For some, perhaps,

Solness and Hilde might seem as capable of existential survival as the Caesar of Shaw's *Caesar and Cleopatra*, who actually rejoices when informed of the burning of the Library at Alexandria. For others, both Solness and Hilde will seem as ill-equipped as Peer Gynt for existential journeys. Venturing into mysteries they can scarcely name, Solness and Hilde certainly have comical as well as heroic aspects in their self-willed isolation.

As though to establish that the heady visions of splendour that are to come should be recognized as of unclear value, Ibsen introduces two keenly ironic elements: one is the issue of what should be done about Ragnar Brovik's demand for recognition; the other is the imaginative use that Ibsen makes of the quarry.

Hilde, having dismissed Solness's library as useless, "turns over some of the papers" in the folder of designs done by Ragnar Brovik. She does not examine them thoroughly—indeed, she says she is incapable of making any decision about him based on "these bits and pieces." But she is sure—if only because he has been a pupil to Solness—that Ragnar must be "frightfully clever." We know that Ragnar is certainly frighteningly clever in the estimation of Solness, who comments cryptically to Hilde about his employee, "I can use him." The ironies run deeper than this, however, for although Hilde takes up Ragnar's cause, knowing as little about architecture as Rebecca West does about politics, it is only seconds after doing so that she informs the master builder, as though she were addressing a Nietzschean superman, that he and he alone should "be allowed to build." Of course there may be no inconsistency here if Hilde's notion of Solness as a builder is as particularized as it certainly seems to have been at Lysanger—and may be again when he ascends his last tower—having more to do, that is, with sublimated sex than with bricks and mortar. Ragnar could be allowed to get on with actual building, and Solness with whatever sexual and spiritual aspects of their relations his high towers symbolically express for Hilde. But even if Hilde sees her master builder as one whose materials are flesh and spirit rather than bricks and mortar, there is still something ludicrous, though both credible and convincing, about her vacillations between the charitable impulses she feels for Ragnar, and later Aline, and the egotism she encourages in Solness no less than in herself.

No one should be surprised at the conflict between pagan (Dionysian or Viking) and residual Christian values that is evident in Hilde, for it has received much critical attention. Its ridiculous aspects appears to have been overlooked, however, as has the sheer ludicrousness of the quarry.

To see the quarry for what it is, one need only recall E. M. Forster's assurances, made in 1928,[24] and the wealth of supporting critical comment made since then, that every aspect of Ibsen's landscapes is charged with significances suggestive of his intense spiritual life. Surely the quarry is not merely realistic. At both the realistic and the symbolic levels, it is a manifestation of the element of the absurd that was a permanent feature of Ibsen's artistic temperament. It is impossible to believe that successful businessmen like Karsten Bernick or Haakon Werle—the sort of people who know much about land, public approbation, and the strength or weakness of the individual will—would have chosen such a site for a house intended to manifest success. Solness's quarry, however, so close to his new house as to constitute a danger to any of its inhabitants—or visitors—is one of Ibsen's best visual jokes. The humour is black, similar to that of the crippling of Little Eyolf, whose bizarre babyhood misfortune it is to fall from a table where he has been left while his unheedful parents give themselves over to sexual abandon. What a fall was there! It is one no more in accordance with good nineteenth-century European taste in matters of high tragedy than the wildest humour of *Peer Gynt*, Vilhelm Foldal's being run over by Fanny Wilton's speeding sleigh as he tries to bid farewell to his fleeing daughter in *John Gabriel Borkman*, or Arnold Rubek and Irene's interruption by an avalanche as they attempt to ascend the peak of mystical love in *When We Dead Awaken*.

It is with precisely such humour that Ibsen continuously deflates heroic pretensions, as we have seen. Tragic heroes commonly fall, metaphorically at least, from the great heights where the gods or Fortune's wheel have placed them; Solness, a tragicomic figure, must fall from the height where his incomprehensible "luck" has placed him, not only the length of a spire and a tower but into the bowels of the earth to a grotesque death in unnatural surroundings. "His head is all smashed in. . . . He fell right into the quarry," people comment, like a distraught Chorus.

When Solness points out to Hilde this singularly unsuitable site for the home of an artist who has seemingly spent most of his career seeking to establish harmony between human and external nature, we are not left to guess what Hilde is looking at. "See there?" says Solness, "Over there in the garden . . .?" And again, "Just beyond where they've been quarrying. . . ." But Hilde makes no comment that might indicate a touch of practical judgement: she is too intent on worming information from Solness about nurseries in the new house. She has begun to suspect his sanity in ways which might make him an unsuitable object of her exclusive attentions. It is important that neither Hilde nor Solness sees anything inherently ridiculous about the site, for their blindness to most external phenomena strengthens the apprehensions one may already have of their immersion in what Begriffenfeldt, in *Peer Gynt*, terms "the barrel of self."

It is important also that when Solness tells her more about his life and career, Hilde sits so that she can see Solness, the garden, and the new house, with the quarry at its foot. Emlyn Williams's adaptation of the play—the text used in Peter Wood's 1964 production—has Solness *stand* between Hilde and the view of the new house, which she can see behind him through the windows of the old. This is entirely appropriate as a means of emphatically placing Solness—now heroically envisioned by Hilde as lover, hero, or superman—against a visual embodiment of his perilous spiritual condition.

What Solness tells Hilde has often, and surely correctly, been interpreted biographically in the sense that the phases of Solness's work as an architect may be seen to parallel those of Ibsen as a playwright. Intriguingly, one of the most convincing of such interpretations goes further than the usual identification of Solness's church-building period with Ibsen's early metaphysical plays (including *Brand* and *Peer Gynt*), his "homes for people" period with the realistic social plays (from *Pillars of Society* to *Hedda Gabler*), and his "castles in the air" period with the four final plays. Arne Røed suggests that the autobiographical allegory is so specific as to equate the Solness twins with *Emperor and Galilean* (the only two-part play Ibsen every wrote, and the one which, though ostensibly regarded by him as his masterpiece, has had an abortive theatrical history), Hilde with the Dionysian aspects of Ibsen's work (which, Røed suggests, Ibsen may have been conscious of betraying in *Rosmersholm*), and Aline with Solness's own innermost poetic powers. This interpretation is particularly interesting in that, unlike so many others, it sees Aline as both a complex and ultimately positive character.[25]

The evidence for biographical interpretation is strong, but it remains for critics espousing the biographical approach to consider fully that the treatment of Solness evinces not only a painful self-analysis by Ibsen but one which is as slyly humorous as should be expected from the author of *Peer Gynt* and *The Wild Duck*. Part of Solness's tragicomic predicament is exactly what he shares with Peer, Borkman, and Rubek, for instance. All are unwilling poets, and all are struck down either because they betrayed their vocations or because their poetry is displeasing to whatever power it is that, in the last plays, appears, unceremoniously, to knock Solness from his perch on top of a tower, to reach out and crush Borkman's heart with an iron hand, and to set thousands of tons of rock and snow in motion to kill Rubek and Irene.

Solness speaks to Hilde in Act II of his supposed guilt, of his attempts to create "warm, cheerful, comfortable homes, where fathers and mothers and their children could live together, secure and happy," and of the price—in the heart's-blood of others and of himself—that he has paid for his supposed good fortune. And at the centre of his brooding is "the great and terrible question" whether in destroying Aline's appetite for life, he is to blame for having destroyed one whose calling was nobler than his own. He hopes he may be innocent while clearly suspecting that he is not. And when he ponders the origin of the mystical "helpers and servants," who, he believes, did for him what he willed but could not execute alone, he describes his anguish as follows:

> ... let me tell you what that sort of luck feels like. It feels as if my breast were a great expanse of raw flesh. And these helpers and servants go flaying off skin from other people's bodies to patch *my* wound. Yet the wound never heals ... never! Oh, if only you knew how it sometimes burns and throbs.

The image recalls Prometheus, of course, in terms which can scarcely be missed. Orley Holtan sees one of Solness's mythic aspects as that of "a Promethean rebel, defying God for the well-being of man."[26] This reading, which mentions also the similarities between the sufferings of Prometheus and those of Christ, is one that has some credibility. And yet it is not really appropriate to allude so certainly to God: Ibsen does not so definitely identify the deity here any more than he does in, for instance, *Brand* or *Peer Gynt*, or in any of the plays which succeeded *The Master Builder*. If he did, much more reference would have to be paid to the specific theology of both the Old and New Testaments in relation to Ibsen's knowledge and use of them. When Solness tells Hilde, in Act III, that he intends again to defy a deity from the tower of his new house, he says he will address a "Great and Mighty Lord." But that Lord is not indisputably Jehovah, or God the Father. Neither does it make good sense simply to equate Solness's unclearly envisioned Lord with Zeus, the latter being signally impossible to associate with either Judaic or Christian ethics, which do seem to play some part in Solness's fall. Solness's "Great and Mighty Lord" has as many possible spiritual identities as Solness himself—including those of total nullity and poet, *digter*.

And if one pays careful attention to what Solness says, the Promethean identity is also less exact than is often supposed. Solness suffers horribly and, he believes, for others, but he does not pay for his supposed disobedience with only his own flesh, ever renewing itself as it is torn away, as Prometheus does; his flesh is, he says, renewed with that ripped by the "helpers and servants" *from the bodies of others*. In other words, his sufferings do not bring solace to mankind, they do not appease any clearly perceived deity, and certainly they bring no clear promise of redemption. Instead, they bring more pain and more doubt to himself and others. And Solness's vision of himself is as much that of unwilling predator as of aspiring saviour. Solness's mythic identity has associations, then, with the god who saved mankind with the gift of fire, with the God who died in agony on the Cross, and, as Holtan interestingly demonstrates, with the sacrificial kings of primitive religions.[27] But his identity is not composite but amorphous, one which, in the end, is as ambivalent—and as much susceptible to the ludicrous—as is that of Solness's "Lord" or Peer Gynt's Great Boyg. It is not for nothing that both Solness and Hilde are fascinated by the lure of "the impossible," which, among other things, may be that which cannot be understood as an integral part of any coherent mythic pattern with an inherent teleology.

It may be precisely because Hilde, with some of Aline's ability to track a wounded creature by its scent, senses the full horror of these ambivalences that she decides to do all she can to reinforce the master builder's will to believe that he is innocent, that his life has made some kind of sense, and that his next ascent shall be a triumph of will. On the other hand, it is equally possible to see Hilde's steeling of Solness's will in negative ways.

What Hilde really makes of Solness's contradictory claims is impossible ultimately to know. He thinks he may be, as he tells her, one of the "people [who] have been singled out, specially chosen, gifted with the power and the ability to *want* something, to *desire* something, to *will* something . . . so insistently . . . and so ruthlessly . . . that they inevitably get it in the end." He insists, in Act II, that his helpers and servants come only when they are summoned. But later, in Act III, he claims that he is possessed by demons and not that he summons them. And he evades Hilde's specific question about their identity. Part of what Hilde does, for whatever motive, is clear, however: she decides to try to convince Solness of the need for a "thoroughly robust" conscience.

Fascinatingly, the situation in Act II in which Hilde embarks upon this task is very close to that in which Solveig comes to Peer to try to provide her faltering hero with a sustaining ideal. Hilde speaks of feeling summoned by Solness, just as Solveig says to Peer that unspoken messages "came [to her] in storm and in stillness." Hilde tells Solness that "leaving Father wasn't all that easy. I'm terribly fond of him," just as Solveig tells Peer that leaving her father was dreadful. And both Hilde and Solveig speak of having left a family home to establish a new, more exalted dwelling. Both heroines believe that their life's work is to restore spiritual wholeness to the man each loves. The vast difference is not, of course, that Solveig's way is undoubtedly right and Hilde's undoubtedly wrong, but that whereas Solveig seems to embody all that is most uplifting about Christian love, Hilde is apparently driven by Dionysian impulses which offer a promise of fulfilment through the uninhibited expression of orgastic desire. And each character may be seen as embodying one element of the religious synthesis which Ibsen's Julian seeks, unsuccessfully, in his "third empire."

Fascinatingly also, Hilde is explicit about being conscious of an element of evil in the summons. "Something inside me forced me, drove me here. Drew me, *tempted* me too" (the Norwegian word is *lokket*, which means "enticed," "tempted," or "seduced"). In Solveig's case we must, from the situation alone, decide whether Peer's attraction for her has a negative constituent.

It is Hilde's declaration that Solness must have a "robust conscience" that prompts Solness to speak of Vikings who "sailed to foreign lands and plundered . . . burned and killed." Hilde is excited by this, as she is also by Solness's references to capture and rape. And she is thinking of the excitement not of "taking women," as Solness specifically asks her, but that of *"being* taken," as she emphatically asserts. When Hilde speaks later in this act, therefore, about her being a predatory bird which can seize prey and hold it firmly in her talons, she is envisioning love-making which has the violence of partners who are both predators and both prey. The image is strikingly similar to that used by the persona of Marvell's "To His Coy Mistress," in which the lovers will, the persona asserts, "tear [their] pleasures with rough strife/Thorough the iron gates of life." Not the least remarkable feature of *The Master Builder* is that it deals with sexual passion with all the forcefulness of Marvell or Donne, and, despite all that Victorian prudery could do, it implies, through symbolism which is as astute in its avoidance of vulgarity as it is candid in its subtlety, that one way to spiritual fulfilment is through physical excess. There is, however, something about the violent athleticism of Hilde's erotic imagery which is, again like that of the imagery of Marvell's persona, comically suggestive of sexual inexperience or, at the very least, immaturity. The idea that spiritual maturity may follow sensual excess is not in itself, of course, an unusual one in the nineteenth century: it is to be found in Kierkegaard, Blake, Wagner, and Shaw, for example. It is not foreign to the Bible itself, as the parable of the Prodigal Son makes clear. What is remarkable about its appearance in *The Master Builder*, therefore, is certainly not its novelty, but, as usual in Ibsen, its ambivalent treatment. Peer may be excluded from hell—which he prefers to extinction—because his sins, as he confesses them, in comical circumstances, do not seem to Satan significant enough to merit Peer's spiritual recognition. Surely we should ask the same question about Solness and Hilde's shared dream and about Solness's enactment of an "impossible" deed which they perceive as defiance: is it significant enough to secure an entrance to any place where souls may be imagined to sustain their identities? Perhaps the best that can be said is that the chances are about even. If nowhere else than in the disunified consciousness of our own culture, Solness and Hilde have attained lasting life as poetic archetypes: one wonders what they would make of such "glory." And even such limited triumph as this (which can hardly have been in the minds of such admittedly non-literary types as Hilde and Solness) does not necessarily exclude an inherent taint of ridicule. All Solness says about Vikings may not be much closer to his actual experience than the fantasies about Mohammed which Peer acts out, with laughable results, for Anitra are to his. And Hilde's ecstatic dreams of being possessed by a "wild brute" she had "grown really fond of" are just as likely to be the overheated products of a too suggestive young woman's muddled imagination as the basis of any kind of ascent to lasting glory.

Even as Solness and Hilde are attaching wings to their romantic dream or illusion—Solness seeing Hilde as a wild, but gentle, forest bird, Hilde insisting on her right to talons—Hilde perceives again a need to do something about Ragnar's drawings. Only if Hilde's renewed concern about the signing of Ragnar's drawings is taken as solely a great romantic urge to rid Solness's path of all trivialities can it be seen as wholly unridiculous. In the context of the more sceptical responses which the play also invites, vacillation is suggested and with more than a touch of the ridiculous; it is part of the evidence that Hilde, for all her wish for the robust conscience of a predator, is sadly confused. She does not seem able to leave Solness's wounded prey alone. She seems to wish, like Gregers Werle, to salvage creatures whom, in some sense, she believes she "knows," from their swamp—and so, with expressions of charitable concern, she obliges Solness to sign the drawings. If she knows she is driving Solness to his death, as seems likely—he tells her that a successful Ragnar would "have [him] down in the dust" and "break" him—Hilde's only rational concern for wishing Ragnar's drawings endorsed is that his father shall die happy. After Solness's approaching death (in the body or spirit or both), Ragnar will have no competition and therefore no need for Solness's signed permission to practice his profession. It seems certain that what Hilde cannot bear is the loss of her dream of Solness. And that, of course, makes her as suitable a target as Solness himself for the ridicule she appears to pour upon his unpracticality. When he speaks of his luck turning—and, again, of retribution being inevitable—Hilde "fearfully, holding her hands over her ears," exclaims, "Don't say things like that! Do you want to kill me? Do you want to rob me of more than life itself?" For Hilde, whatever it is about Solness that transcends living reality is her dream. But the play leaves open the question whether that dream is a vision of ineffable truth or a grotesque delusion.

Solness, towards the end of the act, is aware that the ground is crumbling under him: "Are you quite sure it isn't some kind of dream," he asks Hilde, "some kind of fantasy that's taken hold of you?" He has not yet quite lost his grip on reason, itself no certain guide for the soul. But he is doing so, and in the very same passage, the closing lines of Act II, he sees Hilde as a fairy-tale princess and himself as a knight mounting to the "topmost room in the tower," where she, Rapunzel-like, awaits him. If Åse could return from whatever mysterious regions her soul haunts and be at his elbow, she might have some peasant wisdom to impart about those who take refuge in fairy-stories; on the other hand, the poetry of Solness's air-castle may contain truths not accessible to an old peasant woman who is as preoccupied when dying as when living with social status.

The last part of Act II, after Hilde's passionate outcry about wishing to retain her dreams, is ironically packed with solid mundane concerns: Ragnar's drawings; Aline's shopping; Solness's callous dismissal of Kaja (which looks more like crude brutality than aristocratic transcendence of the manners of the herd); Aline's unintentionally comical observation that Solness gets dizzy on their first-floor balcony. The comedy of all that is incongruous with the sublime aspect of Solness and Hilde's dream reinforces the ambivalence of their last observation in this act: the wreath shall be placed, declares Solness, with more truth than he may know, over the new house, which "will never be a home for [him]." And Hilde finds the prospect "terribly exciting."

Act III moves with great speed towards a climax as vertiginous for spectators as for Solness. But it has intimations of comparative calm. They are present in recollections: in Aline's extraordinary conversation with Hilde about the dolls and in Solness's fullest account to Hilde of what he recalls of his spiritual state when he climbed the tower at Lysanger. As we have already seen, however, these interludes of comparative stillness offer no assurances, no lucid epiphanies.

The setting of the act is entirely appropriate to the border territory between realism and surrealism that the play occupies even more clearly as the action moves to its fullest climax. It is, both visually and symbolically, complex and well worth detailed scrutiny:[28]

A large broad verandah belonging to Solness's house. Left, part of the house can be seen, with a door leading out on to the verandah. Right, the railings of the verandah. At the back, a flight of steps leads down from the narrow end of the verandah to the garden below. Tall old trees in the garden extend their branches over the verandah and towards the house. Extreme right, in among the trees, a glimpse is caught of the lower part of the new villa, with scaffolding round the tower section. In the background, the garden is bounded by an old wooden fence. Beyond the fence is a street with mean dilapidated cottages.

What the eye and the mind are aware of here are contrasts—in height, age, and clarity. The verandah on the house where all the action takes place is at a modest height: the ladies who come to witness the topping-out ceremony with Aline can stand here feeling perfectly secure, though, ironically, it is the one where Solness—even in the usual course of things—has been observed to suffer dizziness. The trees, the oldest things we see, seem to reach out towards this verandah; they remind us of Aline's original home and perhaps, with some shadowy dignity, of Aline's past emotional security. We do not see much of the new house—it is obscured by some of the trees—but the glimpse of the scaffolding around the tower reminds us of heights which are all the more mysterious because not seen. Ibsen, whether conscious of the phallic implications of the tower or not, discreetly avoids crude farce by not allowing the tower to be fully visible or too obviously Rabelaisian. Similarly, the quarry, also not visible but known to be there, should complement the tower by suggesting mystic depths, but again while avoiding explicitness.

There are two surprises about this elaborate set: one is that we see nothing whatever of the "homes for people" that Solness claims to have built at such a cost in human misery and to such financial advantage; the other is that we see, clearly, though in the background, ugly reminders—the "mean dilapidated cottages"—of the lives of a kind of people whom Solness's aspirations seem never to have included at all.

In the foreground, therefore, the verandah suggests the conventional life from which both Solness and Hilde are in full flight. The old trees suggest a way of living—easy, even luxurious, but otherwise uncertain and, in any case, finished with. The implications of the new house and tower, though the centre of interest, are unclear despite the certainty that Solness and Hilde have fixed their fondest hopes there. And the poverty-stricken cottages which were there, it seems, before the Solness marriage, and are still there twelve years later, are either a standing reproach to the high-flown aspirations of Solness, so high above the misery of common humanity, or an indication that a hero in a world such as ours must learn to be unencumbered by pity—as Hilde frequently observes. The total invisibility of the "homes for people," financially "substantial" people that is, for whom Solness claims to have suffered so much, may suggest that Solness is right to have excluded them, as philistines, from his consciousness. It may also suggest his flight from unpleasant reality to "a castle in the air" with no foundation more substantial than the clouds, ever-changing shape, that Peer Gynt describes in one of his most fanciful soliloquies.

When imagining Solness climbing the scaffolding of the tower, we should be aware that in the play that follows, *Little Eyolf*, Borghejm does not feel any compulsion to omit "substantial" people from his vision of things, which seems to have spiritual integrity though no marked aesthetic orientation, and Alfred and Rita Allmers appear to be moving in the right direction when they abandon their previous preoccupations (with abstract ethics and grand erotic passion, respectively) to devote themselves to helping just such people as those who live in the "mean dilapitated cottages" of this set.

The Master Builder does not have a strong social leaning, but Solness and Hilde are not allowed—any more than Rosmer and Rebecca are, for example—to develop their visions in a vacuum. Solness and Hilde seem to believe that their destiny as individuals inevitably removes them from ties with the rest of humanity. But, as is always true in Ibsen—even in *When We Dead Awaken*, which is surely the least socially specific of all Ibsen's works—isolation from people is as likely to indicate egotistical obsession as heroic independence.

As we have seen, Hilde's conversation with Aline about the dolls brings her as close as we ever come to knowing the master builder's wife. And ironically, although it shows Aline's tenderness and her desire to befriend Hilde, it reduces the latter to a state of deep melancholy. Hilde tells Solness, immediately after the conversation and foreshadowing again Irene in *When We Dead Awaken*, that she feels as though she has just arisen from a grave: the frost has seized her bones, she tells him, foreshadowing also the death of John Gabriel Borkman. But the central dramatic importance of Hilde's experience is that it seems to cause her deliberately and knowingly to pollute whatever integrity there is in her relationship with Solness. When he wishes to know whether Aline was grieving about the dead twins, Hilde, seeming to understand fully that Aline was not, first tries to evade an answer in statuesque silence—upon which Solness comments—and then nods her head.

It is impossible to know for sure her motives for this lie. The desire she expresses to leave Solness reminds us of Rebecca West's similar decision in the last act of *Rosmersholm*: it seems like evasion, even panic. Perhaps, on the other hand, she is speaking the truth when she says that she cannot hurt someone she "knows" (Aline). But if this is true, one wonders why she lies about Aline in a way that would seem certain to deprive Aline even more effectively of Solness's understanding, though, as we have seen, there is good reason to doubt whether Hilde does understand Aline's complex state of guilt and unhappiness.

Whether Hilde deliberately suppresses whatever she understands about Aline for reasons we never learn, or is in a state of bemused shock that prevents her from thinking at all, is uncertain. What is sure is that she moves, almost immediately, from an apparent determination not to interfere between husband and wife to what may be a wish, conscious or not, to set free powers that she knows may be murderous.

It seems to be Solness's talk, not now of spirits that do his bidding but of his possession by trolls utterly beyond his control—trolls that, like vampires, "drained [Aline] of all her life's blood," and then chained him alive to the corpse—that decides Hilde's course. She certainly contemplates, momentarily, getting rid of Aline: she reminds us of Rebecca West's virtual murder of Beate Rosmer when she says:

Oh, this whole busines is so stupid, so absolutely stupid. . . .

And again:

This not daring to reach out and lay hold on happiness. On life! Just because standing in the way happens to be somebody one knows!

But the effect of exercising her "robust conscience" so boldly causes her to become exhausted: in this state, she wishes that she could "fall asleep and leave the whole sorry business behind." It is clearly death as an escape—from confusion and from trying to force the refractory material of life's realities into a heroic mould—that she is yearning for here. And this time her own death, not Solness's.

She is roused from this troubled reverie by Solness's asking her, ridiculously enough, whether her home was happy! And it is this question which stirs the fury in Hilde. Her home was the cage, she says, from which she, the bird of prey that Solness ought to recognize, flew. Now comes the great dramatic duet in which Hilde seems, ironically, both to be urging her lover on to the heights of aspiration and demanding from him, like a distraught troll-child, the impossible—her kingdom, her castle in the air, and both immediately:

Hilde. . . . You owe me this kingdom. And surely any kingdom carries a castle with it, doesn't it?

Solness. [more and more animatedly]. Yes, that's generally the way.

Hilde. Good. Then build it for me! Quickly!

Solness. [laughs]. This very minute eh?

Hilde. Of course! Time's up! Ten years. And I'm not waiting any longer. So—bring out the castle, master builder!

Solness. It's no easy matter owing *you* anything, Hilde.

Hilde. You should have thought of that before. Now it's too late! So! [Beating on the table.] Out with the castle! It's *my* castle! I want it at once!

As the state of the lovers becomes ever more rapturous, the air castle becomes, at least as Hilde describes it, a place from which her princely lover can look down, like a superman, on the lowly folk still occupied, unprofitably it would seem, in building churches and houses. But, ironically, this castle will also be a place in which a "stupid" (Hilde's word) master builder may take refuge from reality and his "weak nerves" (Hilde's words again).

That there is an element of vengeance upon Solness—or upon life in general—in Hilde's attitudes to him at this point is impossible to prove or to deny: shortly after this she is incensed to hear from Ragnar that Kaja is claiming that Solness has possessed her mind for ever, and shocked by Ragnar's account of Solness's brutal oppression of himself and his father, the full extent of which she has not, it seems, realized. In this situation, Hilde, egged on by sexual jealousy and, incongruously but feasibly, also by pity for Solness's victims, could just as well be punishing Solness for having failed to live up to her expectations of him as urging him on to some kind of transcendental triumph. Neither can one rule out of consideration the possibility that Hilde may envisage Solness's fall—the risk of which she certainly appears to appreciate—as a kind of forced atonement both to herself and to Aline, the two women he may have immured in their girlhood fancies.

Deliberately, it seems, Ibsen now crowds the act with rapid movement, cursory conversations, and even the openly ridiculous sight of Aline scurrying about so "beset by duties" that she does not know which to attend to first. In the midst of all this, Solness gives Hilde his most detailed account of his defiance of a supposed deity at Lysanger and of his supposed punishment, which was to have a troll set loose within him that could "rampage about as it will." It is tempting to see in Hilde's urging Solness to perform the topping-out ceremony himself the possibility also that she is engineering his death to release him from his own misery.

When Solness climbs, Hilde repeats her behaviour at Lysanger (described by Solness himself as that of a "little devil") so exactly and, it would seem, in such full and certain knowledge of its danger, that it is difficult not to see her as knowingly causing the fall. But even here, we cannot be utterly sure because in Act I, Hilde speaks of her *own* dizziness when Solness was at the top of the tower in Lysanger and refuses to believe that he could have been dizzy. And in Act II, when Hilde is euphoric at the very thought of Solness climbing again, she explicitly states her refusal to believe that he could be a victim of vertigo. The possibility that Hilde deliberately instigates Solness's fall does not, however, strip Solness of conceivable glory in the moments before his death—or even in the fall itself. Nor does it necessarily mean that Hilde, even if she is, like Hjørdis in *Vikings at Helgeland*, a deliberate murderess, is only pretending to see triumph. Solness does stand at the very top of the tower; he does appear to dispute with a deity; Hilde does hear a "mighty song" in the air, and we have no reason to doubt the jubilation behind her ecstatic, "At last, At last! Now I see him great and free again!"

What we cannot be sure of is the nature of the forces which ultimately drive Solness to climb, to behave like a victor on top of his tower—and then to fall. No role that can be defined for him is free from underlying doubts and suggestions of the ridiculous that have accumulated since the moment of his grotesque treatment of Kaja Fosli in the first act. *Peer Gynt* is full of luxuriant visions, grown in Peer's heated imagination, of himself riding high in triumph, a triumph which has such incongruous constituents as imperial splendour, Christian humility, spiritual absolution, and erotic desire. And so it is with Solness, who, also like Peer, is seemingly redeemed when closest to death, within a woman's mind, and perhaps only there.

Ibsen is never more a dramatic poet, and a poet of the sublime and the ridiculous, than he is in presenting the final rise and descent of Solness. Using techniques, in the ending of *The Master Builder*, which are utterly characteristic of his prose plays at their finest and obvious precursors of the poetry in dramatic prose of Beckett and Pinter, for instance, he achieves, with astonishing economy, effects similar to those he attains in *Peer Gynt* through much more varied forms in verse. And it is in the full exploitation of three devices that Ibsen achieves the full range of tragicomic multiplicity at the end of the play: a central image—that of a weathercock; the contrapuntal reiteration of the prepositions and adverbs "up" and "down"; and the schematic juxtaposition of two equally valid but equally unendorsed and utterly irreconcilable views—the apprehensions of Solness's last performance of Hilde and Ragnar Brovik.

The weathercock image is richly suggestive, and it is used repeatedly in association with the two topping-out ceremonies. In Act I, Hilde recalls Solness's ascent at Lysanger as follows:

> Then you climbed straight up the scaffolding. Right to the very top. And you had a big wreath with you. And you hung that wreath right on top of the weathercock.

In Act III the image occurs in the remark which prefaces Solness's fullest acknowledgement of his defiance of supernatural power:

> And as I stood there on high, at the very top, and as I hung the wreath on the weathercock, I spoke to Him: Listen to me, Almighty One! From this day forward, I too will be free. A master builder in his own field, as you are in yours. Never again will I build churches for you. Only homes for the people.

And it occurs in Hilde's insistence, in her penultimate confrontation with Ragnar, upon Solness's imminent triumph:

Ragnar.   [smiles]. Oh? Where will we see him, then?

Hilde.   Right up high! High up by the weathercock is where you'll see him.

Weathercocks inevitably suggest the topmost heights of great churches and palaces, and therefore, symbolically, the pretensions to authority, both divine and human, of those who rule both church and state. But cockerels, brazen or feathered, also have earthier associations than eagles or ducks, for example. Judge Brack wants to be "the only cock in the yard" (literally "the only cock in the basket") for Hedda Gabler, but, in the end, is forced, by the suicide of the hen, from commanding the dirt-heap of his fantasies. Peer struts like a gamecock for Anitra and, with humour that both Ragnar and Solness lack, acknowledges that he ends by getting himself well and truly plucked. Solness's high aspirations do not necessarily obscure, and may indeed be sublimations of, desire and ambitions as proud but as ridiculous as Chanticleer's. And if Solness's aspirations remind us of a strutting rooster as well as of Dionysus and Prometheus, the sound of Hilde's "harps in the air" may clearly issue from lowly carnal as well as exalted spiritual sources. It is, in effect, the multiple, ironically contrasted associations of weathercocks which make the quotation from St. John's Gospel with which Hilde ultimately attests her faith in Solness so "dreadfully thrilling" (to use Hilde's favourite expression) in the most literal sense. The four words "Now it is finished" ("nu er det fullbrakt") as used by a woman who does not accept the validity of Christ's supreme sacrifice and who may, even as she utters the words, be experiencing a perverted form of physical ecstasy, are a fitting consummation to Solness's ambitions. They combine uncertain religious wonder with equally uncertain blasphemous irony. Exactly the same is true of the castles in the air topped with weathercocks that Peer Gynt constructs in his imagination.

In Pinter's works, where the underpinnings of realism are usually substantially demolished, we are used to hearing patterned dialogue in which repeated prepositions and adverbs take on surrealistic overtones and seem to place the action and the fate of characters, however vaguely, in an undefined metaphysical context. Perhaps no better example could be found than the "ups" and "downs" referring to Stanley and Meg Bowles's interest in him which recur in Meg's references to Stanley just before he first appears in *The Birthday Party*. In *The Master Builder* Hilde Wangel and Ragnar Brovik confront each other immediately before Solness climbs and immediately after he falls. And it is in the first of these duologues that we have "ups" and "downs" used as skilfully as they are in Pinter. The frequent use of word "up" together with "high" exactly counterbalances that of "down." *The Oxford Ibsen* translation represents this balance well, though not exactly as in the original, so there is some reason to quote both, with the words "up" (*op* or *oppe*) "high" (*høyt*), and "down" (*ned* or *nede*) italicized. The word *nedenfor* ("below") is included in the count of "downs."

Ragnar.	[with suppressed laughter, in a low voice]. Miss Wangel. . . . Do you see all those people *down* in the street?
Hilde.	Yes.
Ragnar.	They are all the other builders in training, come to watch the master.
Hilde.	What do they want to watch him for?
Ragnar.	They want to see him too scared to climb his own building.
Hilde.	So that's what the lads want, is it?
Ragnar.	[venomously and scornfully]. He's kept us *down* too long. Now we want to watch him having to stay *down*, too.

Hilde.	That's something you won't see. Not this time.
Ragnar.	[smiles]. Oh? Where will we see him then?
Hilde.	Right *up high!* *High up* by the weathercock is where you'll see him!
Ragnar.	[laughs]. Him! Don't you believe it!
Hilde.	He means to get to the top. And that's where you'll see him.
Ragnar.	He means to, yes! I'm prepared to believe that. But he just can't do it. He'll be dizzy long before he's got halfway. He'll have to crawl *down* again on his hands and knees!

In the Norwegian, it will be seen that the first "up" appears earlier:

Ragnar. [med undertrykt latter, halv sagte]. Frøken,—ser De alle de unge folkene *nede* på gaden?

Hilde. Ja.

Ragnar. Det er kammeraterne, som vil sé på mesteren.

Hilde. Hvad vil de sé på ham for da?

Ragnar. De vil sé på at han ikke tør stige *op* på sit eget hus.

Hilde. Nej, vil de det, de gutterne!

Ragnar. [harmfuld og hånlig]. Han har holdt os *nede* så længe, han. Nu vil vi sé på at han også værs 'go' får holde sig *nedenfor*.

Hilde. Det får De ikke sé. Dennegang ikke.

Ragnar. [smiler]. Så? Hvor får vi sé ham henne da?

Hilde. *Højt,—højt oppe* ved fløjen får De sé ham!

Ragnar. [lér]. Han! Jo, det kan De tro!

Hilde. Han vil til toppen. Og altså får De sé ham der også.

Ragnar. Ja, han vil, ja! Det tror jeg så gerne. Men han kan simpelthen ikke. Det vilde gå rundt for ham længe, længe før han kom halvvejs. Han måtte krybe *ned* igen på hænder og knæer!

The two equally valid—or invalid—views of Solness are, of course, those which Hilde and Ragnar express *after* his fall. As Egil Törnqvist has clearly shown, which view we accept, if any, depends upon our own perspective or perspectives.[29] And in the end there is much to be said for accepting neither but appreciating the artistic integrity of the unresolved tension created by the antithesis. But it is when Solness falls to his bizarre death—watched just as attentively by Ragnar as by Hilde—that negative associations of the name "Ragnar" become strongest—and go far to counterbalance whatever glory Hilde sees. The name of Solness's young rival is appropriately close to "Ragnarok," the days of doom which according to Norse mythology would inevitably arrive and destroy everything in heaven and earth, including the gods themselves. Ragnarok suggests some kind of mysterious judgement: Ragnar seems in ordinary human terms, to have a right to demand the punishment of Solness—but his gloating over the prospect of Solness's humiliation suggests a mean and deformed spirit (of which his stoop may be a visual symbol). Perhaps also, Norwegians, hearing Hilde talking with Ragnar about the group of "Lads"—Ragnar's fellow builders in training—who have come with him to taunt Solness, recall the noun *raggar* which, according to Tor Guttu's *Riksmåls Ordboken*, means a young man who is asocial, associates with gangs, and has a distasteful preoccupation with sex. What counts most, of course, is less specific details than the evocations of spiritual squalor and supernatural menace that "Ragnar" may summon up in this context.

In that tension lie similar glories and similar ignominies to those which reside as certainly elsewhere in Ibsen perhaps only in *Peer Gynt*. Solness could be Dionysus resurrected or a shabby adulterer afflicted with satyriasis and megalomania. He could be Prometheus unbound or a hateful predator hiding his cruelty from himself and others in the guise of martyrdom. He could also be, as has been suggested, a Nietzschean superman, but one tragicomically undone by the fascinating young woman he could not keep in her (according to Nietzsche) properly servile place. And whatever he is, in terms of ancient and modern myths, he is undoubtedly as much of an unknown and unknowable quantity as anyone aspiring to heroism of epic proportions in the fragmented culture of Western liberalism.

6

Conclusion: The
Importance of the
Contrary

One of the last observations that Ibsen made in the closing days of his life was "on the contrary."[1] It had seemed to his wife, Suzannah, that his slightly improved condition was a sign of his imminent recovery, or so at least she may, for Ibsen's sake, have pretended to the nurse. But he, having suffered three strokes and, for many months, the anguish of a still active mind in a half-paralyzed body, believed otherwise. Characteristically, he rejected expressions of facile optimism, however well intended. Also, during these last few days, he told his son, Sigurd, "Soon I shall go into the great darkness."[2]

This image, like so much else in Ibsen, seems, initially, ordinary and unremarkable. But also, like so much else in Ibsen, it is not a simpel denial of a hope nourished in illusion. The contrary view to the false optimism of Suzannah Ibsen's bedside manner is not, in Ibsen's terms, the grim certainty of annihilation. It is Ulrik Brendel, who is histrionic and preposterous to the last, and not Ibsen, who sees approaching death as "the mighty nothingness." Ibsen's "great darkness" is as characteristic of its speaker's mode of apprehension as Bjørnson's vision of the world beyond death as a "great whiteness,"[3] and both are quite different from Brendel's sensational view. Uttered, as it was, by one looking mortality in the face, Ibsen's image suggests more than a refusal to be distracted with pleasing fictions of the kind that Peer invents for his dying mother and much more than simple denial of an afterlife. Spoken by a poet who had excelled in nocturnal imagery, Ibsen's final allusion to darkness is as complex in relation to his life and works as it is open.

Beyond the darkness there might have been, so Ibsen seems to suggest, some such certainty, whether terrible or benign, as Peer may come upon if he does meet the Button-Moulder at a final crossroads, or some such positive epiphany as some see in Helene Alving's last moments with Oswald as the sun rises in the mountains and in Hedvig's death in the attic where her world has become heavy with strange darkness. We are reminded of Solness's plunge into the darkness of the quarry after his final possible encounter with an Almighty Someone, or the hopes that some nurture that Rosmer and Rebecca will achieve, in their suicide, the *liebestod* that evades Hjørdis and Sigurd in *The Vikings at Helgeland*. As we have seen, also, the Boyg and trolls of all kinds inhabit the darknesses of Ibsen's poetic drama (in both prose and verse); they are terrible forces capable, it seems, of putting out all lights or of turning them all into false fires. But the lights themselves are none the less defined, in so far as they can be defined, in their contrast to the suggestive darkness of Ibsen's fictive world.

The associations of darkness in Ibsen are, therefore, manifold—as no one was in a better position to understand than his son. When Ibsen wrote *Catiline*, mostly at night, as he recalled twenty-five years afterwards,[4] he created Aurelia, who is associated with dawn, the morning star, and spiritual comfort, as well as Furia, who is the nightmare her name suggests. The question which of these—if either of them—is, as both desire to be, in charge of Catiline's soul when his death approaches is an archetypal instance of fruitful ambivalence in Ibsen—of which the present work has studied four of the most mature and, in Yeats's sense, "multitudinous" examples.[5] There are, as we have seen, many characters in Ibsen whose journeys through the Valley of the Shadow of Death may be more spiritually uplifting than Old Ekdal's. But such journeys have no chance of success unless the shadowy contours of the valley terrain and its elusive terrors are, at some stage, apprehended by whoever seeks salvation, or, less ambitiously, merely a means of making ordinary mortal existence worthwhile as well as endurable.

It is as well, if tempted to quote Ibsen's poem "The Miner" to support the idea that lonely subterranean labours in search of precious metal are guaranteed success by Ibsen, to recall that no certainty of a strike, lucky or otherwise, is offered to the miner of the title despite all his deprivation and effort "hammer blow upon hammer blow." It should not be forgotten that in *John Gabriel Borkman*, the play which draws most clearly on this poem, the title character, whose life is obsessively devoted to exploiting precious ore, is judged guilty of the "sin for which there is no forgiveness" (that of destroying in others the capacity for love) and that, as so rarely happens, Ibsen appears to endorse the poetic justice of the "iron hand" which, in retaliation, mysteriously reaches out to grip Borkman's already frosty heart. And, sometimes, darkness may be merely an escape from truth even, or perhaps especially, for those who profess, like Gregers Werle and Hedda Gabler, a yearning for transcendent heroism. Moreover, though more obviously in some plays that in others, there is the grotesque suggestion that the truths possibly revealed to those capable of enduring the darkest agonies of the soul show that mankind is inescapably at odds with the world, in which he must nevertheless have his inexplicable being. Of all Ibsen's plays, perhaps only *Brand* and *When We Dead Awaken* suggest this as clearly as two of the plays we have examined, *Peer Gynt* and *The Master Builder*.

There is a sense in which virtually every play that Ibsen wrote— whether frothy and juvenile, like *St. John's Night*, or complex and mature, like *Little Eyolf*—is a dramatic structure raised on the foundation of the proposition that humanity does not necessarily know enough about anything to escape Peer's judgement, which appears to apply to him and to Western culture as a whole: "Here No One lies buried." But, unlike some recent writers, Ibsen does not, as we have seen, support a wholly negative view either: if "No One lies buried," many are alive and above the ground to make of their lives what they can and will. We may, if we can reconcile our appraisals of their capabilities with the aspirations they express, think hopefully of Dr. Stockmann and his daughter Petra enlightening the minds of underprivileged children in a village school. And of Alfred and Rita Allmers doing the same—though one may find it difficult to imagine any of them enduring for decades the rigours and the unglamorous aspects of the classroom.

Fittingly, James McFarlane, one of the critics who has written best about the multidimensional nature of Ibsen's themes and characters has also written memorably about Ibsen's suggestive treatment of darkness and light:

> . . . the Light is something to play both hide *and*[6] seek with; the Dark is either a prison or a refuge, something that shuts in or shuts out. On the other hand there are those words of Brand who tells of certain ideas (recurrent in Ibsen) that used to send him into fits of laughter: what if an owl were afraid of the dark, or a fish afraid of water? How they would long for "air and the glad flames of day." And yet this (he says) is the lot of humankind, living between the fact of having to bear and the realization that it is unbearable; imprisoned. But then the Light, as well as being something to be yearned for, can also be something to be feared. In an early poem of Ibsen called "Fear of the Light," he confesses that his courage drains away as the sun rises, that the troubles of the day and the claims of life drip cold terror into his heart so that he hides himself under a flap of the scare-crow veil of the dark, embracing night as a protective shield.[7]

It is ultimately more difficult, because of an absence of an aesthetic form, to know what Ibsen the father meant when he spoke to his son about a "great darkness' than it is to respond to it in his work, which, as we have seen, exploits, daringly and profoundly, modern tragicomic forms. But every question, every antithesis in his work, is rooted in some apprehension of darkness and light in relation to actualities that Ibsen had perceived in the human psyche or the human soul. Many other nineteenth-century writers philosophized about issues similar to those in Ibsen's plays. They produced impressive and sometimes consistent theories—in anthropology, political economy, the natural sciences, psychology, and philosophy—theories which have helped to shape, or misshape, the world in which we live. Ibsen, not a great thinker but an artist who fell passionately the tension arising from antitheses of all kinds, intimated, as we have seen, quintessential realities that tended to evade others more learned, more logical, and more single-minded than he. And if we journey with him, we shall be obliged to question not only all our own intellectual and ethical convictions but also the theory—which lesser artists than Ibsen take for granted—that the poet (*digter*) in an artist and in those responding to his work in truly a guide capable of helping us to keep our footing where the paths we feel bound to follow become most treacherous.

Notes

Some Fundamentals of Vision and Form in Ibsen

1. The statement is quoted, for instance, by Halvdan Koht in the opening chapter of his revised definitive biography, *Life of Ibsen* (English translation by Einar Haugen and A.E. Santiello, New York, 1971), p. 19. James McFarlane also emphasizes its central importance in *Ibsen and the Temper of Norwegian Literature* (London, 1960), p. 68.
2. James McFarlane (ed.), *The Oxford Ibsen* vol. 7 (London, 1966), p. 490. Subsequent references to this edition will use the abbreviation *Oxford*, with appropriate volume and page numbers.
3. The phrase is borrowed from Walter Reed, *Meditations on the Hero* (New Haven, Conn., 1974), which discusses such "meditations" by Kierkegaard, Lermontov, Emily Brontë, and Melville.
4. *Ibsen: A Collection of Critical Essays* (Englewood Cliffs, N.J., 1965), p. 6.
5. *The Modern Ibsen* (1925; rpt. New York, 1960), p. 355.
6. Weigand, p. 23.
7. Weigand, p. 68.
8. *The Dry Mock* (Berkeley, Calif., 1948), pp. 197–244.
9. *Ibsen A Critical Study* (Cambridge, 1973), p. 228.
10. In *Contemporary Approaches to Ibsen*, vol. 1 (Oslo, 1966), pp. 35–50.
11. The phraseology is borrowed from Inga-Stina Ewbank's Inaugural Lecture at Bedford College, *"Shakespeare, Ibsen and the Unspeakable"* (London, 1975).
12. Cocteau's distinction between "poetry *in* the theatre" and "poetry *of* the theatre," made in his Preface to *Les Mariés de la Tour Eiffel* (Paris, 1924), has useful applications in Ibsen criticism: it provides a convenient way of relating Ibsen's visual symbolism to his poetic prose.
13. See Note 11 and "Ibsen and 'The Far More Difficult Art' of Prose," in *Contemporary Approaches to Ibsen*, vol. 2 (Oslo, 1971), pp. 60–83.
14. *A Commentary, Critical and Explanatory on the Norwegian Text of Henrik Ibsen's* Peer Gynt *its Language, Literary Associations and Folklore* (1917; rpt. Westport, Conn. 1970).
15. In *Contemporary Approaches to Ibsen*, vol. 2 (Oxlo, 1971), pp. 42–59.
16. *Ibsen Letters and Speeches*, trans. and ed. Evert Sprinchorn (London, 1965), p. 207. Subsequent references to this work will use the abbreviation *Letters and Speeches*.
17. *Oxford*, vol. 6, p. 440.
18. *Letters and Speeches*, p. 12.
19. *Modern Tragicomedy* (New York, 1966), p. 35.
20. Guthke, p. xiii.

Notes

21 *"Half a Kingdom for a Horse: Ibsenite Tragicomedy,"* *Modern Drama*, 22 (1979), 217–51.
22 The historical information that follows is drawn principally from Guthke.
23 *Tragicomedy: Its Origins and Development in Italy, France and England* (Urbana, Ill., 1962).
24 Guthke, p. 102.
25 Quoted in Guthke, p. 106.
26 Cited by Guthke, p. 169.
27 Brian Johnston, *The Ibsen Cycle* (Boston, 1975).
28 Guthke, p. 43.
29 Guthke, p. 72.
30 Shaw's review, originally for the *Saturday Review*, was reprinted in *Our Theatres in the Nineties* and is quoted in *Oxford*, vol. 6, p. 442.
31 *Ibsen The Norwegian* (London, 1946), p. 98.
32 *In Search of Theater* (1953; rpt. New York, 1954), p. 44.
33 Guthke, p. 144.
34 Guthke, pp. 144–65.
35 *The Dark Comedy* (Cambridge, 1962), p. 39.
36 Styan. p. 40.
37 Styan, p. 40.
38 "Four Elizabethan Dramatists," in *Selected Essays* (London, 1951), p. 113.
39 Eliot, p. 111.
40 *Drama from Ibsen to Eliot* (London, 1952), p. 97.
41 Williams, p. 96.
42 *Letters on the Short Story, the Drama and Other Literary Topics by Anton Chekhov* Louis S. Friedland (ed.), (London, 1965), p. 130.
43 John S. Chamberlain, "Ibsen's 'Vildanden' in Relation to Georg Brandes's 'Gustave Flaubert' and Flaubert's 'Un Cœur Simple,' " *Scandinavica* 14 (1975), 37–43.
44 This view is argued with support from Northrop Frye and Ernst Cassirer, among others. *Mythic Patterns in Ibsen's Last Plays* (Minneapolis, 1970), pp. 11–13.
45 Except as noted subsequently, all quotations from Hoy are from the chapter "The Ekdal Garret," in *The Hyacinth Room* (New York, 1964), pp. 93–115.
46 *Ibsen* (Edinburgh, 1962), p. 109.
47 Northam, p. 11.
48 Guthke, p. 139.
49 Guthke, p. 64.
50 Styan, p. 73.
51 Styan, p. 76.
52 Styan, p. 72.
53 Styan, p. 73.
54 Hoy, p. 289.
55 Hoy, p. 311.
56 See p. 8.
57 An interesting account of this artistic partnership is given by the translator and the director concerned, Inga-Stina Ewbank and Peter Hall, in the Preface to the version of *John Gabriel Borkman* which was used by the National Theatre (London, 1975).

[58] The essay, as quoted here and in the subsequent paragraphs, forms part of an authorized translation, by Rasmus B. Anderson, of a collection of Georg Brandes's critical essays of which the English title is *Creative Spirits of the Nineteenth Century* (New York, 1923). But the essay was written and first appeared (in Danish) in 1882, as William Archer notes in his Introduction to Jessi Muir's translation of it, under the title "Second Impression," for *Henrik Ibsen, A Critical Study* (London, 1899). Anderson's translation (*Creative Spirits of the Nineteenth Century*, pp. 349–96) has the title "Henrik Ibsen."

[59] All the quotations here from Shaw are from the chapter "The Lesson of the Plays," in *The Quintessence of Ibsenism* (1913; rpt. New York, 1957), pp. 147–57.

[60] Koht, p. 18.

[61] H. L. Mencken, extract from the Introduction to *Eleven Plays by Ibsen* (New York, 1935), quoted by James McFarlane, *Henrik Ibsen A Critical Anthology* (Harmondsworth, 1970), pp. 236–42.

[62] Mary McCarthy, "The Will and Testament of Ibsen," *Partisan Review* 23 (1956), 74–80.

[63] One sign of the central importance of John Northam's *Ibsen's Dramatic Method* (London, 1953) is its second edition published by the Norwegian University Press in 1971.

[64] See p. 14 and p. 207, note 43.

[65] *Letters and Speeches*, p. 114.

[66] *Letters and Speeches*, p. 330.

Peer Gynt: Journeys into Uncertainty

[1] *Four Lectures on Henrik Ibsen* (London, 1892), pp. 52–85.

[2] *Spiritual Voices in Modern Literature* (New York, 1919), pp. 41–69. A more recent analysis of the play in Christian terms is Ronald Gaskell, "Symbol and Reality in *Peer Gynt*," *Drama Survey* 4 (1965), 57–64.

[3] *Ibsen the Norwegian*, pp. 53–63.

[4] *Ibsen* pp. 24–29.

[5] *The Drama of Ibsen and Strindberg* (London, 1962), pp. 93–106.

[6] *"Peer Gynt—i dag," Contemporary Approaches to Ibsen* vol. 3 (Oslo, 1977), 91–98.

[7] *Henrik Ibsen, A Critical Study*, trans. Jessie Muir; rev. William Archer (London, 1899), p. 36.

[8] *"Peer Gynt*, dramatisk Digt af Henrik Ibsen," *Fædrelandet*, 30 November 1867.

[9] *Oxford*, vol. 3, pp. 32–33.

[10] "Peer Gynt, Naturalism and the Dissolving Self," *Drama Review* 13, No. 2 (1968), 28–43. The quotation is from p. 39.

[11] See p. 18. Sverre Arestad's skilfully analytic "Peer Gynt and the Idea of Self," *Modern Drama* 3 (1960), 103–22, might farily be taken as representative of the view that while *Peer Gynt* is open-ended, its openness is strictly circumscribed.

[12] Logeman, p. 135.

[13] William Archer quotes Ibsen as follows: " 'Hvirvlens vætter,' [Ibsen] writes, is equivalent to 'Svimmelhedens ånder.' " Archer adds, "i.e. spirits of dizziness or vertigo." Henrik Ibsen, *The Collected Works of Henrik Ibsen*, ed. William Archer, vol. 6, p. 6. Subsequent references to this edition will use the abbreviation "Archer," with appropriate volume and page numbers.

[14] Archer, vol. 4, pp. 272–80, provides a translation of both the Gudbrand Glesne tale and the Peer Gynt tale as they appear in Asbjørnsen, *Norske Huldre-Eventyr og Folkesagn* (Christiania, 1848). Here, as elsewhere, I have, unlike Archer, retained the Norwegian spelling of "Gudbrandsdal."

[15] See p. 19.

[16] Archer, vol. 4, pp. xviii–xix.

[17] Archer, vol. 4, p. xii.

[18] One of the two old women who discover Åse on the millhouse roof uses this expression. According to Logeman (p. 31), it is to be taken both literally and metaphorically. The Archers, however, retain only the metaphorical sense—"to be in an exalted position." There is no reference in the original to the "shingles" which the Archers substitute for "stones" in one of Peer's comments on the millhouse roof.

[19] In Norwegian folktales, the "ashlad" is a common figure. He is a long-headed fellow, despised by two older brothers, who triumphs in the same heroic quest in which they shamefully fail. In some respects, as the name suggests, he is a male version of Cinderella, but it is his shrewdness and imagination which win him his princess and a royal inheritance.

[20] Logeman, p. 65.

[21] See p. 11.

[22] Logeman, pp. 47–48.

[23] *Oxford*, vol. 3, pp. 28–29.

[24] See p. 29.

[25] This point is well and emphatically made by McFarlane. *Oxford*, loc. cit.

[26] *A Study of Six Plays by Ibsen* (Cambridge, 1950), p. 79.

[27] Logeman, p. 87.

[28] Logeman, p. 94.

[29] This production was directed by Alan Cooke.

[30] *Oxford*, vol. 3, p. 289.

[31] Logeman's comments on the nature of linguistic reform in Norway—and the opposed views of Ibsen and Vinje on the subject—are useful. Logeman. pp. 260–64.

[32] Logeman's comments on the Boyg—on which I have drawn extensively—are particularly informative. Logeman, pp. 130–35.

[33] See p. 34.

[34] There are Norwegian folk-tales in the Asbjörnsen and Moe Collection about both the castle west of the moon and east of the sun and Soria Moria Castle. But, as Logeman points out, the latter can be traced to Arabic mythology and is associated with "the islands of the Blessed." Logeman, p. 164.

[35] Logeman mentions a story with Icelandic and Danish sources according to which the woman tricks not only St. Peter but also St. Paul, the Virgin Mary, and Christ himself. Logemand, p. 167.

[36] Logeman, pp. 206–7.

[37] The word *bukk* can refer to a male deer (the English "buck") as well as to a ram or a billygoat.

[38] "Shaw and the Passion of the Mind," *Modern Drama* 16 (1973), 249.

[39] "Mr. James Joyce and the Modern Stage," *The Drama* 6, No. 2 (1916). Reprinted in Ezra Pound, *Pound/Joyce*, ed. Forrest Reed (London 1968), p. 51.

40 Logeman, p. 214.
41 Quoted in H. G. Wells, *The Outline of History*, rev. Raymond Postage, vol. 1 (New York, 1949), p. 485.
42 Wells, vol. 1, p. 483.
43 Logeman identifies the author to whom Peer refers as the German K. F. Becker, whose work *Weltgeschichte*, had been repeatedly translated into Danish.
44 Downs, pp. 99–100.
45 Logeman, pp. 241–43.
46 Logeman, p. 243.
47 In the poem "To my Friend the Revolutionary Orator."
48 Henrik Ibsen, *Peer Gynt*, ed. Daniel Kaakonsen (Solo, 1977), pp. 165–66.
49 Logeman, p. 255.
50 Logeman, pp. 256–57.
51 Intellectual deceit, or "thought-swindling," as Archer translates Clemens Petersen's term "Tankesvindel," is one of the charges made by the noted Danish critic in his review of *Peer Gynt*. See *Archer*, vol. 4, p. xii.
52 *The Quintessence of Ibsenism* p. 65.
53 Logeman, p. 273.
54 Logeman, p. 286–87.
55 The fable used is "Scurra et Rusticus," *The Aesopic Fables*, book V, fable 5.
56 The opinions of Eitrem, Sturtevant, and Woerner are brought together by Logeman, pp. 300–01.
57 Logeman, quoting two authorities, maintains that the word "Subjekter" (which, is Archer, is translated as "talents") means primarily "actors." Logeman, p. 331. Much more recently, however, Daniel Haakonsen in his edition of *Peer Gynt* notes that the word, as used in this context, means "skuespiller"—"plays."
58 Cyrus Hoy, "Beyond Tragedy," in *The Hyacinth Room*, pp. 267–318.

Ghosts: The Vision Blurs

1 In *Henrik Ibsen, A Critical Study*, trans. Jessie Muir, pp. 39–82.
2 *Ibsen A Critical Study*, (Cambridge, 1973), p. 110.
3 "Rosenvold and Rosmersholm: Protagonist Implies Interpretation," *Contemporary Approaches to Ibsen* vol. 4 (Oslo, 1979), 101–19.
4 Northam, pp. 76–112.
5 "The Function of Sacrifice in Ibsen's Realistic Drama," *Contemporary Approaches to Ibsen*, vol. 1 (1966), 21–34.
6 "*Ghosts* Seen from an Existential Aspect," *Ibsen Yearbook* 13 (1974), 118–26.
ox 7 *Henrik Ibsen*, trans. Helen Sebba (New York, 1972) pp. 56–77.
8 "Patterns of Interaction in Ibsen's *Ghosts*," *Ibsen Yearbook* 13 (1974), 89–117.
9 *Oxford*, vol. 5, p. 467.
10 *The Modern Ibsen* (1925; rpt. New York, 1960), p. 71.
11 Quoted in Michael Egan (ed.), *Ibsen The Critical Heritage* (London, 1972), p. 185.
12 Leland quotes Helene's remark, "Dette bæres ikke," in the Norwegian; it is worth noting that Ibsen uses a passive construction, not the active constructions favoured by, for instance, Archer, McFarlane, and Fjelde. To emphasize this point, that to suffer is also to act, Leland echoes Mrs. Alving in his italicized reply, also in Norwegian in the article, "*Det bæres!*" (*It is endured!*) Leland, loc. cit.

13 *The Quintessence of Ibsenism*, p. 90.

14 This 1977 production was directed by John Barton.

15 Anselma Dell'Olio's note was written for the *Caedmon* sound recording of *Ghosts* (New York, 1971).

16 See the chapter on *A Doll's House* in Weigand.

17 The Conversation, of 2 January 1882, was published in *Monthly Review*, June 1906. It is reprinted in *Oxford*, vol. 5, pp. 474–75.

18 Letter from Rome, 6 January 1882. *Letters and Speeches*, pp. 200–1.

19 Letter from Rome, 28 January 1882. *Letters and Speeches*, pp. 202–4.

20 Loc. cit.

21 In a discussion of source material for Strindberg's *The Father*, Martin Lamm mentions Paul Lafargue, the French sociologist, who in March 1886, published an article in *La Nouvelle Revue* claiming that "matriarchy was humanity's original form of social organization and that only by means of violent battles between the sexes was patriarchy established. If an attempt should be made to restore matriarchy, similar violent sexual battles would be risked." Martin Lamm, *August Strindberg*, trans. Harry G. Carlson (New York, 1971), p. 207.

22 Northam, p. 76.

23 *The Idea of a Theater* (1949, rpt. Princeton, N.J. 1968), p. 152.

24 See pp. 84–85 and note 14 above.

25 Letter from Munich, 13 November 1886, *Letters and Speeches*, pp. 260–61.

26 John S. Chamberlain, "*Ghosts* as a Psychological, Social and Existential Work—An Example of Ibsen's Tragicomic Vision," *Contemporary Approaches to Ibsen* vol. 4 (1978), 62–73.

27 Gunnar Ahlström, in his *Det moderna gennombrottet* (Stockholm, 1947), draws attention both to the borrowing of names and to some basic thematic parallels between *The Emigrant Literature and Pillars of Society, A Doll's House*, and *Ghosts*. I have attempted to explore the relationship of *The Emigrant Literature* and *Ghosts* in more detail in "*Gengangere* and *Emigrantlitteraturen*," *Scandinavica* 16 (1977), 1–10.

28 Two Danish editions of *The Emigrant Literature*—the second with substantial revisions and additions—were published before Ibsen commenced work on *Ghosts*. They appeared in 1872 and 1877, respectively. The translations provided here (my own) are of the first edition, which is the one Ibsen praised so enthusiastically. The passage about *Corinne* is from *Emigrantlitteraturen* (Copenhagen, 1872), pp. 206–7.

29 *Henrik Ibsen, A Critical Study*, p. 77.

30 *Emigrantlitteraturen* (1872), p. 125.

31 Leland has written a spirited article which draws attention to Manders's positive attributes, which are often overlooked. See "In Defense of Pastor Manders," *Modern Drama* 21 (1978), 405–20.

32 See p. 96.

33 In *Ibsen's Dramatic Method* (1953; rpt. Oslo, 1971), p. 64, John Northam cites a letter from William Archer to Charles Arches in which the former quotes from a conversation with Ibsen, who said, "my only purpose with the pipe was to show that the only thing Oswald could remember about his father was that he made him vomit—and that, I think, is about the worst thing you *can* remember about someone else. . . ."

[34] Archer, vol. 7, p. xxv.

[35] See p. 211, note 26.

The Wild Duck: All Hope Abandoned?

[1] See p. 8.

[2] All quotations from Guthke in this chapter are from his "Analysis of *The Wild Duck*," in *Modern Tragicomedy* pp. 144–65.

[3] See p. 19 and p. 208, note 62.

[4] Archer, vol. 8, p. xxi.

[5] "The Ekdal Garret," in *The Hyacinth Room* pp. 93–115.

[6] "Tragedie og Komedie—Studie i *Vildanden*," *Ibsen Yearbook* 4 (1955–1956), 29–37. The translations are mine.

[7] "The Wild Duck," *Ibsen A Critical Study*, pp. 113–46.

[8] "*Villanden*—En Innledning og en Kritikk," *Edda* 36 (1936), 269–305.

[9] "Sacrifice and Absurdity in *The Wild Duck*," *Mosaic* 7, No. 4 (1974), 99–107.

[10] "The Emotion of Multitude," in *Essays and Introductions* (London, 1961). All the quotations from it in this paragraph are from pp. 215–16.

[11] Brian Downs observes, "It is just possible that from the mouth of his friend Jens Peter Jacobsen, the Danish translator of Darwin, or otherwise, Ibsen learnt of Darwin's observation: 'We have seen how soon the wild duck, when domesticated, loses its true character, from the effects of abundant or changed feeding, or from taking little exercise." Downs, *A Study of Six Plays by Ibsen*, pp. 148–49. Darwin's remark itself is in *The Variations of Animals and Plants under Domestication*, vol. 2 (London 1868), p. 278.

[12] Cited by Rolf Fjelde, *Henrik Ibsen The Complete Prose Plays* (New York, 1965), p. 7.

[13] See p. 207, note 43.

[14] In condemning the triviality of merely realistic art as "devoid of temperament," Strindberg remarked in his essay "On Modern Drama and Modern Theatre" (1889) that such work "is photography which includes everything, even the grain of dust on the lens of the camera." Extracts from the essay appear in Toby Cole (ed.), *Playwrights on Playwriting* (London, 1960), pp. 15–22.

[15] The translation is literal.

[16] Fjelde, p. 447 (italics mine). Another American translation, that of Dounia B. Christiani (New York, 1968), offers the following: "waddling so cosily in and out in her felt slippers, swaying her hips and making everything nice and comfortable for you."

[17] See p. 19.

[18] Letter to Frederik Hegel, 2 September 1884. *Letters and Speeches*, pp. 236–37.

[19] See the notes for *Ghosts* translated in *Oxford*, vol. 5, p. 467.

[20] The translation of this phrase quoted here is Fjelde's. It is closer to the original than other translations and it conveys better the characteristically grandiose nature of Hjalmar's perception of things.

[21] See p. 96.

[22] *The Quintessence of Ibsenism* p. 175.

[23] Shaw, p. 156.

[24] Forster draws his useful distinction between "flat" and "round" characters and

elaborates it in Chapter 4, "People (continued)," in *Aspects of the Novel* (London, 1949).

[25] This subject is fully discussed by Otto Reinert, "Sight Imagery in *The Wild Duck,*" *Journal of English and Germanic Philology* 55 (1956), 457–62.

[26] Quoted in Michael Egan, p. 185.

[27] Writing from Rome on 14 November 1884, to H. Schröder, the manager of Kirstiania Theatre, Ibsen remarked: "I have been thinking that Hjalmar must be played by Reimers. This part must definitely not be played with any kind of parody of expression; there must be no trace that the actor is conscious of there being any kind of comic element in the lines at all. He has that endearing quality in his voice, says Relling, and that must be maintained above all. His soulfulness is genuine, his moodiness beautiful in its way, not a trace of affectation." Quoted in *Oxford*, vol. 6, p. 439.

[28] Weigand's chapter on *The Wild Duck* develops the thesis that the play "runs through the gamut of comedy, from kindly humor to the bloodiest satire." *The Modern Ibsen* p. 138. All references to Weigand in the present discussion are to this chapter.

[29] Shaw, p. 182.

[30] See p. 11.

[31] See p. 110.

[32] See p. 117.

[33] See p. 212, note 11.

How Firm a Foundation—The Unsound Structures of Master Builder Solness?

[1] *The Flower and the Castle* (New York, 1963), p. 208.

[2] *Mythic Patterns in Ibsen's Last Plays*, pp, 109–10.

[3] *The Death of Tragedy* (London, 1961), p. 294.

[4] *Catiline's Dream; An Essay on Ibsen's Plays* (Urbana, Ill., 1972), p. 169.

[5] The case for considering Solness in this way is cogently argued by Egil Törnqvist, "Individualism in *The Master Builder,*" *Contemporary Approaches to Ibsen* vol. 3 (1975), 134–45.

[6] See the extract from "The Tragic in Daily Life" in Toby Cole (ed.), *Playwrights on Playwriting* (London, 1960), pp. 30–36.

[7] *The Proverb in Ibsen* (New York, 1936), p. 217.

[8] See p. 19.

[9] Hilde's pointed question why he does not call himself an architect elicits Solness's candid reply that he "never really had the proper training." Einar Haugen's *Norsk Engelsk Ordbok* gives only "building contractor" for the Norwegian *byggmester* (though *The Master Builder* is given as the appropriate translation of Ibsen's title *Byggmester Solness*). Otto Reinert is emphatic that Solness is "a Norwegian building contractor." See Reinert, "Ibsen and the Modern Tradition," *Ibsen Yearbook* 13, (1974), p. 17.

[10] Arne Røoed's discussion of the Dionysian aspects of *The Master Builder* is both comprehensive and convincing. See Røoed, "Right to the top,—?" *Ibsen Yearbook* 15 (1977), pp. 122–80. The reference to "sterile sex" is on p. 164.

[11] Solveig's words, as has been pointed out, are reminiscent of St. Luke's Gospel (see p. 34).

[12] Peter Wood's comments on the British National Theatre production of *The Master Builder* in 1964, as they appear in the booklet published with the *Caedmon* sound recording of that production, are an excellent starting point for an exploration of the play's comedy and tragicomic ambivalence.

[13] Hearing Hilde Wangel speak of the "frightfully thrilling" or the "terribly exciting" may remind English audiences too much of contexts in which, especially in upper-class British speech, "frightfully" and "terribly" are pressed into trivial idiomatic service. In Hilde's mouth, the terror and the frightfulness are invariably real.

[14] Holtan, pp. 102 and 196.

[15] In a review of Karl Gutzkow's *Zopf und Schwert*, 13 April 1851. Quoted in James McFarlane (ed.) *Henrik Ibsen*, p. 69.

[16] See p. 209, note 19.

[17] See p. 213, note 5.

[18] Weigand makes the point very directly: ". . . at the climax of his ascent [at Lysanger] her emotions culminated in an orgasm that set free all her motor energies, making her shout and gesticulate like one possessed." *The Modern Ibsen*, p. 291. Described in this way the experience seems so frenetic as to be comic, but that does not appear to be in Weigand's mind.

[19] See p. 213, note 9.

[20] *Letters and Speeches*, p. 122.

[22] *Letters and Speeches*, p. 342–43.

[23] *Letters and Speeches*, pp. 337–38.

[24] "Ibsen the Romantic," (from *Abinger Harvest*, London, 1936), in James McFarlane (ed.), *Discussions of Henrik Ibsen* (Boston, 1962) pp. 66–69.

[25] See p. 213, note 10.

[26] Holtan, p. 109.

[27] Holtan, pp. 106–7.

[28] For once, John Northam's comment does not perceive as much as one expects. *Ibsen's Dramatic Method* p. 181.

[29] See p. 213, note 5.

Conclusion: The Importance of the Contrary

[1] Halvdan Koht, *Life of Ibsen*, p. 463.

[2] Bergliot Ibsen, *The Three Ibsens*, trans. G. Schjelderup (London, 1951), p. 152.

[3] Berliot Ibsen, p. 168.

[4] Preface to the revised edition of *Catiline* (1875), *letters and Speeches*, pp. 8–13. The remark about working at night is on page 10.

[5] See p. 212, note 10.

[6] Author's italics.

[7] James McFarlane, *Ibsen and the Temper of Norwegian Literature* p. 66.

Select Bibliography

Ahlström, Gunnar. *Det moderna genombrottet*. Stockholm, 1947.

Anstensen, Ansten. *The Proverb in Ibsen*. New York, 1936.

Arestad, Sverre. "Peer Gynt and the Idea of Self." *Modern Drama* 3 (1960), 103–22.

Bentley, Eric. *In Search of Theater*. 1953; rpt. New York, 1954.

Bien, Horst. "Peer Gynt—i dag." *Contemporary Approaches to Ibsen* vol. 3 (1977), 91–98.

Bradbrook, Muriel C. *Ibsen the Norwegian*. London, 1946.

Brandes, Georg. *Creative Spirits of the Nineteenth Century*. Trans. Rasmus B. Anderson. New York, 1923.

———. *Henrik Ibsen, A Critical Study*. Trans. Jessie Muir. Rev. William Archer. London, 1899; rpt. New York, 1964.

———. *Hovedströmninger i det 19de Aaarhundredes Litteratur*. 6 vols. Copenhagen, 1872–1890.

Chamberlain, John S. "*Gengangere and Emigrantlitteraturen.*" *Scandinavica* 16 (1977), 1–10.

———. "*Ghosts* as a Psychological, Social and Existential Work—An Example of Ibsen's Tragicomic Vision." *Contemporary Approaches to Ibsen* vol. 4 (1978), 62–73.

———. "Ibsen's 'Vildanden' in Relation to Georg brandes's 'Gustave Flaubert' and Flaubert's 'Un Cœur Simple'. " *Scandinavica* 14 (1975), 37–43.

Chekhov, Anton. *Letters on the Short Story, the Drama and Other Literary Topics by Anton Chekhov*. Ed. Louis S. Friedland. London, 1965.

Cocteau, Jean. Preface to *Less Mariés de la Tour Eiffel* (1924). Trans. Joseph M. Bernstein. In Toby Cole (ed.) *Playwrights on Playwriting*. London, 1960, pp. 240–46.

Cole, Toby (ed.). *Playwrights on Playwriting*. London, 1960.

Darwin, Charles. *The Variation of Animals and Plants under Domestication*. 2 vols. London, 1868.

Davies, Trevor H. *Spiritual Voices in Modern Literature*. New York, 1919.

Dell'Olio, Anselma. Note on *A Doll's House* for the *Caedmon* sound recording. New York, 1971.

Downs, Brian W. *The Intellectual Background*. 1946; rpt. New York, 1969.

———. *A Study of Six Plays by Ibsen*. Cambridge, 1950.

Dukore, Bernard F. "Half a Kingdom for a Horse: Ibsenite Tragicomedy." *Modern Drama* 22 (1979), 217–51.

Durbach, Errol. "Sacrifice and Absurdity in *The Wild Duck*." *Mosaic* 7, No. 4 (1974), 99–107.

Egan, Michael N. (ed.). *Ibsen The Critical Heritage*. London, 1972.

Eliot, T.S. *Selected Essays*. London, 1951.

Ewbank, Inga-Stina. "Ibsen and 'The Far More Difficult Art' of Prose." *Contemporary Approaches to Ibsen* vol. 2 (1971), 60–83.

———. *"Shakespeare, Ibsen and the Unspeakable."* London, 1975.

Fergusson, Francis. *The Idea of a Theater*. 1949; rpt. Princeton, N.J., 1968.

Fjelde, Rolf. (ed.). *Ibsen: A Collection of Critical Essays*. Englewood Cliffs, N.J., 1965.

———. "Peer Gynt, Naturalism and the Dissolving Self." *Drama Review* 13, No. 2 (1968), 28–43.

Forster, E.M. *Abinger Harvest*. London. 1928.

———. *Aspects of the Novel*. London, 1949.

Gaskell, Ronald. "Symbol and Reality in *Peer Gynt*." *Drama Survey* 4 (1965), 57–64.

Guthke, Karl S. *Modern Tragicomedy*. New York, 1966.

Haakonsen, Daniel (ed.). *Contemporary Approaches to Ibsen*. 4 vols. Oslo, 1966–1979.

———. "The Function of Sacrifice in Ibsen's Realistic Drama." *Contemporary Approaches to Ibsen*, vol. 1 (1966), 21–34.

Herrick, Marvin T. *Tragicomedy: Its Origins and Development in Italy, France and England*. 1955; rpt. Urbana, Ill., 1962.

Holtan, Orley I. *Mythic Patterns in Ibsen's Last Plays*. Minneapolis, 1970.

Hoy, Cyrus. *The Hyacinth Room*. New York, 1964.

Hurt, James. *Catiline's Dream; An Essay on Ibsen's Plays*. Urbana, Ill. 1972.

Ibsen, Bergliot. *The Three Ibsens*. Trans. G. Schjelderup. London, 1951.

Ibsen, Henrik. *The Collected Works of Henrik Ibsen*. Ed. William Archer. Trans. William Archer et al. 12 vols. London, 1906–1912.

———. *Henrik Ibsen The Complete Prose Plays*. Trans. Rolf Fjelde. New York, 1965.

———. *Ibsen Letters and Speeches*. Trans. Evert Springchorn, London, 1965.

———. *John Gabriel Borkman*. Trans. Inga-Stina Ewbank and Peter Hall. London, 1975.

———. *The Oxford Ibsen*. Ed. James Walter McFarlane. Trans. James Walter McFarlane et al. 8 vols. London, 1960–1977.

———. *Samlede Verker*. Ed. Francis Bull, Halvdan Koht, and Didrik Arup Seip. 21 vols. Oslo, 1928–1957.

———. *The Wild Duck*. Trans. Dounia B. Christiani. New York, 1968.

Johnston, Brian. *The Ibsen Cycle*. Boston, 1975.

Knight, G. Wilson. *Ibsen*. Edinburgh, 1962.

Koht, Halvdan, *Life of Ibsen*, Trans. Einar Haugen and A.E. Santiello. New York, 1971.

Kruuse, Jens. "The Function of Humour in the Later Plays of Ibsen." *Contemporary Approaches to Ibsen*, vol. 2 (1971), 42–59.

———. "Tragedie og Komedie—Studie i *Vildanden*." *Ibsen Yearbook* 4 (1955–1956), 29–37.

Lamm, Martin. *August Strindberg*. Trans. Harry G. Carlson, New York, 1971.

Leland, Charles. "*Ghosts* Seen from an Existential Aspect." *Ibsen Yearbook* 13 (1973–1974), 118–26.

———. "In Defense of Pastor Manders." *Modern Drama* 21 (1978), 405–20.

Logeman, Henri. *A Commentary, Critical and Explanatory on the Norwegian Text of Henrik Ibsen's* Peer Gynt *Its Language, Literary Associations and Folklore*. 1917; rpt. Westport, Conn., 1970.

Lucas, F.L. *The Drama of Ibsen and Strindberg*. London, 1962.

Maeterlinck, Maurice. "The Tragical in Daily Life." In *The Treasure of the Humble*. Trans. Alfred Sutro. New York, 1916.

McCarthy, Mary. "The Will and Testament of Ibsen." *Partisan Review* 23 (1956), 74–80.

McFarlane, James (ed.). *Discussions of Henrik Ibsen*. Boston, 1962.

———. (ed.). *Henrik Ibsen A Critical Anthology*. Harmondsworth, 1970.

———. *Ibsen and the Temper of Norwegian Literature*. London, 1960.

———. "Meaning and Evidence in Ibsen's Drama." *Contemporary Approaches to Ibsen*, vol. 1 (1966), 35–50.

Meyer, Hans Georg. *Henrik Ibsen*. Trans. Helen Sebba. New York, 1972.

Northam, John. *Ibsen A Critical Study*. Cambridge, 1973.

———. *Ibsen's Dramatic Method*. 1953; rpt. Oslo, 1971.

Petersen, Clemens. "*Peer Gynt*, dramatisk Digt af Henrik Ibsen." *Fœdrelandet*, 30 November 1867.

Pound, Ezra. *Pound/Joyce*. Ed. Forrest Read. London, 1968.

Reed, Walter. *Meditations on the Hero*. New Haven, Conn., 1974.

Reinert, Otto. "*Ibsen* and the Modern Tradition." *Ibsen Yearbook* 13 (1973–1974), 9–27.

———. "Sight Imagery in *The Wild Duck*." *Journal of English and Germanic Philology* 55 (1956), 457–62.

Røed, Arne. "Right to the top'—?" *Ibsen Yearbook* 15 (1977) 122–80.

Saari, Sandra E. "Rosenvold and Rosmersholm: Protagonist Implies Interpretation." *Contemporary Approaches to Ibsen* vol. 4 (1979), 101–19.

Salmon, Eric. "Shaw and the Passion of the Mind." *Modern Drama* 16 (1973), 239–50.

Shaw, Bernard. *The Quintessence of Ibsenism*. 1913; rpt. New York, 1957.

Steiner, George. *The Death of Tragedy*. London, 1961.

Strindberg, August. *Samlade Skrifter af August Strindberg*. Ed. John Landquist. 55 vols. Stockholm, 1912–1919.

Styan, J.L. *The Dark Comedy*. Cambridge, 1962.

Thomas, David. "Patterns of Interaction in Ibsen's *Ghosts*." *Ibsen Yearbook* 13 (1973–1974), 89–117.

Thompson, Alan Reynolds. *The Dry Mock*. Berkeley, Calif., 1948.

Törnqvist, Egil. "Individualism in *The Master Builder*." *Contemporary Approaches to Ibsen* vol. 3 (1975), 134–45.

Valency, Maurice. *The Flower and the Castle*. New York, 1963.

Weigand, Hermann J. *The Modern Ibsen*. 1925; rpt. New York, 1960.

Well, H.G. *The Outline of History*. Rev. Raymond Postgate. 2 vols. New York, 1949.

Wicksteed, Philip H. *Four Lectures on Henrik Ibsen*. London, 1892.

Williams, Raymond. *Drama from Ibsen to Eliot*. London, 1952.

Woods, Peter. Director's commentary for the *Caedmon* sound recording of the British National Theatre production of *The Master Builder*. New York, 1965.

Wyller, Anders. "*Villanden*—En Innledning og en Kritikk." *Edda* 36 (1936), 269–305.

Yeats, W.B. *Essays and Introductions*. London, 1961.

INDEX